Praise from the Experts

"If you are a SAS Enterprise Guide user at any level, this book is essential. It is written in plain English, easy-to-follow, and well illustrated. *The Little SAS Book for Enterprise Guide 4.2* is thorough, with well-explained examples that give the user the ability to utilize the software efficiently. As with all of the 'Little SAS Books' authored by Susan Slaughter and Lora Delwiche, the care and attention given to the creation of the indexes stands above other technical books, making its effectiveness quite appreciated by the reader. If someone asks me a SAS Enterprise Guide question, this is the resource I will point them to!"

Jenine Milum
President of the Charlotte (NC) SAS Users Group

"*The Little SAS Book for Enterprise Guide 4.2* is an effective resource for learning and using this powerful and productive SAS product. Susan and Lora divide their book into tutorial and reference sections. The tutorials have good screenshots and clearly walk you through four projects. This makes getting started with SAS Enterprise Guide easy and fast. The reference section takes you beyond 'getting started' and gives you a deeper understanding of SAS Enterprise Guide. It includes new features, such as task templates. This is a book that we will recommend to our students and clients."

Ginger Carey and Helen Carey
SAS Enterprise Guide Instructors

"Once again Susan and Lora have produced a book that will be a 'must-have' for new users to SAS Enterprise Guide 4.2, whether they are new to the SAS Enterprise Guide family or, like me, making the move from earlier versions of SAS Enterprise Guide."

Peter Eberhardt
Fernwood Consulting Group Inc.

"Lora and Susan's latest addition to their popular 'Little SAS Book' series brings the power and flexibility of SAS Enterprise Guide 4.2 capabilities to the desktops of both new and experienced users of this latest update to menu-driven business intelligence tool from SAS. Their real-world experience as SAS programmers and trainers is reflected on every page of their book. Intuitive step-by-step tutorials and easy-to-understand explanations enable novice SAS Enterprise Guide 4.2 users to apply powerful data management, reporting, analysis, and graphing features within minutes of starting their first session with the product. And, experienced SAS Enterprise Guide users and SAS programmers will appreciate how well the book enables them to apply their existing skill via this new graphical interface to longstanding SAS tools. You'll want to keep this text within easy reach as you apply SAS Enterprise Guide 4.2 capabilities to your projects and programs."

Andrew H. Karp
Principal Consultant, Sierra Information Services
www.SierraInformation.com

"*The Little SAS Book for Enterprise Guide 4.2* guides you through the multiple functionalities of SAS Enterprise Guide in a logical, stepwise manner. First, you complete a specific job via tutorials. Then you extend your scope and gain flexibility by being introduced to more advanced methods. Learning by doing is an invaluable benefit of the book tutorials. The many screen captures provided allow you to learn away from your computer. The side-by-side page formatting provides short-term goals to optimize your time. *The Little SAS Book for Enterprise Guide 4.2* is the reference for learning about SAS Enterprise Guide on your own."

Véronique Bourcier
www.sasreference.com

SAS Publishing

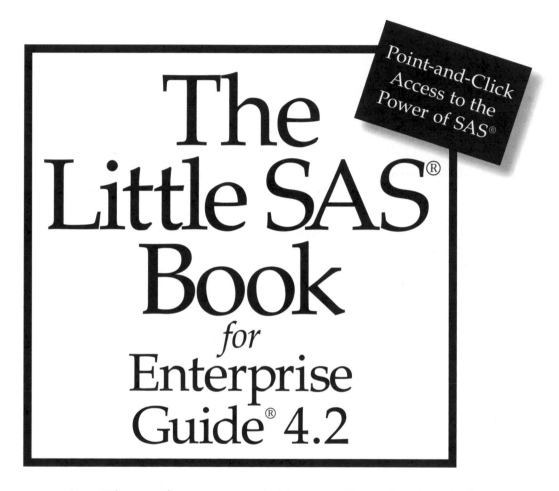

The Little SAS® Book

for

Enterprise Guide® 4.2

Point-and-Click Access to the Power of SAS®

Susan J. Slaughter and *Lora D. Delwiche*

The correct bibliographic citation for this manual is as follows: Slaughter, Susan J., and Lora D. Delwiche. 2010. *The Little SAS® Book for Enterprise Guide® 4.2.* Cary, NC: SAS Institute Inc.

The Little SAS® Book for Enterprise Guide® 4.2

Copyright © 2010, SAS Institute Inc., Cary, NC, USA

ISBN 978-1-59994-726-6
ISBN 978-1-60764-575-7 (electronic book)

All rights reserved. Produced in the United States of America.

SAS Institute Inc., SAS Campus Drive, Cary, North Carolina 27513.

1st printing, March 2010
2nd printing, March 2011
3rd printing, September 2011

SAS® Publishing provides a complete selection of books and electronic products to help customers use SAS software to its fullest potential. For more information about our e-books, e-learning products, CDs, and hard-copy books, visit the SAS Publishing Web site at **support.sas.com/publishing** or call 1-800-727-3228.

Contents

About SAS Enterprise Guide

For over three decades, SAS software has been used by programmers, analysts, and scientists to manipulate and analyze data. Today, SAS (pronounced sass) is used around the world in 120 countries and at more than 45,000 sites. SAS users stay with SAS year after year because they know its broad flexibility and depth of functionality will enable them to get the work done. However, not everyone wants to write programs.

What SAS Enterprise Guide is SAS Enterprise Guide gives you access to the power of SAS via a point-and-click interface. SAS Enterprise Guide does not itself analyze data. Instead, SAS Enterprise Guide generates SAS programs. Every time you run a task in SAS Enterprise Guide, it writes a SAS program. The List Data task, for example, writes a PROC PRINT. The Summary Tables task writes a PROC TABULATE. There are over 80 such tasks offered within SAS Enterprise Guide. When you click **Run** in SAS Enterprise Guide, it submits the program to SAS. SAS runs the program, and then sends the results (such as reports, graphs, data tables, and SAS logs) back to SAS Enterprise Guide so that you can see them.

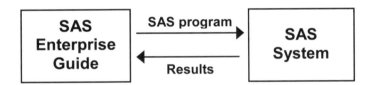

You don't have to be a programmer to use SAS Enterprise Guide, but, if you would like to see the SAS program that SAS Enterprise Guide writes for you, you can do that too. You can also edit the programs written by SAS Enterprise Guide, or open an empty Program window and write a SAS program from scratch using a syntax-sensitive editor similar to the one in Base SAS. Then you can run your SAS program, and view the SAS log and output. So, SAS Enterprise Guide meets the needs of programmers and non-programmers alike.

What software you need To run SAS Enterprise Guide, you need, of course, SAS Enterprise Guide software. SAS Enterprise Guide runs in only the Windows operating environment. Because SAS Enterprise Guide writes programs and submits them to SAS, you also need a machine on which Base SAS is installed. That machine is called a SAS server, and it may be the same machine where SAS Enterprise Guide is installed (in which case, it is called a local server) or it may be a separate machine (called a remote server). SAS runs in many operating environments and on many types of computers. Any computer running SAS can be a SAS server as long as you have access to that machine.

You may have more than one SAS server. For example, you might have SAS installed on both your desktop computer and on a mainframe computer. In that case, you can use SAS Enterprise Guide to run analyses on either computer. When you run a SAS program, you can specify which server you want to use. When you submit a task, it will run on the server where the data table is stored.

SAS has many different products. To run SAS Enterprise Guide, you need only a few. You must have Base SAS software installed on your SAS server. If you have a remote SAS server, you may need a product called SAS Integration Technologies. If you want to run statistical analyses, then you must also have SAS/STAT software. For running econometric time series analyses, you need SAS/ETS software. For graphics, you need SAS/GRAPH software. Except in special cases, you probably won't need SAS/ACCESS software. (See section 2.1 for more information about uisng SAS/ACCESS software with SAS Enterprise Guide.)

Getting Help We have tried to design this book to answer any questions you are likely to have. In addition, SAS Enterprise Guide has extensive built-in help (accessible via the Help menu). If you still have questions, you may want to contact SAS Technical Support. With some software companies, very little technical support is available, or the support is available but only for an extra charge—not so with SAS. All licensed SAS sites have access to SAS Technical Support.

There are several ways to contact SAS Technical Support, including via their Web site, **support.sas.com**, or via phone at (919) 677-8008. Before you contact SAS Technical Support you must know your site number and the version of SAS Enterprise Guide that you are running. To find these, start SAS Enterprise Guide and select **Help ▶ About SAS Enterprise Guide**. The About SAS Enterprise Guide window will open, displaying both the version of software and your site number.

About This Book

This book is divided into two distinct but complementary sections: a tutorials section and a reference section. Each tutorial is designed to give you a quick introduction to a general subject. The reference section, on the other hand, gives you focused information on specific topics.

Tutorials section If you are new to SAS Enterprise Guide, you'll probably want to start with the tutorials. Each of the four tutorials leads you step-by-step through a complete project, from starting SAS Enterprise Guide to documenting what you've done before you exit. The tutorials are self-contained so you can do them in any order. People who know nothing about SAS or SAS Enterprise Guide should be able to complete a tutorial in 30 to 45 minutes.

Reference section Once you feel comfortable with SAS Enterprise Guide, you'll be ready to use the reference section. This is where you'll turn when you need a quick refresher on how to join data tables, or a detailed explanation of filtering data in a query. With 12 chapters and 93 topics, the reference section covers more information than the tutorials, but each topic is covered in just two pages so you can read it in a few minutes.

The data for this book The data used for the examples in this book revolve around a theme: the Fire and Ice Tours company, a fictional company offering tours to volcanoes around the world. Using a small number of data sets over and over saves you from having to learn new data for every example. The data sets are small enough that you can type them in if you want to run the examples, but to make it even easier, the data are also available for downloading via the Internet. Appendix A contains both the data and instructions on how to download the data files.

Acknowledgments

How do you describe something that is dynamic and graphical with mere printed words and static screen shots? That's the fundamental challenge we have faced in writing this book. We have struggled at every point: finding the best and most useful features, discovering all those little points of confusion that are likely to trip up users of the software, and wrestling with sentences in an effort to express ideas clearly within the confines of a two-page format. Now that we are nearing the completion of this project, we offer this quote to describe our feelings:

Zounds! I was never so bethump'd with words.
William Shakespeare, King John

Fortunately, we've had plenty of help with those words. Among the many people we'd like to thank are our software installation team: David Gray, Chris Hemedinger, and Shelly Sessoms; our technical reviewers: Marilyn Adams, David Bailey, Marie Dexter, Paul Grant, Chris Hemedinger, Rich Papel, Stacey Syphus, Jennifer Tamburro, and Cynthia Zender; our technical publishing specialist, Candy Farrell; our designers: Patrice Cherry and Jennifer Dilley; our marketing specialists: Stacey Hamilton and Shelly Goodin; our copy editor, Kathy Underwood; our managing editor, Mary Beth Steinbach; and Julie Platt , Editor-in-Chief. All these people worked hard to ensure that this book is accurate and appealing. Special thanks go to Stephenie Joyner, our acquisitions editor.

And, as always, we thank our families for everything.

TUTORIALS SECTION

A

" Dimidium facti qui coepit habet. "

" What's well begun is half done. "

HORACE

From *Epistolae*, I. 2. 40, 20 BC. As quoted in *The Cyclopedia of Practical Quotations: English, Latin, and Modern Foreign Languages* by Jehiel Keeler Hoyt, 1896.

A ▶ Getting Started with SAS Enterprise Guide

This first tutorial will give you a basic understanding of how SAS Enterprise Guide works and how quickly tasks can be accomplished. The following topics will be covered:

- Starting SAS Enterprise Guide

- A quick tour of SAS Enterprise Guide windows

- Data types

- Entering data into the Data Grid

- Using SAS Enterprise Guide tasks

- Making changes to tasks

The data for this tutorial come from the Fire and Ice Tours company, a fictional company that arranges tours of volcanoes around the world. For each tour, the company keeps track of the name of the volcano, the city from which the tour departs, the number of days of the tour, and the price. Because the tours can require some physical exertion, the company gives each tour a difficulty rating: easy, moderate, or challenging.

Desktop

✓ Double-click SAS Enterprise Guide 4.2 icon

Starting SAS Enterprise Guide

Start SAS Enterprise Guide by either double-clicking the **SAS Enterprise Guide 4.2** icon on your desktop, or selecting **SAS Enterprise Guide 4.2** from the Windows **Start** menu. Starting SAS Enterprise Guide brings up the SAS Enterprise Guide windows in the background, with the Welcome window in the foreground. The Welcome window allows you to choose between opening an existing project or starting a new project. Click **New Project**.

SAS Enterprise Guide Projects

SAS Enterprise Guide organizes all your work into projects. You can work on only one project at a time, and each project is stored in a single file. A project will contain all the reports that you produce, plus shortcuts to all the data files that you use.

Welcome Window

✓ Click New Project

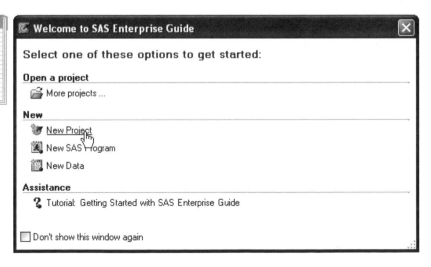

SAS Enterprise Guide
windows When you first start SAS Enterprise Guide, your screen should look something like the following. There are several parts to the SAS Enterprise Guide window: some are visible, while others may be hidden or temporarily closed.

Resetting the SAS Enterprise Guide Windows

Does your screen look like this? If not, it may be because someone has already used SAS Enterprise Guide on your computer, and made some changes to the initial settings. To reset the windows, select **Tools ▶ Options** from the menu bar. Then click **Restore Window Layout**.

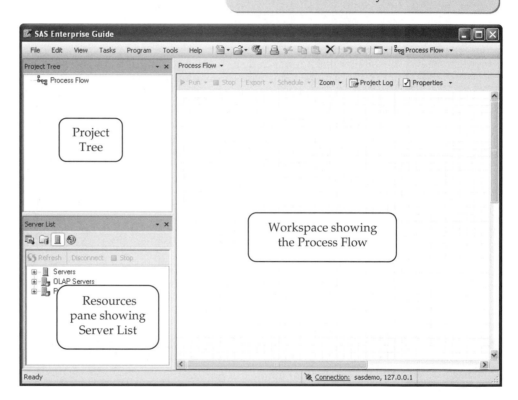

Basic elements of SAS Enterprise Guide

Project Tree: This window displays your project in a hierarchical tree diagram.

Workspace: This is a container for the Process Flow, results from tasks that you run, Data Grids, SAS code, SAS logs, and Notes.

Process Flow: This window displays a graphical representation of your project.

Resources pane: This pane shows either the Server List, Task List, SAS Folders, or Prompt Manager windows. The Server List window displays all the SAS servers that you can access during your SAS Enterprise Guide session. A SAS server is any computer on which SAS software is installed. The Task List displays all available tasks. The SAS Folders contain links to all your stored processes, information maps, and projects. The Prompt Manager displays all available prompts. To switch between the windows, click their icons at the top of the pane: ▯ for the Server List, 📠 for the Task List, 📁 for SAS Folders, or 🧩 for the Prompt Manager.

Task Status (not shown): When you are running a task, messages about the progress of the task appear in the Task Status window. To open the Task Status window, select **View ▶ Task Status** from the menu bar.

Entering data

There are many ways to get data into SAS Enterprise Guide, and SAS Enterprise Guide can use data from a variety of sources, including SAS data sets, Microsoft Excel files, and plain text files. For this example, you are simply going to type the data directly into SAS Enterprise Guide. To bring up the Data Grid so you can enter the data, select **File ▶ New ▶ Data** from the menu bar.

Menu Bar
✓ Select
File ▶ New ▶
Data

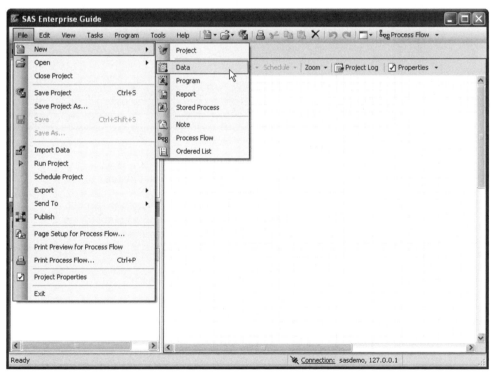

This opens the New Data wizard. In the first window of the wizard, SAS Enterprise Guide asks what you want to name the data table and where you want to save the data you are about to type. Initially, the location for the data table is set to the WORK library and the name is Data.

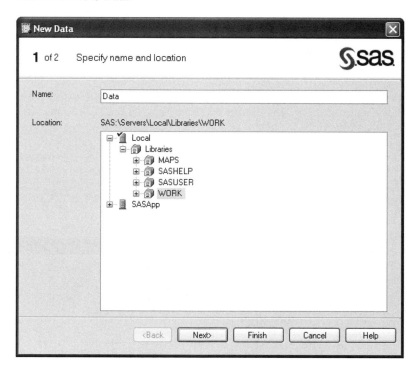

SAS Data Sets or SAS Data Tables?

A SAS data set and a SAS data table are the same thing. The two terms are used interchangeably, and you will see both terms used in this book.

Give the new data table the name Tours by typing **Tours** in the **Name** box. Then, because WORK is a temporary storage location, choose an alternate library. For this example, save the data in the SASUSER library. Click **SASUSER** to select the SASUSER library. The SAS Enterprise Guide administrator at your site may have set up the SASUSER library so that you cannot save files there. If this is the case for you, choose an alternate library that is available to you.

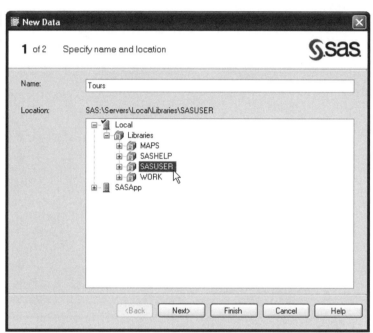

Click **Next** to open the second window of the New Data wizard.

Libraries

SAS Enterprise Guide and SAS organize SAS data sets into libraries. Libraries are locations, or folders, where data sets are stored. Instead of referring to the folders by their full path, SAS Enterprise Guide gives the folders short nicknames, called librefs. The WORK library points to a temporary storage location that is automatically erased when you exit SAS Enterprise Guide. The SASUSER library is a permanent storage location. If the EGTASK library is defined for your site, then data sets produced by tasks will be stored in the EGTASK library. If the EGTASK library is not defined, then data sets produced by tasks will be stored in the SASUSER library. Libraries can be created using the Assign Project Library task available from the Tools menu.

The second window of the New Data wizard is where you assign names and properties to the columns in your data table. As a starting point, the New Data wizard sets up six columns with one-letter names from A to F. All these initial columns have the same properties.

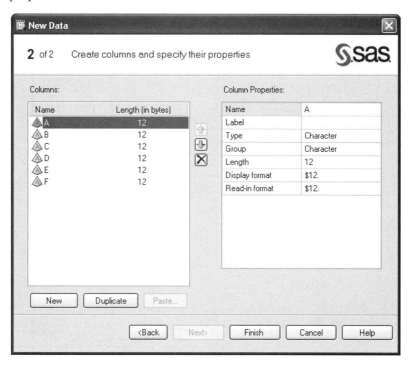

Column Names

You can give your columns almost any names you want, but the names must be 32 characters or fewer in length. While it is possible to have special characters (including spaces) in your names, you may want to stick with just letters, numerals, and underscores. These characters are all that are allowed under the default naming rules for SAS programs. In addition, names must start with a letter or underscore. Using these rules will make it easier if you ever want to refer to your data in SAS programs that you or someone else writes.

In the Column Properties box, you can assign each column a name, label, type, group, length, display format, and read-in format. The first column will contain the names of the volcanoes, so type **Volcano** in the box next to **Name**.

New Data
Wizard

✓ In Name
box, type
Volcano

✓ Press Enter

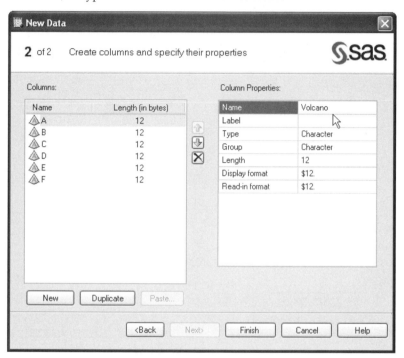

When you press **Enter**, the name you typed in the Name box will replace the name, in this case A, in the Columns box on the left. Because the names of the volcanoes contain characters, as opposed to numbers, leave the **Type** and **Group** properties as **Character**, and because none of the volcano names are longer than 12 characters, leave the **Length** set to **12**.

> ## Lengths of Character Columns
>
> The New Data wizard in SAS Enterprise Guide gives character columns a length of 12. If your character data are longer than 12 characters, you need to change the length of the column to be at least as long as the longest data value. When you do this, you also need to change the length of the display and read-in formats to match the length of the column. If all your data values are shorter than 12 characters, you can shorten the length for the column. Using shorter lengths for character data decreases the storage space needed for the data table. If you shorten the column length, make sure you also change the display and read-in formats to the same length.

Now click the column named **B** in the **Columns** box on the left. This column will contain the name of the departure city for the tour, so type the word **Departs** next to **Name** in the **Column Properties** box on the right. Leave the other settings as they are.

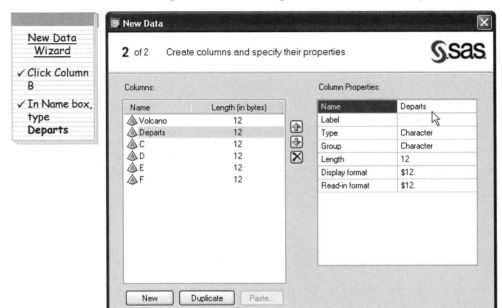

New Data
Wizard

✓ Click Column
B

✓ In Name box,
type
Departs

The third column contains the number of days the tour lasts. Give it the name **Days**, and because the values in this column are numbers, use the pull-down list to select **Numeric** for the **Type** property.

New Data Wizard

✓ Click Column C

✓ In Name box, type **Days**

✓ From Type list, select Numeric

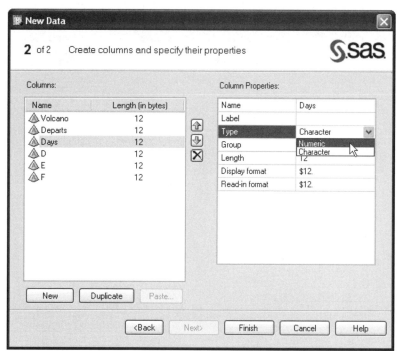

Notice that when you set the column type to numeric, the icon next to the column name changes from the red pyramid 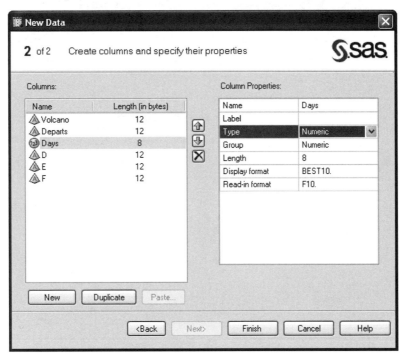 (character) to the blue ball ⑫ (numeric). The length of **8** is the default for all numeric columns and means that the numbers will be stored with maximum precision. Generally, there is no need to change the length of numeric columns.

Character versus Numeric

How do you decide if a column should be character or numeric? If the values for the column have letters or special characters in them, then the column must be character. If the column contains only numerals, then it could be either character or numeric. Generally, if it does not make sense to add or subtract the values, then the column should be character.

Name the fourth column **Price** and give it the type **Numeric**. When you choose the numeric type, you have several options for **Group**: numeric, date, time, and currency. Because Price will contain currency values, select the group **Currency**.

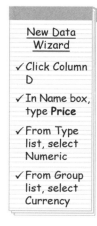

New Data
Wizard

✓ Click Column
D

✓ In Name box,
type **Price**

✓ From Type
list, select
Numeric

✓ From Group
list, select
Currency

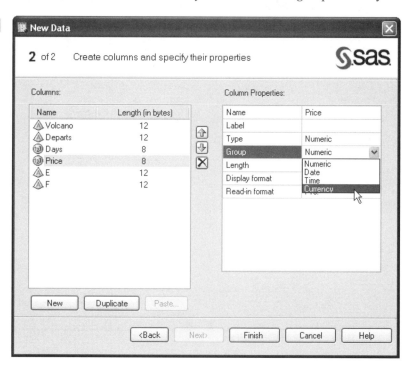

Numeric Groups

By choosing a group for your numeric column, what you are doing is assigning your column a format. A format is a way of displaying the values in the column. If you choose currency, then when you type a number like 1200, SAS Enterprise Guide will automatically display the number as $1,200. SAS Enterprise Guide has made it easy for you to assign some of the frequently used formats to your columns.

Notice that when you do this, the icon changes from the blue ball to the currency icon $¥/€.

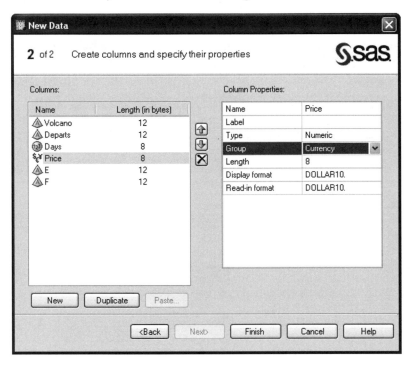

The final column will contain the difficulty ratings of each tour. The most challenging tours have values of **c**, the moderately challenging tours have values of **m**, while the easiest tours have values of **e**. Give the column the name **Difficulty** and select **Character** as the type.

New Data
Wizard

✓ Click Column
E

✓ In Name box,
type
Difficulty

✓ Press Enter

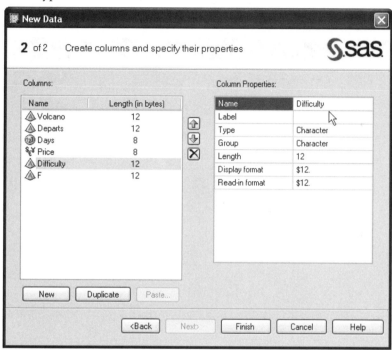

Now the properties for all the columns have been set. However, there is one extra column: column F. Delete the unnecessary column by clicking it in the **Columns** box and then clicking the delete button  to the right of the **Columns** box.

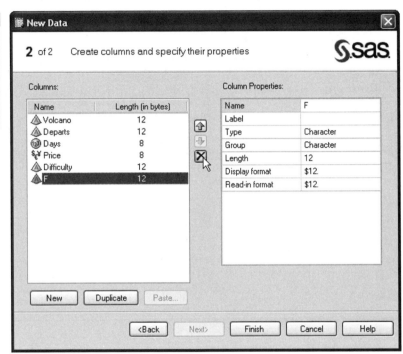

Now all the columns have been given names and properties, and there are no extra columns.

New Data
Wizard

✓Click Finish

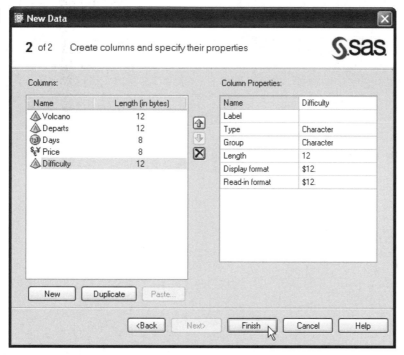

Click **Finish** to create the new data table. The Tours data table appears in a Data Grid in the workspace with all the columns that you just defined. There is also an icon for the Tours data table in the Project Tree under the words Process Flow.

Notice that the numeric columns, Days and Price, have periods in the data cells. This is because in SAS Enterprise Guide missing numeric values are represented by a single period, whereas missing character values are represented by blanks. Because no data have been entered into the Data Grid, all the values are missing.

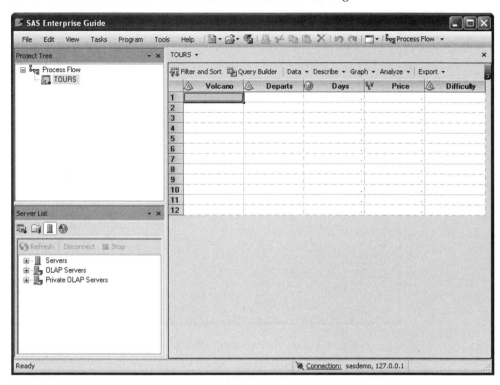

You can now start entering the data into the Data Grid. To enter data into the Data Grid, simply click a cell and start typing the data. Click the first cell in the **Volcano** column and type the volcano name **Etna**.

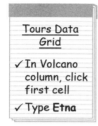

Tours Data Grid

✓ In Volcano column, click first cell

✓ Type **Etna**

	Volcano	Departs	Days	Price	Difficulty
1	Etna		.	.	
2			.	.	
3			.	.	
4			.	.	
5			.	.	
6			.	.	
7			.	.	
8			.	.	
9			.	.	
10			.	.	
11			.	.	
12			.	.	

TOURS ▾

Filter and Sort   Query Builder | Data ▾ Describe ▾ Graph ▾ Analyze ▾ | Export ▾

To move over to the next column, press the **Tab** key. To move down to the cell below, press the **Enter** key. You can also use the arrow keys to move around in the Data Grid, or you can simply click the cell where you want to type. Enter all the data for the volcano tours so that your Data Grid looks like the following. Notice that when you enter the data for the Price column, you do not need to enter the dollar signs and commas. Simply enter the numerals that make up the number, and then when you move on to another cell, SAS Enterprise Guide will give your number the proper formatting.

Tours Data Grid

✓ Enter data into columns

TOURS ▾

Filter and Sort   Query Builder | Data ▾ Describe ▾ Graph ▾ Analyze ▾ | Export ▾

	Volcano	Departs	Days	Price	Difficulty
1	Etna	Catania	7	$1,075	m
2	Fuji	Tokyo	2	$225	c
3	Kenya	Nairobi	6	$830	m
4	Kilauea	Hilo	1	$55	e
5	Kilimanjaro	Nairobi	9	$1,310	c
6	Krakatau	Jakarta	7	$895	e
7	Poas	San Jose	1	$65	e
8	Reventador	Quito	4	$575	m
9	St. Helens	Portland	2	$167	e
10	Vesuvius	Rome	6	$985	e
11			.	.	
12			.	.	

If you need to go back and make any changes, just click the cell and make the necessary changes.

By default, SAS Enterprise Guide provides 12 rows for data entry. If you have more than 12 rows of data, then you can press the **Enter** key from any cell in the last row and SAS Enterprise Guide will automatically generate a new blank row for you. Because there are only 10 tours in this data file, you will need to delete the two extra blank rows. If you don't delete the blank rows, then all the values for those rows will be missing and these missing values will appear in any report or analysis you perform. Highlight both blank rows by clicking row 11 and dragging the cursor to row 12. Then right-click one of the rows and select **Delete rows**.

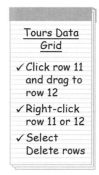

Tours Data Grid

✓ Click row 11 and drag to row 12

✓ Right-click row 11 or 12

✓ Select Delete rows

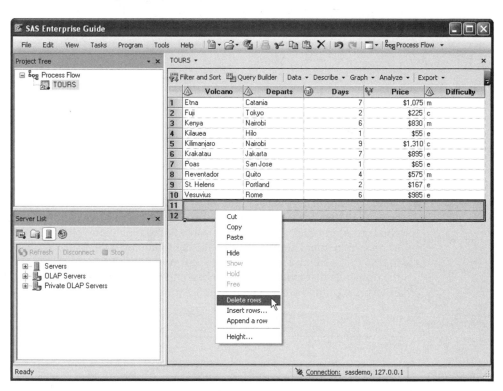

Confirm that you want to delete the rows by clicking **Yes** in the pop-up dialog box.

Delete Rows?

✓ Click Yes

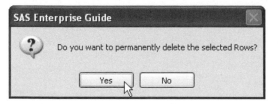

Now the Data Grid is completely filled without any extra rows or columns.

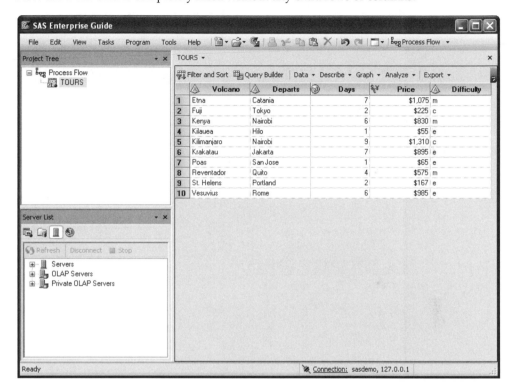

Creating a frequency report To create a simple frequency report that will show the number of easy, moderate, and challenging tours, use the One-Way Frequencies task. Select **Describe ▶ One-Way Frequencies** from the workspace toolbar located just above the data.

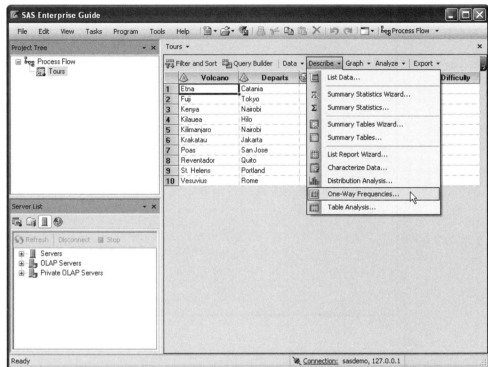

Opening Tasks and Wizards

You can open tasks by selecting them from the workspace toolbar of a Data Grid, the **Tasks** item on the menu bar, or the Task List window. Use whichever method feels more comfortable for you. In the tutorials, we describe how to open tasks using the workspace toolbar. But it's fine if you want to use the Task List or menu item instead.

Some tasks have wizards in addition to the regular task window. A wizard guides you through the task one window at a time and gives access to many of the features of the task. Not all tasks have wizards, but if a task does have a wizard, it will be listed next to the task in the pull-down list.

Because the data have just been entered into the Data Grid, the following dialog box appears.

Continue?

✓Click Yes

Data must be protected before you can perform any task on your data. Protecting the data ensures that the data cannot be accidentally changed. If your data are not protected, SAS Enterprise Guide will prompt you. Click **Yes**.

This opens the One-Way Frequencies task window, which has six pages: Data, Statistics, Plots, Results, Titles, and Properties. When you first open the task, the Data page will be displayed. All six pages for the task are listed in the selection pane on the left, with the displayed page highlighted.

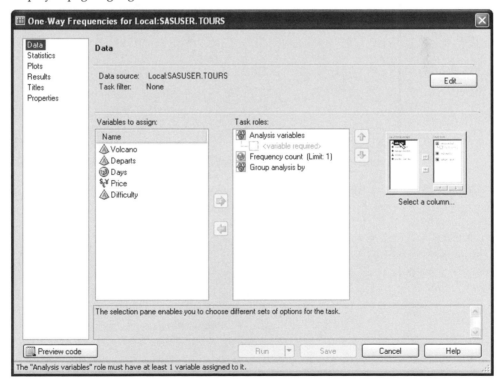

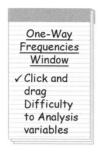

For most tasks that you perform in SAS Enterprise Guide, you will need to assign variables to roles. To produce a report with the number of tours in each category of the variable Difficulty, click the variable **Difficulty** and drag it to the **Analysis variables** role.

One-Way
Frequencies
Window

✓ Click and
  drag
  Difficulty
  to Analysis
  variables

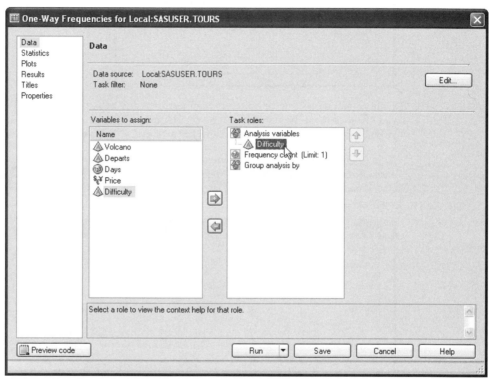

Click **Run** to run the task and produce your report.

One-Way
Frequencies
Window

✓ Click Run

Columns or Variables?

A column and a variable are the same thing. The two terms are used interchangeably, and you will see both terms used in SAS Enterprise Guide. For example, the One-Way Frequencies task uses the term "variable," while the Scatter Plot task uses the term "column." Just remember, a variable is a column, and a column is a variable.

Tutorial A

The results from the task appear in the workspace on the Results tab. Along with the Results tab, the task has also generated an Input Data tab, a Code tab, and a Log tab. The Input Data tab contains the data used in the task. The Code tab shows the SAS code generated by the task, and the Log tab shows the code along with any messages SAS produced while running the task. The results show that two tours are challenging, five are easy, and three are moderate.

Workspace
Toolbar

✓ Click Modify
Task

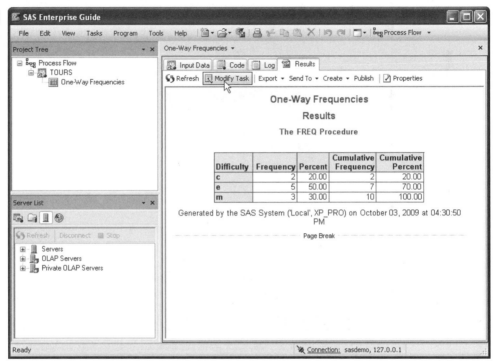

To make changes to the task and modify the results, click **Modify Task** on the workspace toolbar to reopen the task. This reopens the One-Way Frequencies task.

Workspace Toolbar

The workspace toolbar gives you quick access to many features you might want when viewing a particular item in the workspace. For example, the **Modify Task** button appears on the toolbar when you are viewing the results, log, or code for a task.

Notice that when you reopen the task, all the choices you made are still there. For this example, we are going to remove the cumulative statistics from the table, so click **Statistics** in the selection pane on the left to open the Statistics page.

One-Way
Frequencies
Window

✓Click
Statistics

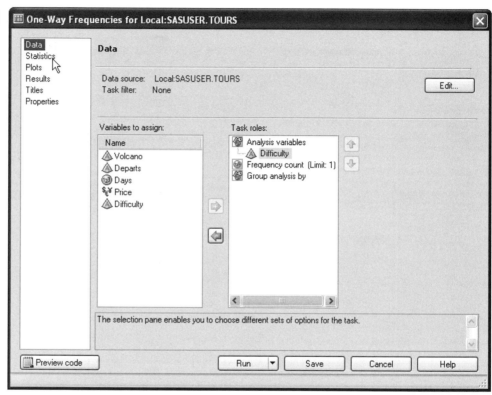

There are many options in the Statistics page. In the area labeled **Frequency table options**, you can choose which frequencies and percentages will appear in the table. By default, frequencies, percentages, cumulative frequencies, and cumulative percentages will appear in the table. To exclude the cumulative statistics, check **Frequencies and percentages**.

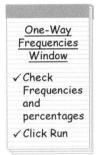

One-Way
Frequencies
Window

✓ Check
Frequencies
and
percentages

✓ Click Run

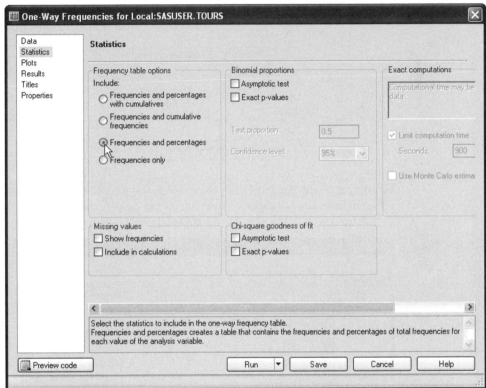

Rerun the task by clicking the **Run** button at the bottom of the window. When you do this, SAS Enterprise Guide gives you a choice. You can either replace the results that you generated the last time you ran the task, or you can create new results.

Replace
results?

✓ Click Yes

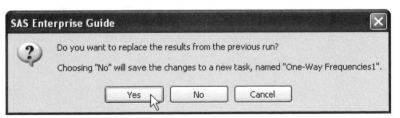

In this case, there is no reason to keep the old results, so click **Yes**.

Here are the results that will appear in the workspace showing just the frequencies and percentages without the cumulative statistics.

One-Way Frequencies
Results
The FREQ Procedure

Difficulty	Frequency	Percent
c	2	20.00
e	5	50.00
m	3	30.00

Generated by the SAS System ('Local', XP_PRO) on October 03, 2009 at 04:39:53 PM

———— Page Break ————

Creating a scatter plot To generate a scatter plot of the data, you will need to use a different task. First reopen the Tours data set to display the data. Right-click the **TOURS** data set icon in the Project Tree and select **Open TOURS**.

Project Tree
- ✓ Right-click TOURS icon
- ✓ Select Open TOURS

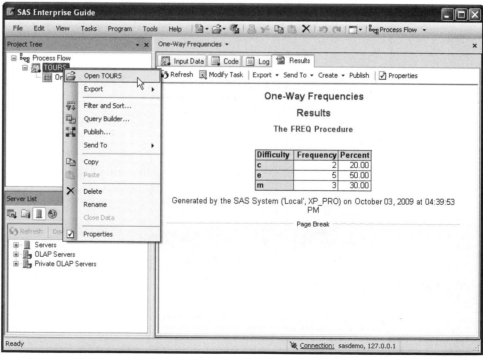

With the Tours data set open in the workspace, the workspace toolbar now shows menu items that apply to data. Select **Graph ▶ Scatter Plot.**

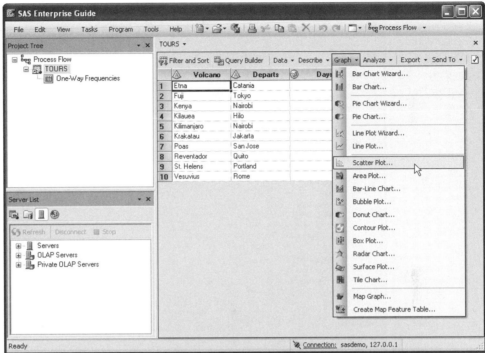

Opening Data Tables in the Workspace

There are several ways to display data tables in the workspace. You can right-click the data table icon in the Project Tree or Process Flow and select Open. You can double-click the data table icon in the Project Tree or Process Flow. Or, if you have run a task using the data, you can click the **Input Data** tab in the workspace to view the input data for the task.

This opens the Scatter Plot window. Before assigning roles to columns, you need to choose the type of scatter plot to produce. A simple two-dimensional scatter plot is appropriate for this report, so click **2D Scatter Plot**.

Scatter Plot
Window

✓ Click 2D
  Scatter Plot

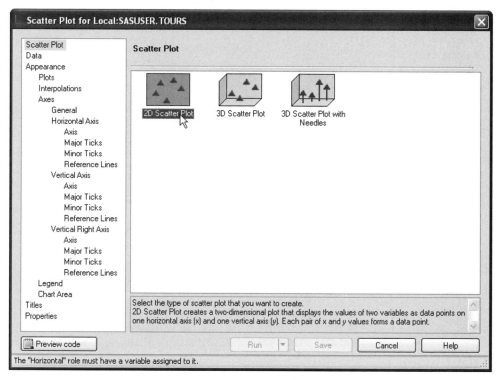

Next, click **Data** in the selection pane on the left to assign columns to roles.

Scatter Plot
Window

✓ Click Data

For this plot, the column Days should be on the horizontal axis, and the column Price on the vertical axis. So, click **Days** and drag it to the **Horizontal** task role, and click **Price** and drag it to the **Vertical** task role.

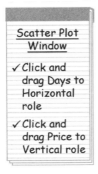

Scatter Plot Window

✓ Click and drag Days to Horizontal role

✓ Click and drag Price to Vertical role

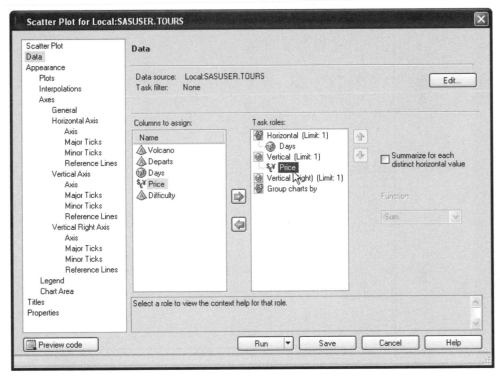

The Scatter Plot task has many groups of options, but to produce a simple plot, there is no need to change anything else. Click **Run**.

Scatter Plot Window

✓ Click Run

Here are the results of the Scatter Plot task that appear in the workspace.

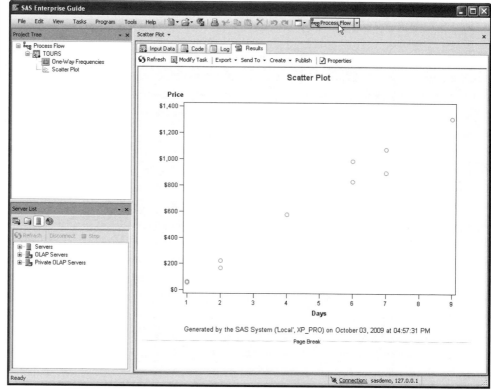

Now click **Process Flow** on the menu bar and take a look at the Process Flow.

Displaying the Process Flow

There are several ways to display the Process Flow in the workspace. You can select it from the Process Flow drop-down list on the menu bar, double-click its name in the Project Tree, select it from the **View** menu, select it from the drop-down list located above the workspace but below the main toolbar, or press **F4**.

Both the Project Tree and the Process Flow show the various parts of your project and how they are related. In the Process Flow, you can see that there are two arrows coming from the Tours data set. There is an arrow for the One-Way Frequencies task and one for the Scatter Plot task. Each task produces a report. The Process Flow makes it easy to see how the different parts of the project are related.

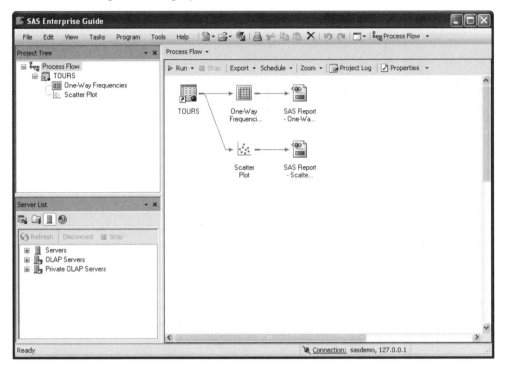

An alternate view of your project can be found in the Project Tree. The Project Tree displays the same elements as the Process Flow, except they are arranged in a hierarchical tree diagram. The Project Tree is always visible, but since the Process Flow is in the workspace, it sometimes gets displaced by other items.

Tutorial A

Project Tree

✓ Click
  Process Flow

Menu Bar

✓ Select
  File ▶ New
  ▶ Note

Adding a note to the project A nice feature of SAS Enterprise Guide is that you can add notes to your projects to document them. To add a note to the project, click the words **Process Flow** in the Project Tree so that the note will be associated with the entire process flow instead of a particular item. Then select **File ▶ New ▶ Note** from the menu bar.

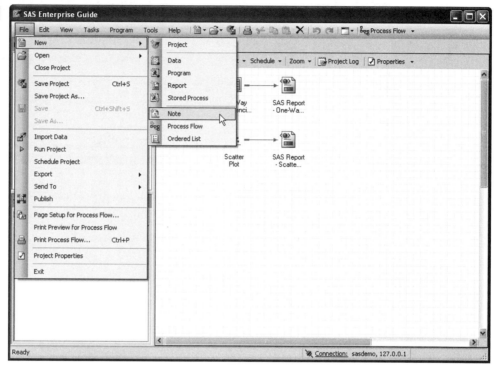

Enter a brief description of the project in the Note window that appears in the workspace.

Note

✓Type
descriptive
text

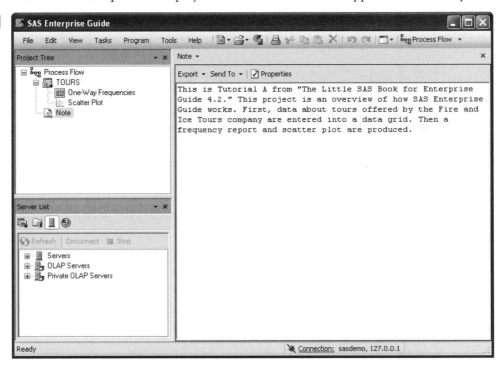

Saving the project SAS Enterprise Guide will always ask if you want to save any changes before allowing you to exit. Of course, you can save your work at any time before exiting. All the tasks created in your project, along with the results and any notes, are saved in the project. The data files are saved outside the project file—only the shortcuts to the data files are saved in the project. To save the project, select **File ▶ Save Project As** from the menu bar.

Menu Bar

✓ Select
File ▶ Save
Project As

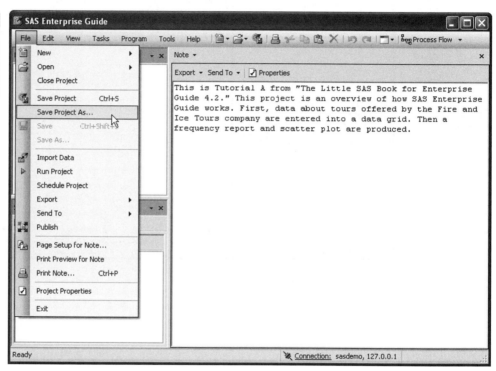

Navigate to the location where you want to save the project. Give the project the filename **TutorialA** and click **Save**.

Now you can exit SAS Enterprise Guide and all your work and data will be saved. From the menu bar, select **File ▶ Exit** to exit SAS Enterprise Guide and complete the first tutorial.

B

" The obvious is that which
is never seen until someone
expresses it simply. "

KAHLIL GIBRAN

From *Sand and Foam: A Book of Aphorisms*, 1926.

B ▶ Creating Reports

In this tutorial, you will create a basic report using the List Data task. Then using several of the options in the List Data task, you will make modifications to the report. Also, you will learn ways of formatting data that apply to most tasks. Here are the topics covered in this tutorial:

- Creating list reports

- Titles, footnotes, and labels

- Display formats

- User-defined formats

- Styles

- Result types

Desktop

✓ Double-click SAS Enterprise Guide 4.2 icon

Before beginning this tutorial This tutorial uses the Tours data set, which contains information about the volcano tours offered by the Fire and Ice Tours company. The Tours data set is created as part of Tutorial A. If you did not complete Tutorial A, see Appendix A for the data and instructions for downloading the Tours data set.

Starting SAS Enterprise Guide Start SAS Enterprise Guide by either double-clicking the **SAS Enterprise Guide 4.2** icon on your desktop, or selecting **SAS Enterprise Guide 4.2** from the Windows **Start** menu. Starting SAS Enterprise Guide brings up the SAS Enterprise Guide windows in the background, with the Welcome window in the foreground. The Welcome window allows you to choose between opening an existing project or starting a new project. Click **New Project**.

Welcome Window

✓ Click New Project

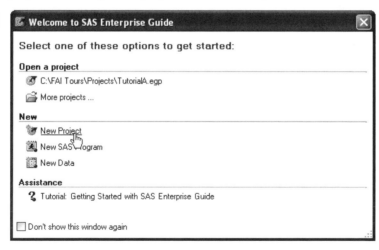

Opening the Tours data set Open the Tours data set created in Tutorial A by selecting **File ▶ Open ▶ Data** from the menu bar.

Menu Bar

✓ Select
File ▶ Open ▶
Data

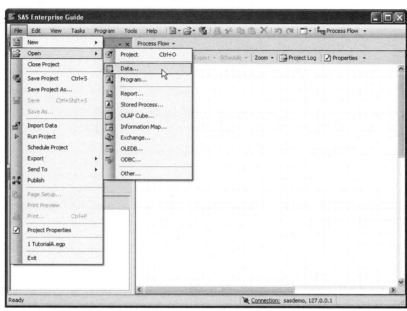

This opens the Open Data window. In the panel on the left, you can choose to open files from your Local Computer, Servers, or SAS Folders. The Tours data set from Tutorial A was stored in the SASUSER library. The easiest way to access SAS libraries in the Open Data window is through the servers view, so click **Servers**. The servers view shows two servers (you may have additional servers, or only one), Local and SASApp.

Open Data
Window

✓ Click
  Servers

✓ Click Local

✓ Click Open

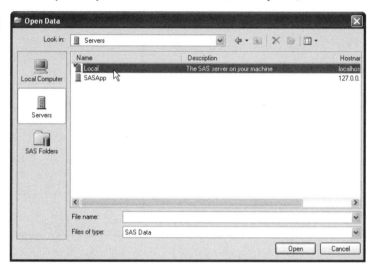

Then click **Local** to select it (if your SASUSER library is not on your local computer, then choose the appropriate server), and click **Open**.

Open Data
Window

✓ Click
  Libraries

✓ Click Open

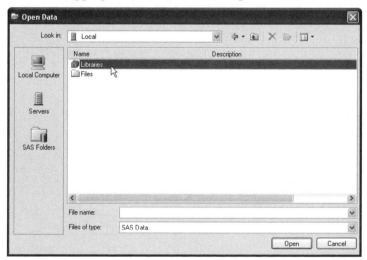

Click **Libraries**, then click **Open** to display all the defined SAS libraries for your computer.

Tutorial B

There are four libraries defined in this example: MAPS, SASHELP, SASUSER, and WORK. You may have additional libraries defined.

Open Data
Window

✓ Click
SASUSER

✓ Click Open

Click **SASUSER,** then click **Open** to view the data sets in the SASUSER library.

Open Data
Window

✓ Select
Tours

✓ Click Open

Select the **Tours** data set and click **Open**. You may have additional data sets in your SASUSER library.

After you open the Tours data set, your screen should look like the following.

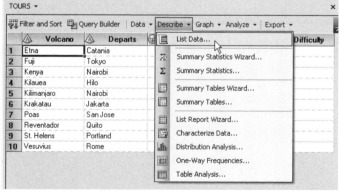

Creating a simple report To produce a price list of all the tours offered by the Fire and Ice Tours company, use the List Data task. Select **Describe ▶ List Data** from the workspace toolbar for the Tours data set.

Workspace
Toolbar

✓ Select
  Describe ▶
  List Data

This opens the List Data window. Before doing anything else, you need to assign variables to task roles. For a price list, all the variables in the data set should be listed, so assign all the variables to the **List variables** role. You can drag each variable separately, or you can highlight all the variables, and then drag the group to the List variables role. The order of the variables under List variables will be the order that the variables will appear in the report. To change the order, click and drag the variables up or down the list, or highlight the variable and use the up or down arrow buttons next to the **Task roles** box.

List Data
Window

✓ Drag
variables to
List variables
role

✓ Click Run

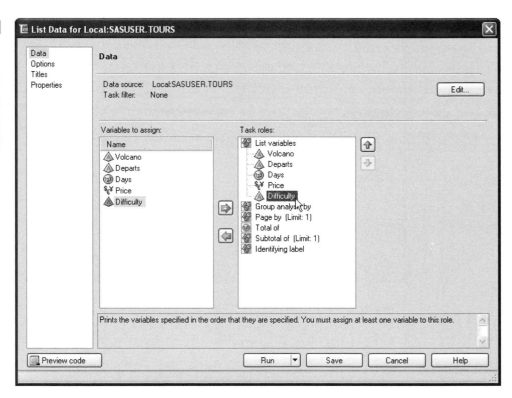

When you have all the variables under List variables in the proper order, click **Run**.

This produces a list of all the data in the Tours data set with some simple formatting. The result appears in the workspace, and, by default, the result will be in SAS Report format.

Report Listing

Row number	Volcano	Departs	Days	Price	Difficulty
1	Etna	Catania	7	$1,075	m
2	Fuji	Tokyo	2	$225	c
3	Kenya	Nairobi	6	$830	m
4	Kilauea	Hilo	1	$55	e
5	Kilimanjaro	Nairobi	9	$1,310	c
6	Krakatau	Jakarta	7	$895	e
7	Poas	San Jose	1	$65	e
8	Reventador	Quito	4	$575	m
9	St. Helens	Portland	2	$167	e
10	Vesuvius	Rome	6	$985	e

Generated by the SAS System ('Local', XP_PRO) on July 18, 2009 at 01:53:03 PM

························· Page Break ·························

SAS Report Results Format

SAS Report Format is a special format that can be used to generate custom reports. These reports can combine multiple results, text, and images. Elements from results in SAS Report format can also be copied and pasted into other applications such as Microsoft Word and Excel.

Tutorial B

Changing titles and footnotes The report contains all the information needed for the price list, but it could use some improvements. There are many parts of this simple listing that can be changed to meet specific needs. The first change to be made is to edit the title and footnote for the report. To change the titles and footnotes, reopen the List Data task by clicking **Modify Task** on the workspace toolbar for the results.

Workspace Toolbar

✓Click Modify Task

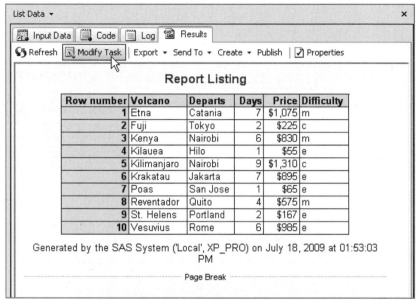

Reopening Tasks

There are several ways you can reopen tasks to make modifications. You can click **Modify Task** on the workspace toolbar for the task result, or you can right-click the task icon in either the Process Flow or the Project Tree and select **Modify *task-name*** from the pop-up window.

**List Data
Window**

✓Click Titles

Click **Titles** in the list of options in the selection pane on the left of the List Data window. You can make changes to both the titles and the footnotes in this window. When you click **Report Titles** in the box labeled **Section**, the current title is displayed in the box on the right side of the window. SAS Enterprise Guide has default text it will use for your report for both titles and footnotes. To change the title for your report, uncheck the box to the left of **Use default text**. Now you can edit the default text that SAS Enterprise Guide supplied. Delete the default text and replace it with **Fire and Ice Tours** on one line, followed by **Price List** on the second line. This produces a two-line title with both lines centered at the top of the report.

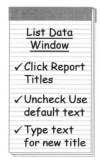

**List Data
Window**

✓Click Report
Titles

✓Uncheck Use
default text

✓Type text
for new title

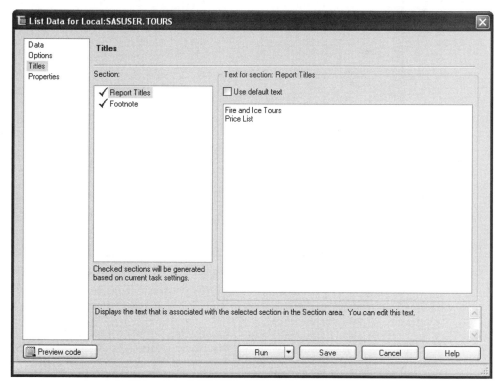

To make changes to the footnote, click **Footnote** in the box labeled **Section**.

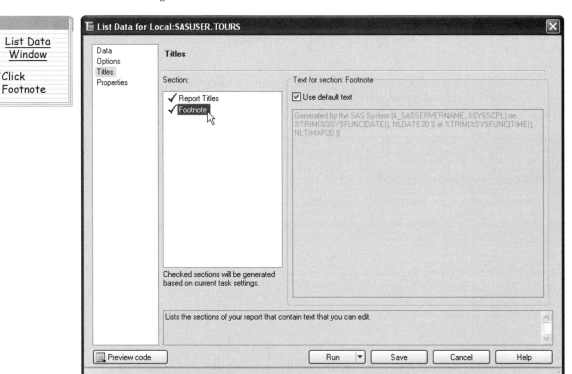

Why Does the Default Footnote Text Look So Odd?

If you take a close look at the default text for the footnote, you will notice that it does not look much like the footnote that appears at the bottom of your reports. The default text contains calls to SAS macros (starting with %) and macro variables (starting with &). These calls generate the actual text for the footnote, and the text that is generated depends on the date and time the report was produced, and the name and type of SAS server that generated the report. You can change the default footnote text by selecting **Tools ▶ Options** from the menu bar and selecting the **Tasks General** page. Enter the desired text in the **Default footnote text for task output** box. Then all tasks run after this change will have the new footnote text, even if you open a new project.

Change the footnote the same way you changed the title. Uncheck **Use default text**. Then because no footnote is necessary for this report, simply delete the text that SAS Enterprise Guide supplied.

List Data Window

✓ Uncheck Use default text

✓ Delete text

✓ Click Run

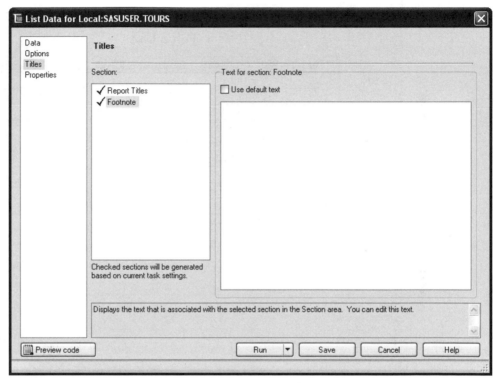

Click **Run** to produce a revised report with a new title and no footnote. When SAS Enterprise Guide asks if you want to replace the previous results, click **Yes**.

Replace Results?

✓ Click Yes

Tutorial B

The following report will appear in the workspace. Note the new title and the lack of a footnote.

Fire and Ice Tours
Price List

Row number	Volcano	Departs	Days	Price	Difficulty
1	Etna	Catania	7	$1,075	m
2	Fuji	Tokyo	2	$225	c
3	Kenya	Nairobi	6	$830	m
4	Kilauea	Hilo	1	$55	e
5	Kilimanjaro	Nairobi	9	$1,310	c
6	Krakatau	Jakarta	7	$895	e
7	Poas	San Jose	1	$65	e
8	Reventador	Quito	4	$575	m
9	St. Helens	Portland	2	$167	e
10	Vesuvius	Rome	6	$985	e

Page Break

Workspace
Toolbar

✓ Click Modify
Task

Changing column labels and formatting values To make more changes to the report, open the List Data task window again by clicking **Modify Task** on the workspace toolbar for the results. Click **Options** in the selection pane on the left. By default, SAS Enterprise Guide will show the row number in the report and give it the label Row number. You can choose not to show the row numbers by unchecking **Print the row number**. For this report, keep the row numbers, but replace the label for the column heading with the word **Tour**.

List Data
Window

✓ Click Options

✓ Type **Tour**
in Column
heading box

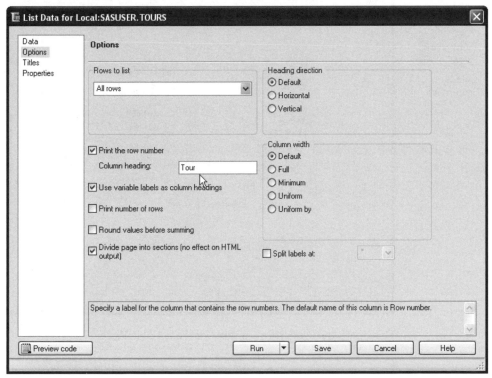

Tutorial B

Now click **Data** in the selection pane on the left. Each variable in the task has properties associated with it and you can make changes to the properties. Right-click the variable **Price** and select **Properties** from the pop-up menu.

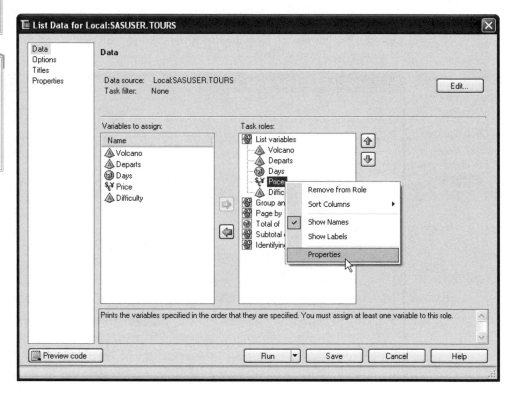

This opens the Properties window for the variable Price.

There are six properties listed in the Properties window, two of which you can change in the window: the Label and the Format. Changes that you make in this window will affect only the results of the List Data task. The changes are not stored with the data. The Label is text that can be used for labeling the variable in the report. If the variable does not have a label, then SAS Enterprise Guide will use the variable's name as a label. Give the variable Price the label "Price USD" by typing **Price USD** in the box next to the word **Label**.

Properties
Window

✓ Type **Price USD**

✓ Click Change

The current format for Price is the DOLLAR10. format. Click **Change** to change the format for Price. This opens the Formats window.

Formats determine how values for the variable will be displayed. The format DOLLAR10. that was assigned to Price displays values with dollar signs and commas. The number at the end of the format name determines how many spaces to allow for the value, including any commas, decimal places, and dollar signs. If decimal places are to be displayed, then the number of decimals follows the period at the end of the format name. Because there is no number after the period in the DOLLAR10. format, no decimal places will be displayed. Change the number of decimal places displayed for Price to **2** in the box next to **Decimal places**. Notice that when you do this, an example of how values will be displayed using this format appears at the bottom of the Formats window.

Formats
Window

✓ Change
Decimal
places to 2

✓ Click OK

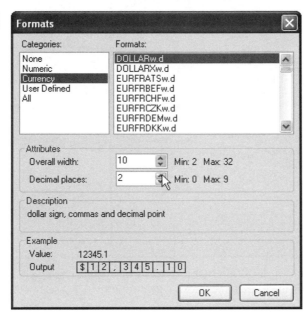

Click **OK** to close the Formats window.

Now Price has a label and will be formatted with the DOLLAR10.2 format.

Properties
Window

✓Click OK

Price Properties ⊠

General

$¥€ Price

Label:	Price USD ⌄
Type:	Currency
Length:	8
Format:	DOLLAR10.2 [Change...]
Informat:	DOLLAR10.
Sorted:	No

[OK] [Cancel]

List Data
Window

✓Click Run

Click **OK** to close the Properties window, and then click **Run** in the List Data window.

Select **Yes** when SAS Enterprise Guide asks if you want to replace the previous results.

Replace
Results?

✓Click Yes

The following report will appear in the workspace. Notice the column heading for the row number and the Price variable, and that the values for Price are now displayed in dollars and cents.

Fire and Ice Tours
Price List

Tour	Volcano	Departs	Days	Price USD	Difficulty
1	Etna	Catania	7	$1,075.00	m
2	Fuji	Tokyo	2	$225.00	c
3	Kenya	Nairobi	6	$830.00	m
4	Kilauea	Hilo	1	$55.00	e
5	Kilimanjaro	Nairobi	9	$1,310.00	c
6	Krakatau	Jakarta	7	$895.00	e
7	Poas	San Jose	1	$65.00	e
8	Reventador	Quito	4	$575.00	m
9	St. Helens	Portland	2	$167.00	e
10	Vesuvius	Rome	6	$985.00	e

Page Break

Defining your own formats Many different formats come with SAS Enterprise Guide, but sooner or later you will have a particular need for which there is no format defined. Fortunately, SAS Enterprise Guide provides a way for you to create your own formats. This type of format is called a user-defined format. For example, the variable **Difficulty** has coded values of c, e, and m. These single-letter values are too cryptic for a price list; it would be better to spell out the values: Challenging, Easy, and Moderate. To create a user-defined format, select **Tasks ▸ Data ▸ Create Format** from the menu bar to open the Create Format window.

Menu Bar

✓ Select
  Tasks ▸
  Data ▸
  Create
  Format

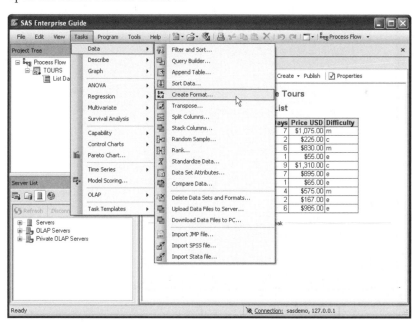

Tutorial B

Location for Storing Formats

Formats can be temporary or permanent. If they are temporary, they are stored in the WORK library and are automatically deleted when you exit SAS Enterprise Guide. If you have a temporary format in your project that you want to use, then you will need to rerun the Create Format task every time you open SAS Enterprise Guide. You can save a format permanently by choosing a library other than WORK. Then the format will not only be available for the project in which it was created, it will also be available for other projects. If you have access to more than one SAS server, store the format on the same server that is used for the task. To see which server is used for a task, place the cursor over the task icon in the Process Flow and the server name will be displayed in the pop-up window. The server is also displayed in the Properties window for the task.

Give the format a name by typing **Diff** in the box under **Format name**. Because this format will be used for a character variable, leave the **Format type** as **Character**.

Create Format
Window

✓ Type **Diff**

✓ Click Define
formats

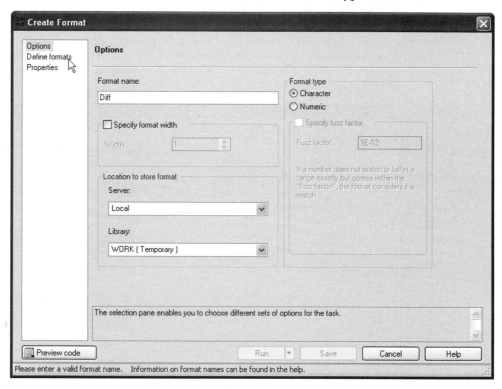

Click **Define formats** in the selection pane on the left to set values and ranges for the format.

Format Names

Character format names must be 31 characters or fewer in length, while numeric format names must be 32 characters or fewer. For both format types, names must contain only letters, numerals, or underscores, and cannot start or end with a numeral.

There are instructions in this window telling you how to define your format. First, click **New Label** and type **Easy** in the box under the word **Label** in the Label definition portion of the window. As you type the label, the label appears in the Label box at the top of the window.

Create Format
Window

✓ Click New
  Label

✓ Type **Easy**

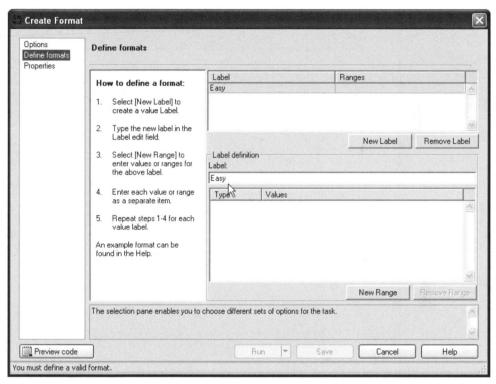

Next click **New Range**. In the box under **Values**, type the lowercase letter **e**, which is the value to be associated with the label Easy. When you enter text values, it is important that the case of the text matches the case of the actual value. Character formats are case sensitive. As you type the value, it will appear in the Ranges box at the top of the window, beside the label Easy.

Create Format
Window

✓ Click New
Range

✓ Type **e**

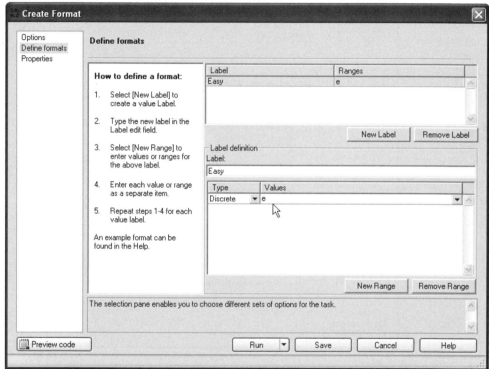

Multiple Ranges for a Label

You can enter more than one range for a label by clicking **New Range** again before adding another new label. For example, you might want the months SEP, OCT, and NOV to all be given the label Fall (or Spring if you are in the southern hemisphere). If you have a consecutive range of values that should all have the same label, then select **Range** from the **Type** drop-down list. For example, you might want the values 13 to 19 to all have the label Teenager. If your format is character and you use the Range type, then all values that fall alphabetically between the end points of the range will be included.

Now add labels for the other two values, m and c. Click **New Label** and type **Moderate** in the box under the word **Label** in the Label definition portion of the window. Click **New Range** and in the box under **Values**, type the letter **m**. Next click **New Label** and type **Challenging** in the box under **Label** in the Label definition portion of the window. Click **New Range** and type the letter **c** in the box under **Values**.

Create Format Window

✓ Create labels for m and c ranges

✓ Click Run

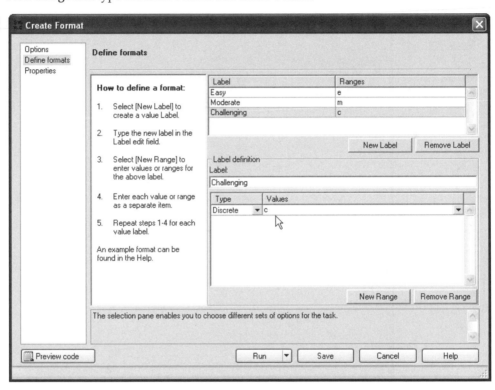

When you have all the labels and ranges defined, click **Run**.

Since there is no output from the Create Format task, after running, the SAS log is displayed in the workspace. Click **Process Flow** on the menu bar to view the Process Flow. An icon for the Create Format task appears in the Project Tree and the Process Flow. Notice that the Create Format task is not connected to anything in the Process Flow, and nothing in the report changed.

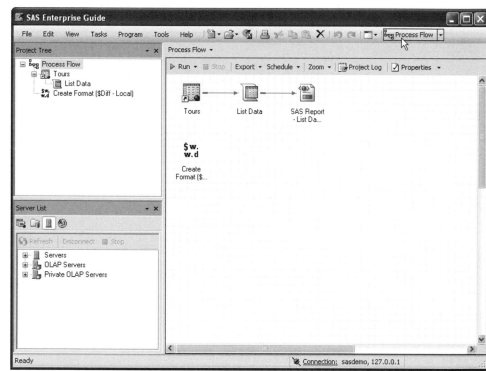

You created the format, but the format has not been associated with any variables yet. To associate the new format with the Difficulty variable, reopen the List Data window by right-clicking the **List Data** icon in the Project Tree or Process Flow and selecting **Modify List Data**. Then right-click the **Difficulty** variable and select **Properties**.

Project Tree
- ✓ Right-click List Data icon
- ✓ Select Modify List Data

List Data Window
- ✓ Right-click Difficulty
- ✓ Select Properties

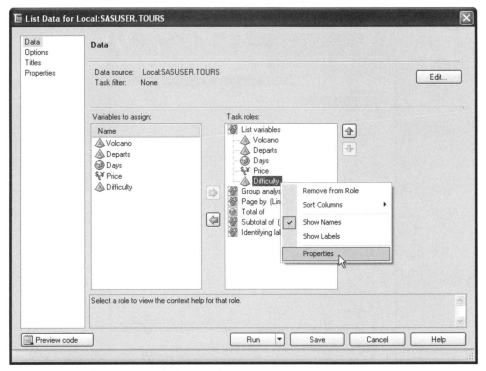

This opens the Properties window for the variable Difficulty.

Properties Window
- ✓ Click Change

Click **Change** to open the Formats window.

Tutorial B

From the **Categories** list, select **User Defined**. Any formats defined in the current SAS Enterprise Guide session or any formats that have been saved in a permanent location appear in the list of formats. The format $DIFF. should be in your list and you may or may not have additional formats. The $ in the format name indicates that the format is for character values. Click the **$DIFF.** format.

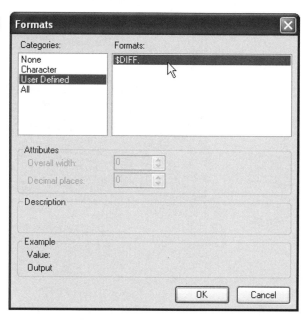

Click **OK** to close the Formats window, and then click **OK** again in the Properties window to return to the List Data window. Click **Run** in the List Data window, and click **Yes** to replace the previous results.

The following report will appear in the workspace, showing the formatted values for the Difficulty variable.

Fire and Ice Tours
Price List

Tour	Volcano	Departs	Days	Price USD	Difficulty
1	Etna	Catania	7	$1,075.00	Moderate
2	Fuji	Tokyo	2	$225.00	Challenging
3	Kenya	Nairobi	6	$830.00	Moderate
4	Kilauea	Hilo	1	$55.00	Easy
5	Kilimanjaro	Nairobi	9	$1,310.00	Challenging
6	Krakatau	Jakarta	7	$895.00	Easy
7	Poas	San Jose	1	$65.00	Easy
8	Reventador	Quito	4	$575.00	Moderate
9	St. Helens	Portland	2	$167.00	Easy
10	Vesuvius	Rome	6	$985.00	Easy

Page Break

Selecting a style for the report Every report that you produce in SAS Enterprise Guide has a style associated with it (except for results produced in text format which have no style). All the reports that you have produced so far have been in SAS Report format, and the default style for SAS Report results is Analysis. The style of the report includes the color scheme, fonts, and the size and style of the font. You do not have to use the default style for your reports. SAS Enterprise Guide comes with many different styles for you to choose from, and if you can't find one that suits your needs, you can create your own.

To change the report style for SAS Report (and HTML) results, click **Properties** on the workspace toolbar for the List Report results.

Workspace
Toolbar

✓Click
Properties

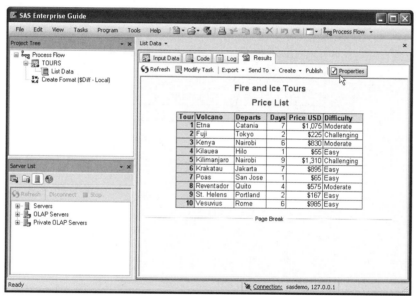

Changing the Default Style Used for SAS Enterprise Guide

If you find a style that you want to use for all your SAS Enterprise Guide projects, you can set it to be the default. Select **Tools ▶ Options** from the menu bar. In the selection pane on the left, select a result format: SAS Report, HTML, RTF, or PDF. Then select the style from the **Style** drop-down list.

This opens the Properties window for the SAS Report results created from the List Data task. Select the **BarrettsBlue** style from the drop-down **Style** menu.

Properties for
SAS Report
Window

✓ Select
BarrettsBlue
from Style
drop-down
menu

✓ Click OK

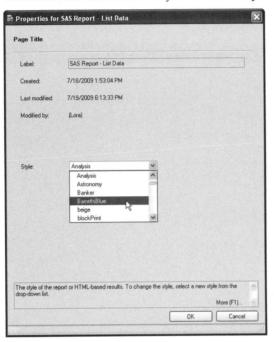

Click **OK**. Your report should look like the following, except that yours will be in shades of blue.

Fire and Ice Tours
Price List

Tour	Volcano	Departs	Days	Price USD	Difficulty
1	Etna	Catania	7	$1,075.00	Moderate
2	Fuji	Tokyo	2	$225.00	Challenging
3	Kenya	Nairobi	6	$830.00	Moderate
4	Kilauea	Hilo	1	$55.00	Easy
5	Kilimanjaro	Nairobi	9	$1,310.00	Challenging
6	Krakatau	Jakarta	7	$895.00	Easy
7	Poas	San Jose	1	$65.00	Easy
8	Reventador	Quito	4	$575.00	Moderate
9	St. Helens	Portland	2	$167.00	Easy
10	Vesuvius	Rome	6	$985.00	Easy

Page Break

Tutorial B

Workspace
Toolbar

✓Click Modify
Task

Changing the output format for the report So far all the results we have produced have been in the SAS Report format. But you can also produce results in HTML, RTF, PDF, or text format. Reopen the List Data task by clicking **Modify Task** on the workspace toolbar for the List Data result. Then click **Properties** in the selection pane on the left.

List Data
Window

✓Click
Properties

✓Click Edit

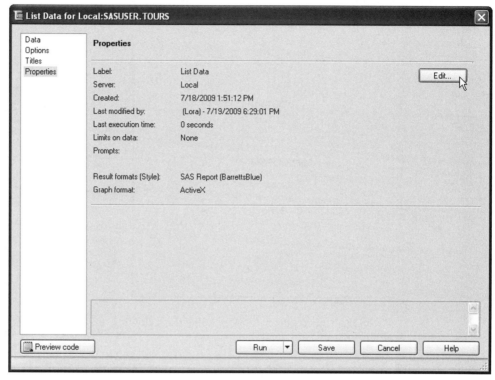

Click **Edit** to make changes to the properties of the task.

This opens the Properties window for the List Data task. Click **Results** in the selection pane on the left. On the Results page you can choose from several different result formats, as well as choose alternate styles for the task result. Click the box next to SAS Report to turn off the SAS Report result format, then check PDF.

Properties for
List Data
Window

✓ Click Results

✓ Uncheck
  SAS Report

✓ Check PDF

✓ Click OK

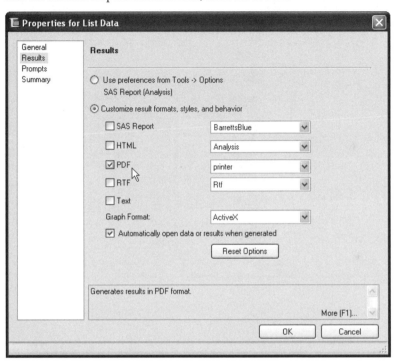

Click **OK** to close the Properties window, click **Run** in the List Data window, and click **Yes** to replace the previous results.

List Data
Window

✓ Click Run

Replace
Results?

✓ Click Yes

> **Choosing Default or Custom Result Formats and Styles**
>
> To use the default format and style, check **Use preferences from Tools -> Options** in the Results page of the Properties window for the task. To customize the format and style for the result of the task, check **Customize result formats, styles, and behavior**. Because we already changed the style for this task, the results are customized. Normally, if no changes were made to the task formats or styles, **Use preferences from Tools -> Options** will be checked.

If the results do not appear in the workspace, click the **Results** tab to view the PDF results.

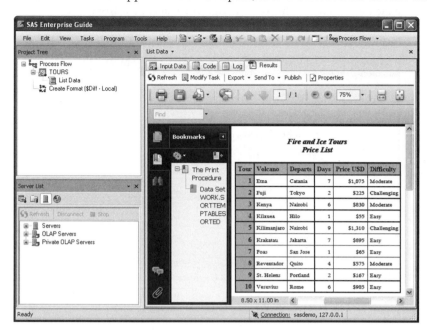

Completing the tutorial To complete the tutorial, add a note to the project with a project description. Click **Process Flow** in the Project Tree, and then select **File ▶ New ▶ Note** from the menu bar. Enter a brief description of the project in the Note window that appears in the workspace.

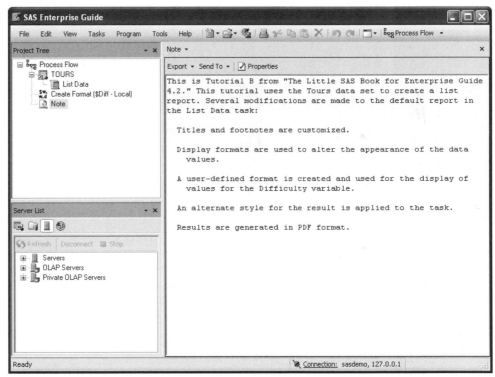

Now save the project and exit SAS Enterprise Guide. Select **File ▶ Save Project As** from the menu bar. Navigate to the location where you want to save the project, give the project the name **TutorialB**, and click **Save**. Select **File ▶ Exit** from the menu bar to close SAS Enterprise Guide.

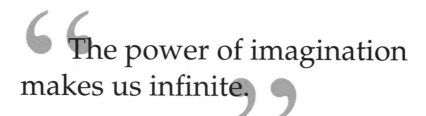

"The power of imagination makes us infinite."

JOHN MUIR

From *John of the Mountains: The Unpublished Journals of John Muir*, 1938.

Working with Data in the Query Builder

Often the data tables you have are not exactly what you want. You may need to compute a new column based on existing columns, or you may need just part of the data table for your analysis. Using SAS Enterprise Guide, there are many ways in which you can manipulate your data. This tutorial covers the following topics in the Query Builder:

- Selecting columns

- Using the Expression Editor to create new columns

- Filtering rows

- Sorting data

Before beginning this tutorial This tutorial uses the Volcanoes SAS data table, which contains information about volcanoes around the world. The data and instructions for downloading the file can be found in Appendix A.

Starting SAS Enterprise Guide Start SAS Enterprise Guide by either double-clicking the **SAS Enterprise Guide 4.2** icon on your desktop, or selecting **SAS Enterprise Guide 4.2** from the Windows **Start** menu. Starting SAS Enterprise Guide brings up the SAS Enterprise Guide windows in the background, with the Welcome window in the foreground. The Welcome window allows you to choose between opening an existing project or starting a new project. Click **New Project**.

Desktop

✓ Double-click SAS Enterprise Guide 4.2 icon

Welcome Window

✓ Click New Project

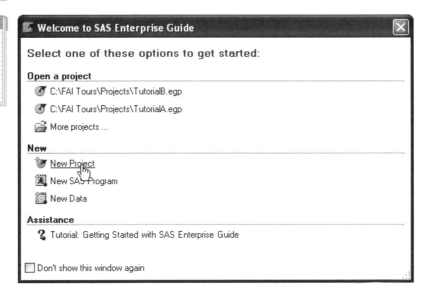

This opens an empty SAS Enterprise Guide window.

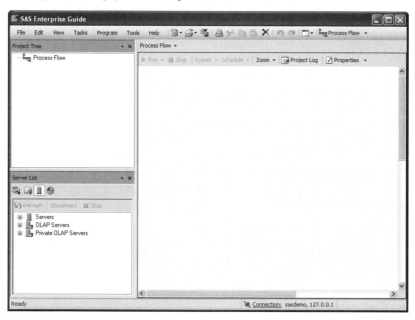

Opening the Volcanoes SAS data table Open the Volcanoes SAS data table by
selecting **File ▶ Open ▶ Data** from the menu bar. Because the Volcanoes data table is not
stored in a defined SAS library, click **Local Computer** in the selection pane on the left.

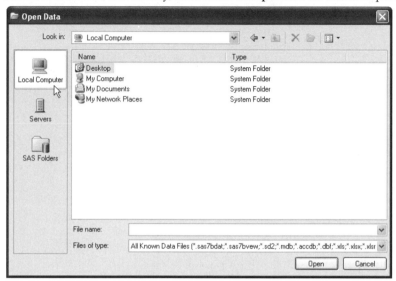

Navigate to the location where you stored the Volcanoes file and click on its name to
select it.

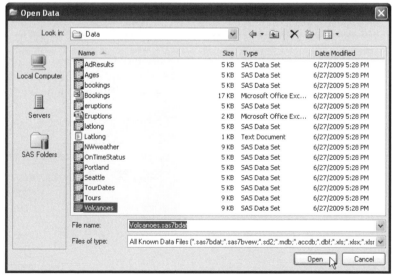

Click **Open**.

After you open the Volcanoes SAS data table, your screen should look like the following.

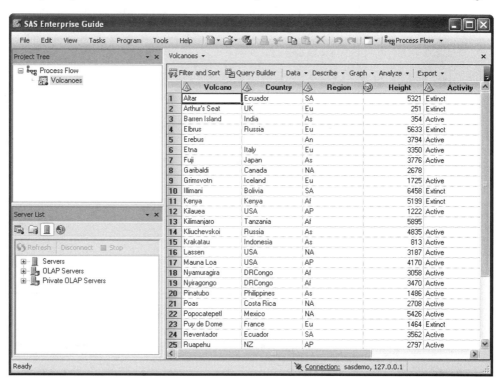

Opening the Query Builder The Query Builder is a powerful tool for data manipulation. In the Query Builder, you can filter and sort data, create new columns, and join tables. To open the Query Builder, click **Query Builder** on the workspace toolbar for the Volcanoes data table.

Workspace
Toolbar

✓ Click Query
Builder

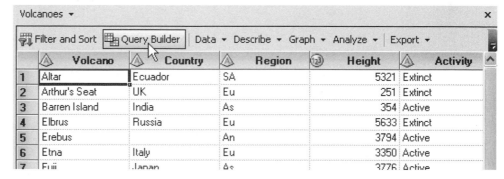

The Query Builder window has three tabs for different tasks: Select Data, Filter Data, and Sort Data. In addition, there are several buttons including Add Tables, Delete, Join Tables, Computed Columns, and Prompt Manager. So, you can see there is a lot going on in the Query Builder. The name of the active data table appears in the list on the left, along with all the columns in the data table. The Query Builder opens with the Select Data tab on top and no columns selected.

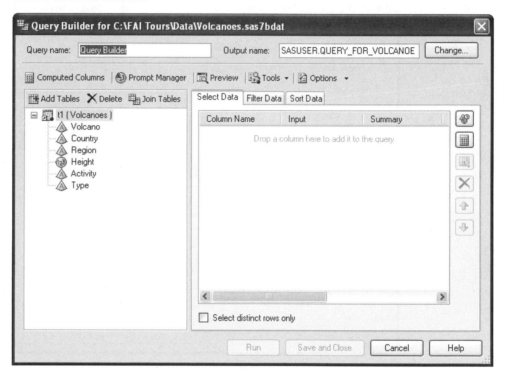

Selecting columns To select columns for your query, click the column name in the box on the left and drag it over to the box on the right on the Select Data tab. For this query, select all the columns except Type. You can select them individually, or you can select the whole group at once by clicking Volcano, and then holding down the shift key and clicking Activity. Drag the selected columns to the Select Data tab.

Query Builder
Window

✓ Click Volcano

✓ Drag to
   Select Data
   tab

✓ Repeat for
   Country,
   Region,
   Height, and
   Activity

✓ Click Preview

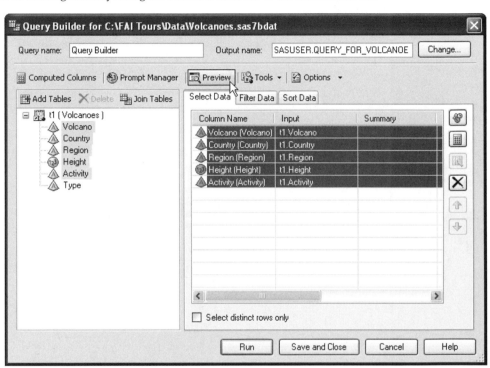

At this point, you could click Run to see the results of this simple query. However, the Query Builder has a Preview window that allows you to see the results, or a sample of the results, without having to exit the Query Builder. To open the Preview window, click **Preview** near the top of the Query Builder window.

> **Alternate Methods for Selecting Columns**
>
> In addition to clicking and dragging columns, you can double-click column names to select them. After you double-click it, the column name will appear on the Select Data tab. To select all columns from a data table, click and drag the table name to the Select Data tab.

In addition to showing a preview of the query results, the Preview window can also display the code that the Query Builder generates as well as the SAS log for the query. The log contains notes about how the query ran as well as any warnings or errors. The code and log may be of particular interest to people familiar with SAS programming. Normally you do not need to concern yourself with the code and log.

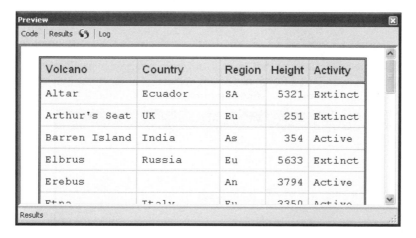

Click **Results** to see a preview of the query results. Notice that all the columns from the Volcanoes data table are in the result except the Type column.

You can choose to leave the Preview window open at this time, or you can close it by clicking the **×** in the top right corner of the window. To reopen the Preview window, simply click **Preview** again in the Query Builder window.

Tutorial C

Creating a new column Sometimes you want to create a new column based on values in an existing column. For example, the Height column in the Volcanoes data table contains the height of each volcano in meters. You can create a new column that uses the values in the Height column to compute a new column containing the height in feet.

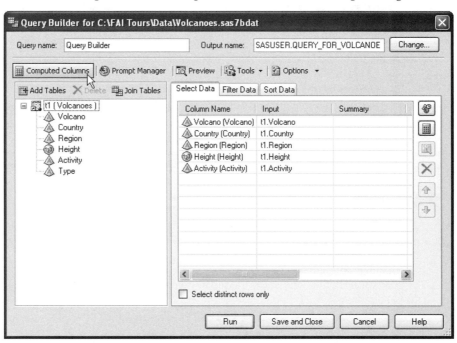

To create a new column that contains the height in feet, click **Computed Columns**. This opens the Computed Columns window where you can create new columns as well as edit, delete, or rename existing computed columns.

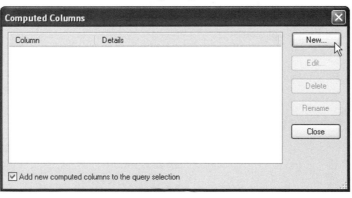

To create a new computed column, click **New.**

This opens the New Computed Column wizard. There are four types of computed columns to choose from: Summarized column, Recoded column, Advanced expression, and From an existing computed column (if there are any). Click **Advanced Expression**.

New Computed
Column Wizard

✓ Click
  Advanced
  expression

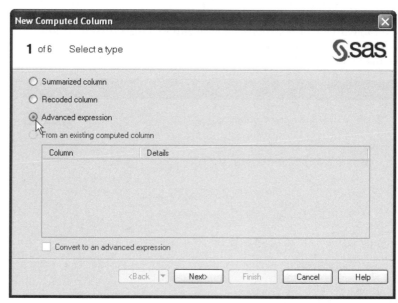

What Is a Summarized Column?

Use the Summarized column option when you want to compute a summary statistic such as mean, minimum, sum, or count for a column. By default, the chosen statistic is produced for the summarized column for each combination of all other selected columns in the query. To specify which columns to use to group statistics, use the Summary Groups area of the Query Builder window located on the Select Data tab.

What Is a Recoded Column?

If you create a new column by building an expression, then all values in the new column will be generated using that expression. But what if you want to take an existing column and change only some of the values, or treat a group of values differently from others? For example, the Activity column has some missing values. You could recode those missing values as "Unknown." Or, say you want to group the volcanoes according to height: short, medium, and tall. To do these types of operations, you would choose **Recoded column**.

The next window is where you build your expression. The empty box at the top of the window is where the expression is displayed. If you know the expression you want to use, you can type it directly in the box. But, if you are unsure exactly what the expression should look like, you can get some help from SAS Enterprise Guide. Under the box are several mathematical symbols you can add to the expression. Below the symbols are folders for Functions and Tables and a node for Selected Columns. Expand the Selected Columns node by clicking the + symbol located to the left of the Selected Columns icon.

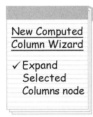

New Computed
Column Wizard

✓ Expand
    Selected
    Columns node

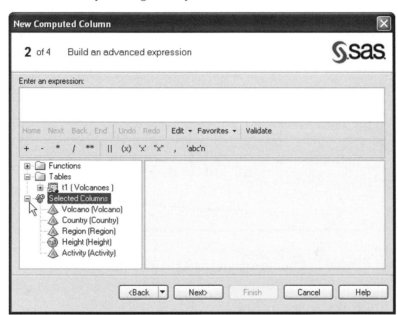

What Are Functions?

If you find you can't build the expression you want using the simple mathematical operators, then chances are SAS Enterprise Guide has a function that can help. Functions take a value and turn it into another related value. For example, the ABS function takes a number and returns the absolute value of that number. There are hundreds of functions available to you in several categories including: arithmetic, character, mathematical, date, and time.

To calculate the volcano's height in feet, you need to multiply the Height column by 3.25. Double-click **Height** in the Selected Columns list. When you do this, the full name of the Height column is inserted into the expression text box at the top of the window. The full name, t1.Height, includes the source for the column, which is table one (Volcanoes).

New Computed
Column Wizard

✓Double-click
Height

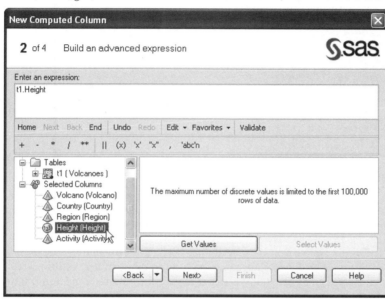

Now click the multiplication button under the Expression text box. Notice that the asterisk is inserted after the column name in the Expression text box.

New Computed
Column Wizard

✓Click *

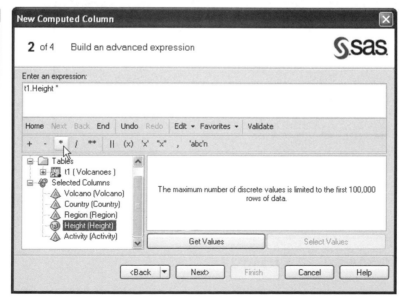

To complete the expression, type the number **3.25** in the Expression text box after the asterisk.

New Computed
Column Wizard

✓ Type **3.25**

✓ Click Next

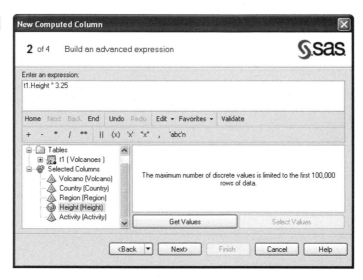

Click **Next**. Notice that the column has been given the name _Calculation and the alias Calculation. The alias will become the column name in the resulting data table. You could leave these as they are, but it is better to give the column a meaningful name. In both the Column text box and Alias text box, enter **HeightInFeet**.

New Computed
Column Wizard

✓ Type
HeightInFeet
in Column box

✓ Type
HeightInFeet
in Alias box

✓ Click Next

Click **Next**.

The final window of the New Computed Column wizard simply gives a summary of the new computed column.

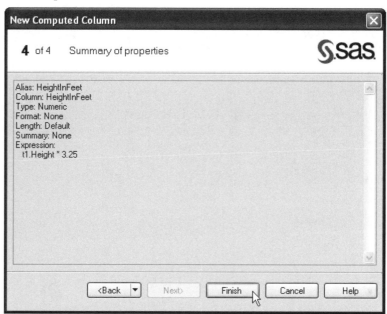

Click **Finish** to return to the Computed Columns window.

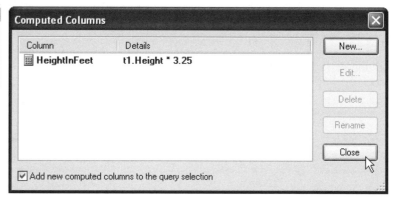

Click **Close**.

Notice that the new column, HeightInFeet, appears in the list of columns on the Select Data tab as well as under Computed Columns in the list on the left.

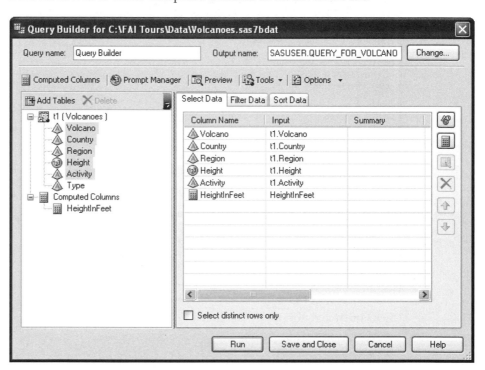

Click the Refresh icon 🔄 in the Preview window to preview the result of the query with the newly computed column.

The values for HeightInFeet are correct, but they could use some formatting. It is not necessary to show fractions of feet, and it would be nice to have commas in the numbers to make them easier to read. To change the display format of the HeightInFeet column, open the Properties window for the column. Click **HeightInFeet** in the list of column names on the Select Data tab.

Query Builder
Window

✓ Click
HeightInFeet

✓ Click
Properties
icon

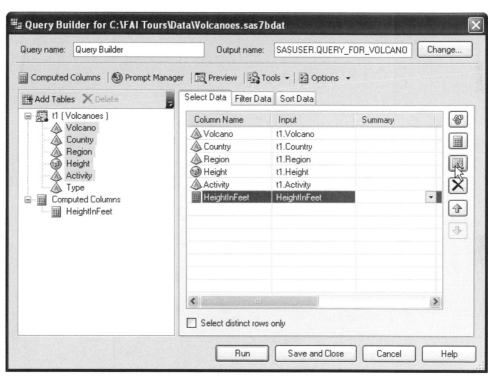

Then click the Properties icon 🖼 located on the right side of the Query Builder window.

The HeightInFeet column currently has no format associated with it.

Properties Window

✓ Click Change

Properties for HeightInFeet

Alias: HeightInFeet

Label:

Format: None   Change...

Summary: None   Length (in bytes):

Expression: t1.Height * 3.25

                                                      Edit...

Input: HeightInFeet

                        OK   Cancel   Help

Click **Change**. This opens a window where you can select a format for the column. Select the **COMMAw.d** format from the **Numeric** group. The default width of 6 is fine for this column because the heights of all the volcanoes are at most 6 digits including the comma. Make sure that the number of decimal places is set to **0**.

Formats Window

✓ Click Numeric

✓ Click COMMAw.d

✓ Click OK

Formats

Categories: Formats:
None   BESTw.d
Numeric   BESTXw.d
Date   BINARYw.d
Time   COMMAw.d
Date/Time   COMMAXw.d
Currency   CRSPDRAw.
User Defined   CRSPDRDw.
All   CRSPDRMw.

Attributes
Overall width: 6   Min: 1 Max: 32
Decimal places: 0   Min: 0 Max: 5

Description
commas in numbers

Example
Value: 12345.1
Output   1 2 , 3 4 5

                        OK   Cancel

Click **OK** to return to the Properties window.

Now the format for the column, COMMA6., appears in the Format area of the Properties window.

Properties for HeightInFeet

Alias:	HeightInFeet
Label:	
Format:	COMMA6. [Change...]
Summary:	None Length (in bytes):
Expression:	t1.Height * 3.25
	[Edit...]
Input:	HeightInFeet

[OK]   [Cancel]   [Help]

Click **OK**, then click the Refresh icon in the Preview window to see the result of setting the format for the HeightInFeet column.

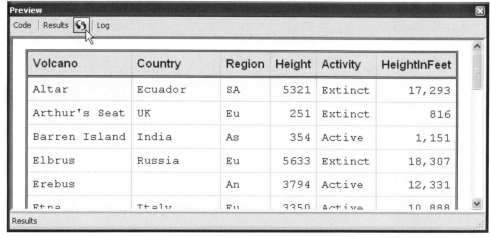

Preview

Code | Results | Log

Volcano	Country	Region	Height	Activity	HeightInFeet
Altar	Ecuador	SA	5321	Extinct	17,293
Arthur's Seat	UK	Eu	251	Extinct	816
Barren Island	India	As	354	Active	1,151
Elbrus	Russia	Eu	5633	Extinct	18,307
Erebus		An	3794	Active	12,331
Etna	Italy	Eu	3350	Active	10,888

Results

Ordering and removing columns Now that you have the HeightInFeet column, you no longer need the Height column. To remove it from the query, first select it by clicking **Height** in the list of columns on the Select Data tab.

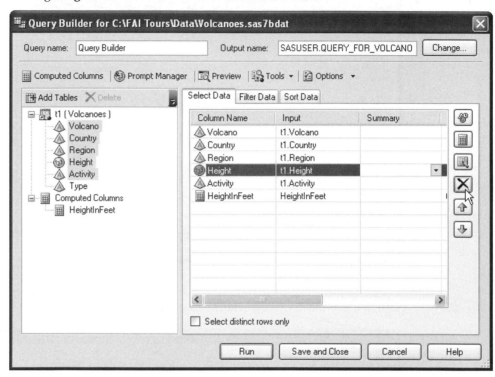

Then click the Delete icon located on the right side of the Query Builder window. It is important to note that deleting the column from the query result does not delete the column from the original data table.

In the results, the columns will be listed in the order that they appear in the Query Builder. You can change the order on the Select Data tab. Click the new column

HeightInFeet and then click the up-arrow icon located on the right side of the Query Builder window until the column is listed just above the column Activity.

Query Builder
Window

✓ On Select
Data tab,
click
HeightInFeet

✓ Click
up-arrow
icon

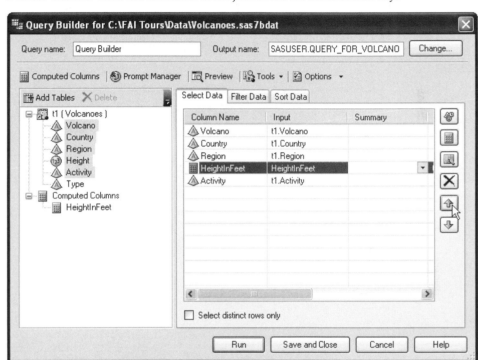

Click the Refresh icon in the Preview window. Notice that HeightInFeet now appears before Activity and the Height column is no longer in the result.

Preview Window

✓ Click Refresh
icon

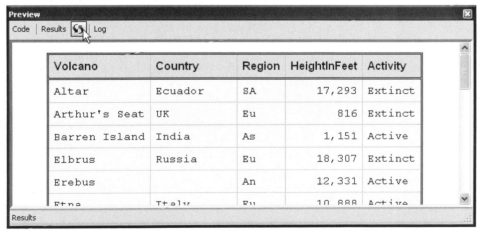

Filtering data To filter or create subsets of your data, use the Filter Data tab of the Query Builder. Click the **Filter Data** tab to bring it forward. To create a filter, drag the column that you want to use as the basis of your filter over to the Filter Data tab. For this example, use the HeightInFeet column to select only the volcanoes with heights over 12,000 feet.

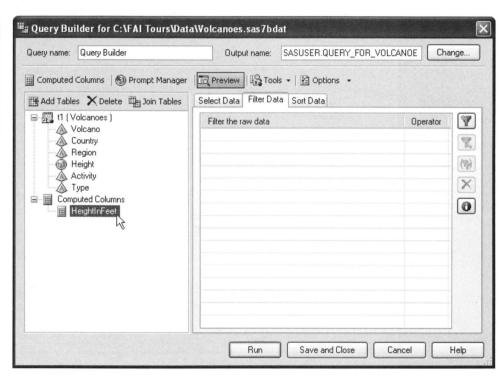

Click the **HeightInFeet** column on the left side of the window and drag it over to the **Filter Data** tab.

Other Ways to Filter Data

In addition to the Filter Data tab in the Query Builder, you can filter data using the Filter and Sort task accessible by clicking **Filter and Sort** on the workspace toolbar for Data Grids, or by selecting **Tasks ▶ Data ▶ Filter and Sort** from the menu bar. You can also filter data used for tasks by clicking the **Edit** button located near the top of the Data page for tasks. This opens the Edit Data and Filter window where you can define your filter.

As soon as you release the mouse button, the New Filter wizard will open. The column for the filter is automatically set to HeightInFeet, and the Operator is initially set to Equal to.

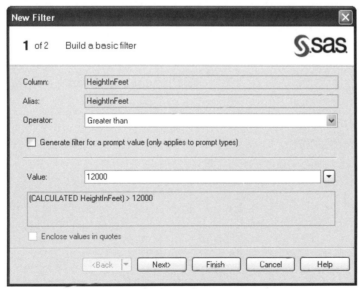

Because you want all volcanoes with a height over 12,000 feet, you need to select a different operator. Click the down-arrow to the right of **Operator** to display the drop-down list of operators. Select the **Greater than** operator. Next, type the value **12000** in the box labeled **Value**. When you enter numeric values, do not enter any commas or dollar signs.

> **New Filter Wizard**
>
> ✓ From Operator list, select Greater than
>
> ✓ In Value box, type **12000**
>
> ✓ Click Next

Click **Next** to display a summary of the filter.

Tutorial C

New Filter
Wizard

✓Click Finish

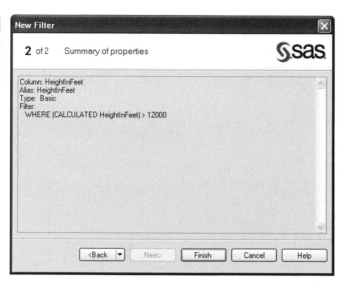

Click **Finish**.

Now the Filter Data tab shows the filter you created.

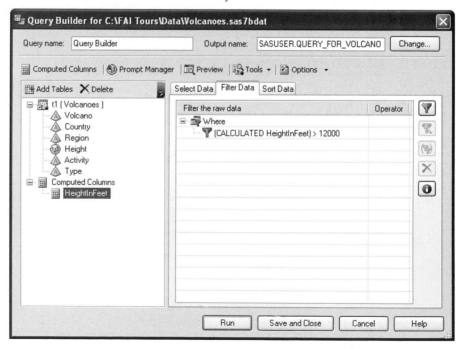

Click the Refresh icon in the Preview window and see that now all the volcanoes listed are over 12,000 feet.

Volcano	Country	Region	HeightInFeet	Activity
Altar	Ecuador	SA	17,293	Extinct
Elbrus	Russia	Eu	18,307	Extinct
Erebus		An	12,331	Active
Fuji	Japan	As	12,272	Active
Illimani	Bolivia	SA	20,989	Extinct
Kenya	Kenya	Af	16,897	Extinct

You can create more complicated filters by adding more conditions to your filter. Add the Activity column to the filter to create a data table having only volcanoes that are over 12,000 feet and are active.

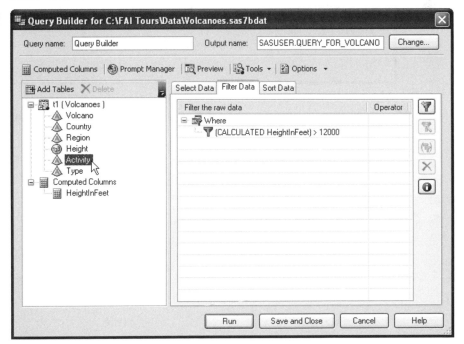

Click the column **Activity** and drag it over to the **Filter Data** tab.

When you release the mouse button, the New Filter wizard will open. This time, there is no need to change the operator because you want all volcanoes where the column Activity equals Active. At this point, you could type the value **Active** (paying attention to the casing of the letters) in the **Value** box to complete the filter. However, SAS Enterprise Guide gives you the option of choosing from a list of values for the column. Choosing the value from a list has the advantage that you can't accidentally misspell the value or use lowercase where it should be uppercase. But use caution if your data tables are very large, as it may take a long time to generate the list of values.

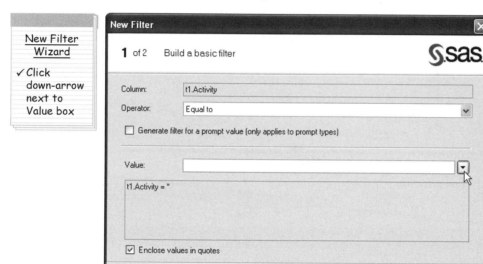

New Filter
Wizard

✓ Click
 down-arrow
 next to
 Value box

Click the down-arrow next to the **Value** box to open a new window where you can view the values for the Activity column.

Values Tab

✓ Click Get Values

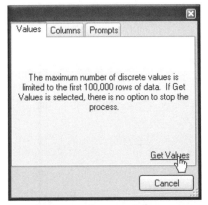

Click **Get Values** to load all possible values for Activity.

Values Tab

✓ Click Active

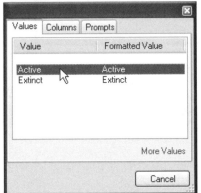

The Activity column has three values: Active, Extinct, and a null or missing value. Click **Active** in the list of values. The window will close, and the value will appear in the Value box of the New Filter window.

New Filter Wizard

✓ Click Next

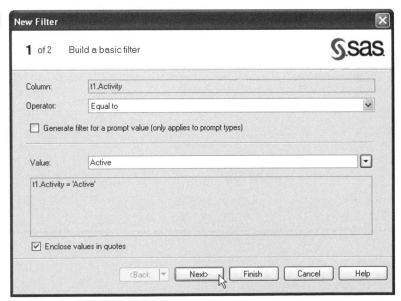

Click **Next** to display a summary of the filter.

Tutorial C

**New Filter
Wizard**

✓Click Finish

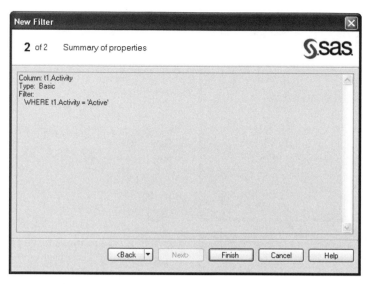

Click **Finish**.

Notice that a new condition has been added to the filter on the Filter Data tab.

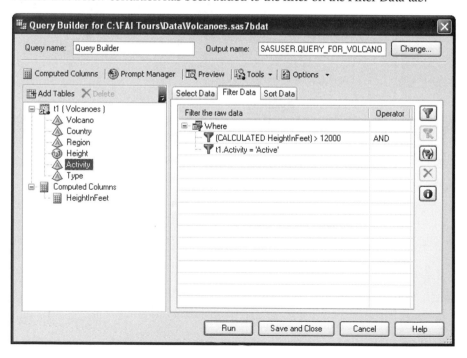

If you wanted to change either filter condition, you could simply double-click the condition to reopen the Edit Filter window, or highlight the filter on the Filter Data tab and click the Edit Filter icon located on the right side of the window.

Now click the Refresh icon in the Preview window and notice that all the volcanoes listed are over 12,000 feet and are active.

Preview Window

✓ Click Refresh icon

Preview

Code | Results | ⟳ | Log

Volcano	Country	Region	HeightInFeet	Activity
Erebus		An	12,331	Active
Fuji	Japan	As	12,272	Active
Kliuchevskoi	Russia	As	15,714	Active
Mauna Loa	USA	AP	13,553	Active
Popocatepetl	Mexico	NA	17,635	Active
Sabancaya	Peru	SA	19,422	Active

Results

AND or OR?

In this example, you want all rows that meet two conditions: volcanoes over 12,000 feet and Active. Because the volcano must pass both conditions, you use the AND operator (the default). But suppose you are not such a thrill seeker, and you would rather just look at volcanoes that are either extinct or less than 8,000 feet. The volcano has to meet only one of the conditions to be included. For this type of filter, use the OR operator. To change the operator from AND to OR, click the AND operator and choose OR from the drop-down list that appears after you click AND.

Tutorial C

Sorting the data rows There is one last change to make to this query. The data came sorted alphabetically by the name of the volcano. For this list, it would be better to sort the volcanoes by height, showing the tallest volcano at the top of the list. To sort the data, click the **Sort Data** tab.

Query Builder Window

✓ Click Sort Data tab

✓ Click HeightInFeet

✓ Drag to Sort Data tab

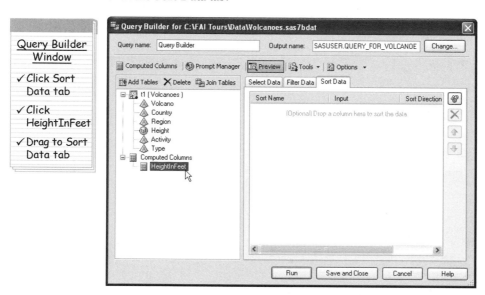

Click and drag the **HeightInFeet** column over to the **Sort Data** tab.

Initially, the sort direction for the column is set to Ascending. To change the sort direction so that the tallest volcano will be first, click **Ascending** and select **Descending** from the drop-down list.

Sort Data Tab

✓ In Sort Direction box, click Ascending

✓ Select Descending

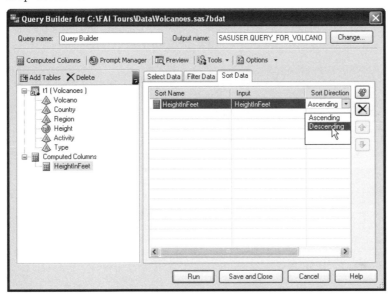

Click the Refresh icon in the Preview window and notice how the volcanoes are now sorted according to height, with the tallest volcano listed first.

Preview Window

✓ Click Refresh icon

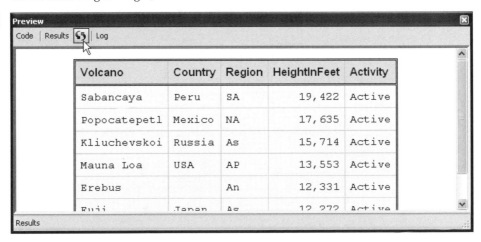

Volcano	Country	Region	HeightInFeet	Activity
Sabancaya	Peru	SA	19,422	Active
Popocatepetl	Mexico	NA	17,635	Active
Kliuchevskoi	Russia	As	15,714	Active
Mauna Loa	USA	AP	13,553	Active
Erebus		An	12,331	Active
Fuji	Japan	As	12,272	Active

Tutorial C

Query Builder
Window

✓ Click Run

You have no more changes to make to this query, so click **Run** in the Query Builder window to run the query and close the window.

When you run the query, SAS Enterprise Guide will create a SAS data table by default. The new data table is given a name starting with Query, and is stored in a default location. The data table is displayed in the workspace. This data table is now ready for any other tasks that you may want to perform.

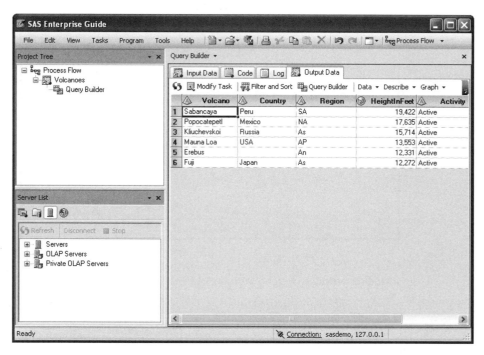

If you want to make any changes to the query, click **Modify Task** on the workspace toolbar for the query result to reopen the Query Builder.

Specifying the Format, Name, and Location for the Results of a Query

In this example, you are creating a SAS data table as a result of the query. If you want, you can create a report instead. Also, you may want to specify a meaningful name for your results, or store the results in a different location. To change the name and/or storage location for the resulting data table, click the Change button located in the upper right corner of the Query Builder window next to the Output Name. To change the result type of the query from data table to report, select **Options for this query** from the Options drop-down menu in the Query Builder window. On the Results page of the Query Options window that opens, check **Override the corresponding default settings in Tools -> Options**. Then check **Report**.

Project Tree

✓ Click
 Process
 Flow

Completing the tutorial To complete the tutorial, add a note documenting the project. Click the words **Process Flow** in the Project Tree, and then select **File ▶ New ▶ Note** from the menu bar. Type comments about the project into the Note window in the workspace.

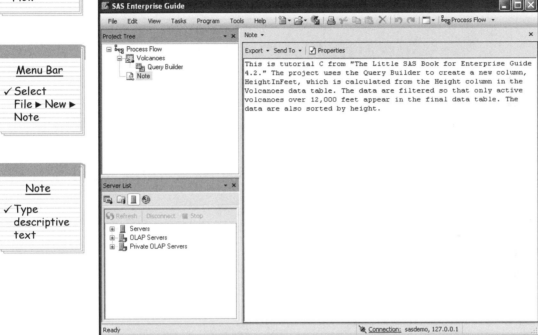

Menu Bar

✓ Select
 File ▶ New ▶
 Note

Note

✓ Type
 descriptive
 text

Menu Bar

✓ Save project

✓ Exit

Now save the project and exit SAS Enterprise Guide. Select **File ▶ Save Project as** from the menu bar. Navigate to the location where you want to save the project, give the project the name **TutorialC**, and click **Save**. Then select **File ▶ Exit** from the menu bar to close SAS Enterprise Guide.

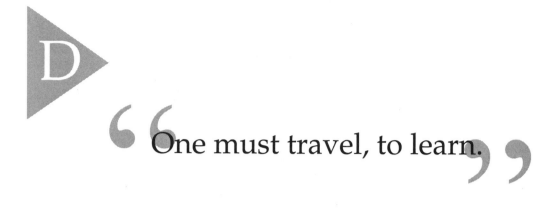

"One must travel, to learn."

Mark Twain

From *The Innocents Abroad: or, The New Pilgrim's Progress*, 1869.

Joining Two Data Tables Together

Often the data you need for a particular analysis are in more than one table. To perform the analysis, you need to join tables together. In this tutorial, you will be joining together two data tables, and then manipulating the data after the join. Here are the topics covered in this tutorial:

- Joining two tables together

- Filtering data after the join

- Selecting which data rows to keep

Before beginning this tutorial This tutorial uses the Volcanoes SAS data table, which contains information about volcanoes around the world. This tutorial also uses the Tours data table, which contains information about the volcano tours offered by the Fire and Ice Tours company. The data and instructions for downloading the data tables can be found in Appendix A.

The Fire and Ice Tours company wants to produce a list of tours for all volcanoes in Europe. The problem is that the Tours data set does not contain information about the region of the volcano. The region of the volcano is contained in the Volcanoes file. So, for the company to produce the desired list, the Volcanoes data and the Tours data must be joined together.

Starting SAS Enterprise Guide Start SAS Enterprise Guide by either double-clicking the **SAS Enterprise Guide 4.2** icon on your desktop, or selecting **SAS Enterprise Guide 4.2** from the Windows **Start** menu. Starting SAS Enterprise Guide brings up the SAS Enterprise Guide windows in the background, with the Welcome window in the foreground. The Welcome window allows you to choose between opening an existing project or starting a new project. Click **New Project**.

Desktop

✓ Double-click SAS Enterprise Guide 4.2 icon

Welcome Window

✓ Click New Project

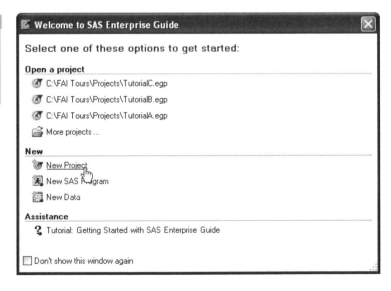

This opens an empty SAS Enterprise Guide window.

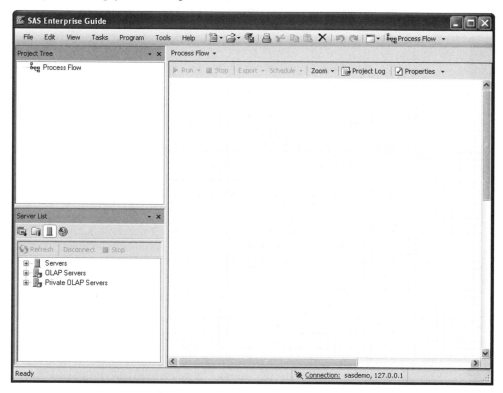

Menu Bar

✓ Select File ▶
Open ▶ Data

✓ Click Local
Computer

✓ Open
Volcanoes
and Tours

Opening the two data files to be joined
Open the Volcanoes and Tours data tables by selecting **File ▶ Open ▶ Data** from the menu bar, clicking **Local Computer**, and navigating to the location where you saved the data for this book. You can select both tables at once by clicking one table, holding the control (CTRL) key down and then clicking the other table. Click **Open**. (If you created the Tours data table in Tutorial A and saved it in the SASUSER library, you may prefer to open your version instead by selecting **File ▶ Open ▶ Data** from the menu bar, clicking **Servers**, and navigating to the SASUSER library.)

After opening both files, your SAS Enterprise Guide window should look like the following.

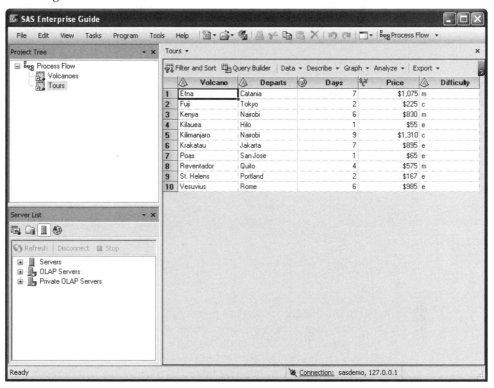

Here is what the Tours data table looks like. The Tours data contain information about the tour: the name of the volcano, the city where the tour departs, the number of days the tour lasts, the price, and a difficulty rating for the tour. The region of the volcano is not part of the Tours data table, so it would not be possible, using this data table alone, to produce a list of volcano tours in Europe.

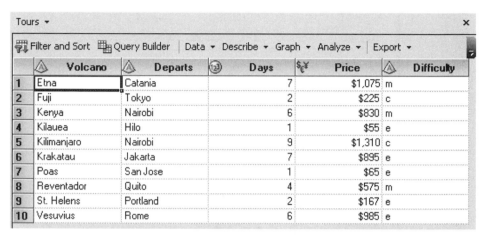

Here is a partial listing of the Volcanoes data table. This table includes the country and region of the volcano, as well as the height, activity, and type of volcano. While the two data tables contain different information, they do have one column in common, the name of the volcano. To join data tables together in a meaningful way, the tables must have at least one column that appears in both data tables. The common column does not have to have the same name in both data tables, but it must contain the same information and have the same possible values.

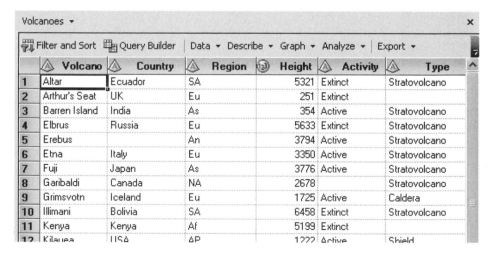

Joining tables   You join tables using the Query Builder. In the Query Builder, in addition to joining tables, you can filter and sort data, and create new columns. To open the Query Builder, click **Query Builder** on the workspace toolbar for the Volcanoes data table. Or, you can right-click the **Volcanoes** data icon in the Project Tree or Process Flow and select **Query Builder**.

Workspace Toolbar

✓ Click Query Builder

Volcanoes ▾   ✕

⯆ Filter and Sort   🖿 Query Builder   Data ▾   Describe ▾   Graph ▾   Analyze ▾ │ Export ▾

	⚠ Volcano	⚠ Country	⚠ Region	🔢 Height	⚠ Activity	⚠ Type
1	Altar	Ecuador	SA	5321	Extinct	Stratovolcano
2	Arthur's Seat	UK	Eu	251	Extinct	
3	Barren Island	India	As	354	Active	Stratovolcano
4	Elbrus	Russia	Eu	5633	Extinct	Stratovolcano
5	Erebus		An	3794	Active	Stratovolcano
6	Etna	Italy	Eu	3350	Active	Stratovolcano
7	Fuji	Japan	As	3776	Active	Stratovolcano
8	Garibaldi	Canada	NA	2678		Stratovolcano
9	Grimsvotn	Iceland	Eu	1725	Active	Caldera
10	Illimani	Bolivia	SA	6458	Extinct	Stratovolcano
11	Kenya	Kenya	Af	5199	Extinct	
12	Kilauea	USA	AP	1222	Active	Shield

Tutorial D

The Query Builder window has three tabs: Select Data, Filter Data, and Sort Data. In addition, in the box on the left side of the Query Builder, you can choose: Add Tables, Delete, and Join Tables. The name of the data table appears in the list on the left, along with all the columns in the data table.

Query Builder
Window

✓Click Add
Tables

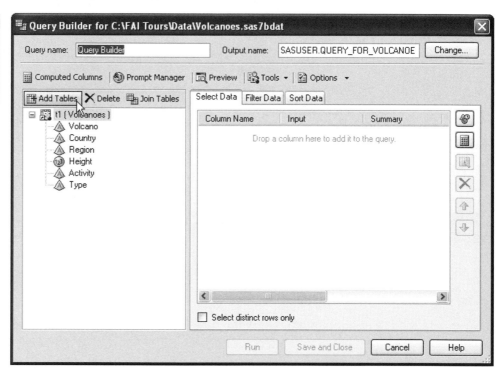

Even though both the Tours and the Volcanoes data tables are in the project, only the Volcanoes table is in the current query. In order to join the two tables together, you must add the Tours table to the query. Click **Add Tables**.

Tutorial D

In the Open Data window, you can choose to add data from your Local Computer, Servers, SAS Folders, or the Project. Both data tables are open in your project, so click **Project** in the selection pane on the left.

Open Data
Window

✓ Click Project

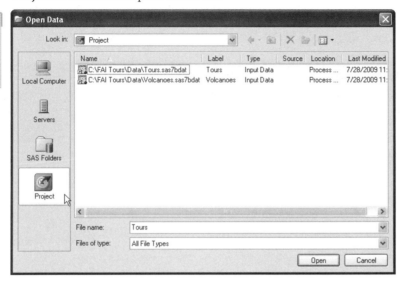

All the tables open in the project are listed in the Open Data window. The name includes the full path for the data and the extension for SAS data tables (sas7bdat).

Open Data
Window

✓ Click Tours
data set

✓ Click Open

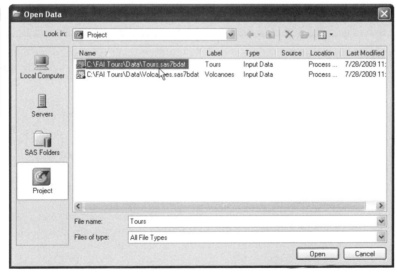

Add the Tours table to the query by clicking **Tours**, and then clicking **Open**.

Tutorial D

When you add data tables to the query, SAS Enterprise Guide checks to see if the data tables have a column in common. Common columns must have the same name and be the same type (numeric or character). If there is a common column, SAS Enterprise Guide will automatically use that column for the join. Because the Volcanoes data table and the Tours data table both have a character column named Volcano, SAS Enterprise Guide will use it to find matching rows.

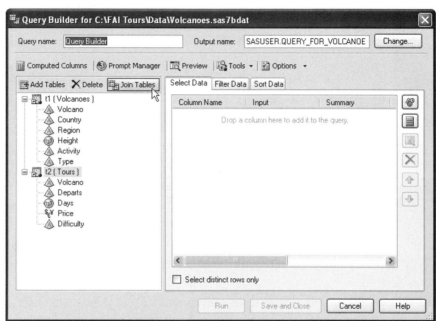

It's not obvious from the Query Builder window that SAS Enterprise Guide has found common columns for the join. To see what the join looks like, click **Join Tables** to open the Tables and Joins window.

What If the Common Columns Have Different Names?

No problem! When you try to join the two tables, SAS Enterprise Guide will let you know that it cannot determine how to join them and that you will need to do it manually. Click **OK**, and the Tables and Joins window will open automatically. Click the first table, then right-click the common column, select **Join With** from the pop-up menu, and select the column from the second table. Next, choose a join type from the Join Properties window, and click **OK**. SAS Enterprise Guide will draw a line between the two columns, and the columns will be linked.

In the Tables and Joins window, both tables are visible along with the columns in the tables. Notice the line drawn between the Volcano column in the Volcanoes table and the Volcano column in the Tours table. This shows how the tables will be joined. Also, there is a diagram on the line that shows the type of join. In this case, only rows found in both tables will be included in the resulting table.

Tables and
Joins Window

✓Click Close

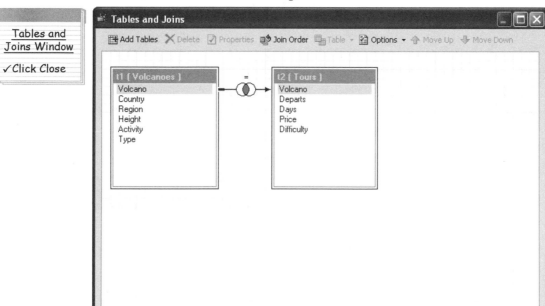

Click **Close** to close the Tables and Joins window and return to the Query Builder.

Tables with More Than One Common Column

It is possible to join data tables that have more than one common column. For example, you may have year and month columns in both data tables, and you want to match the tables based on the values of both columns. SAS Enterprise Guide does not handle this type of join automatically, but it is easy to do it yourself. SAS Enterprise Guide will link the first pair of columns for you. To link the second pair, open the Tables and Joins window by clicking **Join Tables** in the Query Builder window. Create another link by clicking the first table, then right-clicking the column name, choosing Join With in the pop-up menu, and selecting the column from the second table.

Before you can run the query, you must select the columns you want in the result. To select columns, click the column in the box on the left and drag it over to the Select Data tab. For this query, select the **Volcano**, **Country**, **Region**, **Height**, and **Activity** columns from the Volcanoes table. Then select the **Departs**, **Days**, and **Price** columns from the Tours table.

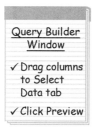

Query Builder Window

✓ Drag columns to Select Data tab

✓ Click Preview

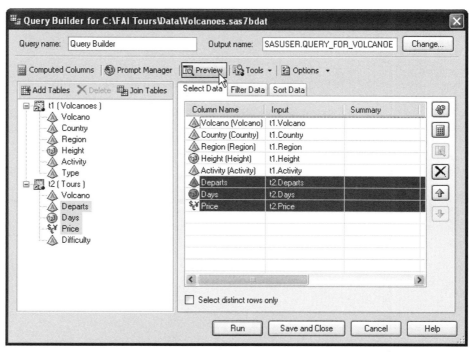

To get an idea of what the results of the join will look like, click the **Preview** button near the top of the Query Builder window. Then click the **Results** tab in the Preview window.

Preview Window

✓ Click Results tab

What If One Table Has Repeated Values of the Common Column?

In this example, each table has only one entry for each volcano, so there is a one-to-one match between the tables. But suppose the Tours table had two tours for one volcano. Then the values for the columns in the Volcanoes data table will be repeated for these two tours for the same volcano.

When you preview the results of a query, usually you will not see the complete result. The Preview window is designed to show you what to expect from your join without having to complete the entire join. With these small data tables, it wouldn't take long to perform the join, so the Preview window does not save you much time. But if you have very large data tables, it can take a long time for SAS Enterprise Guide to complete the join, so the Preview window allows you to make sure the query is correct before starting the join.

Notice that the volcanoes from the Volcanoes data table have been matched with the corresponding row from the Tours data table.

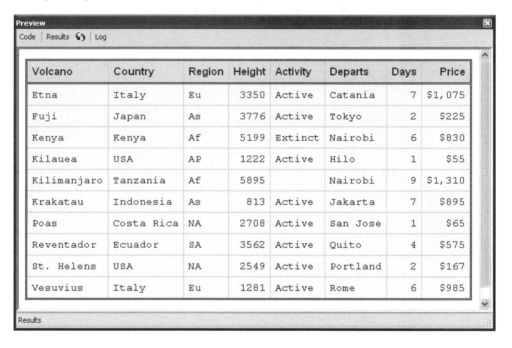

Volcano	Country	Region	Height	Activity	Departs	Days	Price
Etna	Italy	Eu	3350	Active	Catania	7	$1,075
Fuji	Japan	As	3776	Active	Tokyo	2	$225
Kenya	Kenya	Af	5199	Extinct	Nairobi	6	$830
Kilauea	USA	AP	1222	Active	Hilo	1	$55
Kilimanjaro	Tanzania	Af	5895		Nairobi	9	$1,310
Krakatau	Indonesia	As	813	Active	Jakarta	7	$895
Poas	Costa Rica	NA	2708	Active	San Jose	1	$65
Reventador	Ecuador	SA	3562	Active	Quito	4	$575
St. Helens	USA	NA	2549	Active	Portland	2	$167
Vesuvius	Italy	Eu	1281	Active	Rome	6	$985

Tutorial D

Click **Run** in the Query Builder window to run the query. The data table created by the query will display in the workspace. Notice that only the rows that appear in both data tables are part of the result. This is the default type of join for SAS Enterprise Guide. Because all the volcanoes in the Tours data table also appear in the Volcanoes data table, all the tours are represented here. However, some volcanoes do not have matching tours, and so they are not included in the result.

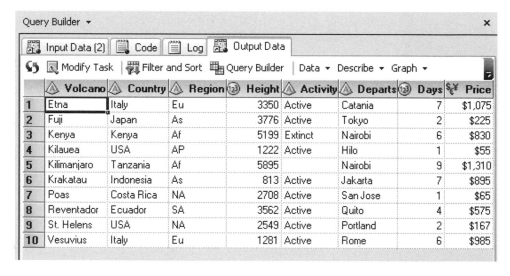

	Volcano	Country	Region	Height	Activity	Departs	Days	Price
1	Etna	Italy	Eu	3350	Active	Catania	7	$1,075
2	Fuji	Japan	As	3776	Active	Tokyo	2	$225
3	Kenya	Kenya	Af	5199	Extinct	Nairobi	6	$830
4	Kilauea	USA	AP	1222	Active	Hilo	1	$55
5	Kilimanjaro	Tanzania	Af	5895		Nairobi	9	$1,310
6	Krakatau	Indonesia	As	813	Active	Jakarta	7	$895
7	Poas	Costa Rica	NA	2708	Active	San Jose	1	$65
8	Reventador	Ecuador	SA	3562	Active	Quito	4	$575
9	St. Helens	USA	NA	2549	Active	Portland	2	$167
10	Vesuvius	Italy	Eu	1281	Active	Rome	6	$985

Click the **Process Flow** button to view the Process Flow for the project. It is not obvious from the Project Tree that the query uses both the Tours and the Volcanoes tables, but in the Process Flow it is easy to see that both tables contribute to the query. By default, results of queries are given an arbitrary name starting with the letters QUERY and are stored in a default location.

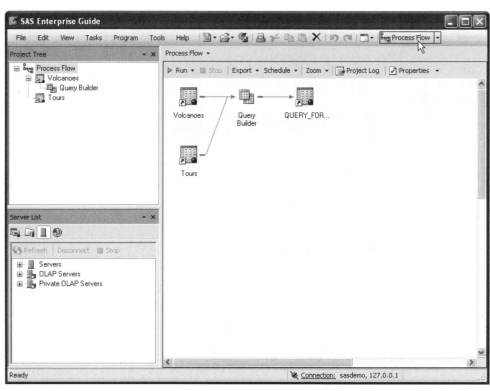

Filtering the data Now that the Tours data table and the Volcanoes data table have been joined together, it is possible to create a data table of tours for volcanoes in Europe. To do this, you create a filter as part of the same query that you used to join the data tables.

Project Tree

✓ Right-click
   Query
   Builder icon

✓ Select
   Modify
   Query
   Builder

Right-click the Query Builder icon in the Project Tree or Process Flow and select **Modify Query Builder** to reopen the query. The Query Builder window opens with the Select Data tab on top. Click **Filter Data** to open the Filter Data tab. The Region column in the Volcanoes data table gives the general location of the volcano: North America, South America, Europe, Asia, Australia Pacific, Africa, or Antarctica.

Query Builder
Window

✓ Click Filter
   Data tab

✓ Drag Region

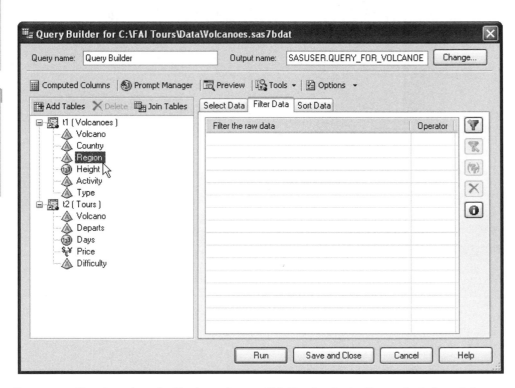

To create a filter based on the Region column, click **Region** in the list on the left, and drag it to the **Filter Data** tab.

This automatically opens the New Filter wizard with Region from the Volcanoes data table (table 1) listed as the Column.

New Filter Wizard

✓ Click down-arrow

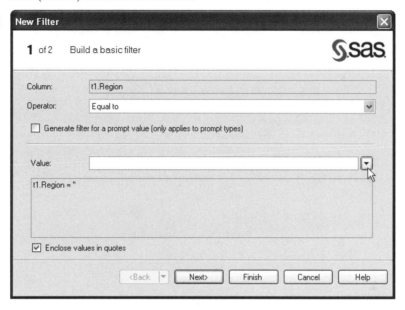

Click the down-arrow next to the **Value** box to open a window where you can display all possible values for Region. Click **Get Values**.

Values Box

✓ Click Get Values

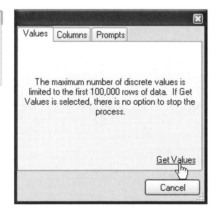

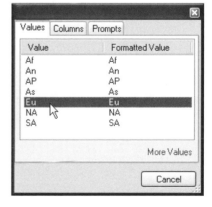

Values Box

✓ Click Eu

The values for Region are coded, and the code for Europe is Eu. Click the value **Eu** in the list of column values.

Tutorial D

After you select Eu from the list of values, the window will close and Eu will appear in the box next to Value in the New Filter wizard.

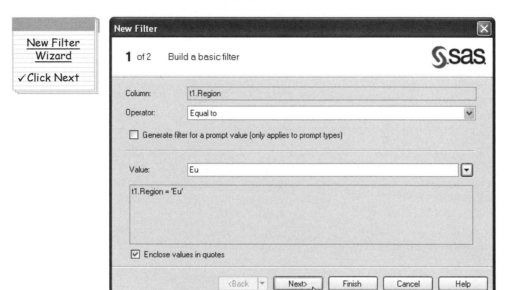

New Filter
Wizard
✓ Click Next

Click **Next.**

Choosing an Operator

In this example, you want all the volcanoes whose region equals Eu, so you use the **Equal to** operator. The **Equal to** operator is the default operator, so you didn't need to change it. But you can change it if you want. To choose a different operator, click the down-arrow in the **Operator** box, and choose from the list. For example, if you wanted all volcanoes in North and South America, you would use the **In a list** operator. The **In a list** operator selects all rows in a table whose values for the column are contained in the specified list.

The final window of the New Filter wizard shows a summary of the filter you just created.

Click **Finish** to complete the filter condition and return to the Query Builder.

Tutorial D

Now the filter appears on the Filter Data tab of the Query Builder window.

Query Builder
Window

✓ Click Run

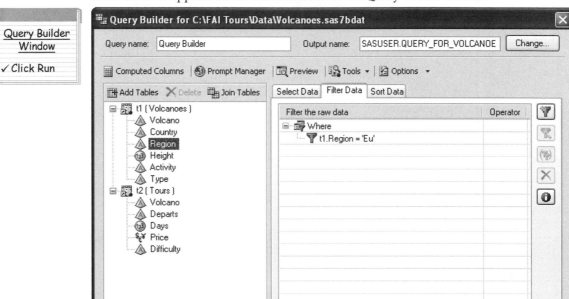

Click **Run** to see the results of this change to the query.

Replace
Results?

✓ Click Yes

When SAS Enterprise Guide asks if you would like to replace the results from the previous run, click **Yes**.

Look at the resulting data table and note that only the tours of volcanoes in Europe appear in the data table.

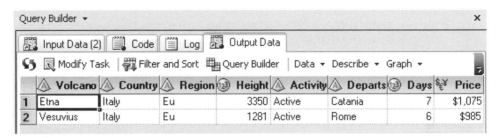

Selecting which rows to keep Suppose the Fire and Ice Tours company wants to expand the number of tours that it offers in Europe. The company wants to include in the list all the volcanoes in Europe, not just volcanoes that currently have tours. In SAS Enterprise Guide, the default action of a join is to include only the rows that appear in both tables. To change this default action, you need to change the type of join.

To reopen the query, right-click the Query Builder icon in the Project Tree or Process Flow and select **Modify Query Builder** or simply click **Modify Task** on the workspace toolbar for the query result.

Workspace Toolbar

✓ Click Modify Task

Query Builder Window

✓ Click Join Tables

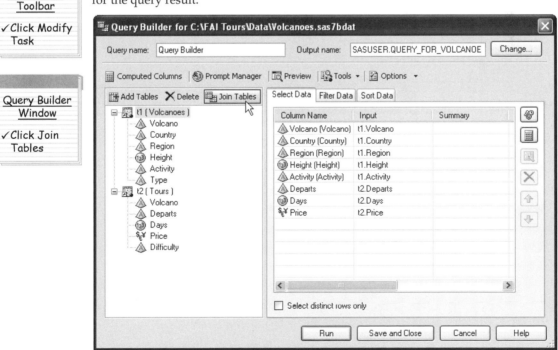

Click **Join Tables** to open the Tables and Joins window.

In the Tables and Joins window, notice the diagram 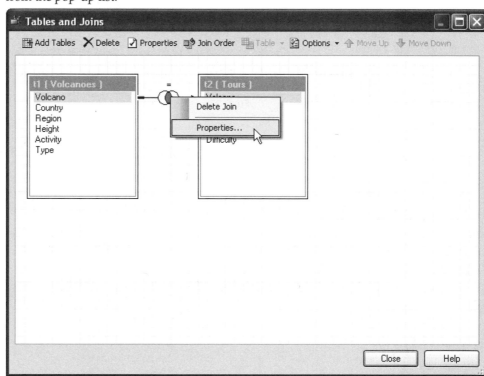 with the equal sign (=) above it on the line connecting the two tables. Right-click this join indicator and select **Properties** from the pop-up list.

This opens the Join Properties window. There are several types of joins listed under Join type. Each type of join has its own diagram using overlapping circles. For the **Matching rows only given a condition (Inner Join)** type of join, only the intersection of the two circles is filled with black.

For this join, you want all the rows from each data table, even if there is no match. So, select **All rows from both tables given a condition (Full Outer Join)**.

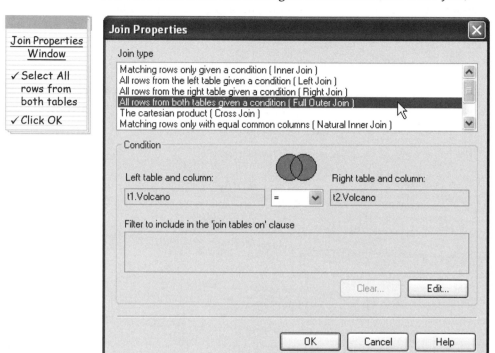

Notice that the join symbol has changed so that now both circles are completely filled with black. Click **OK**.

The join indicator in the Tables and Joins window has changed to reflect the type of join you just selected.

Tables and Joins Window

✓ Click Close

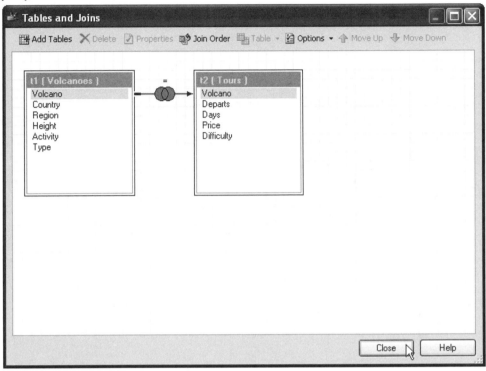

Click **Close** to return to the Query Builder window.

In the Query Builder window, click **Run** to see the results.

Query Builder Window

✓ Click Run

Click **Yes** when SAS Enterprise Guide asks if you would like to replace the previous results.

Replace Results?

✓ Click Yes

Tutorial D

Look at the resulting data table in the workspace. Now the data include all the volcanoes in Europe, even if they don't have tours. Notice that all the columns from the Tours data table (Departs, Days, and Price) have missing values for the volcanoes for which there are no tours. Because all the volcanoes in the Tours data table also appear in the Volcanoes data table, all the columns from the Volcanoes data table have values.

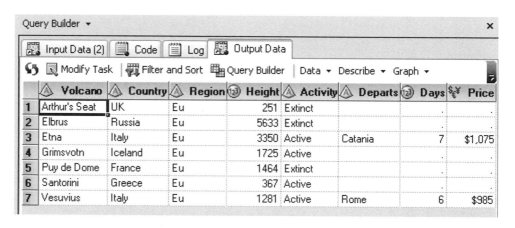

Query Builder ▾   ✕

| Input Data (2) | Code | Log | Output Data |

🔁 Modify Task | Filter and Sort Query Builder | Data ▾ Describe ▾ Graph ▾

	Volcano	Country	Region	Height	Activity	Departs	Days	Price
1	Arthur's Seat	UK	Eu	251	Extinct		.	.
2	Elbrus	Russia	Eu	5633	Extinct		.	.
3	Etna	Italy	Eu	3350	Active	Catania	7	$1,075
4	Grimsvotn	Iceland	Eu	1725	Active		.	.
5	Puy de Dome	France	Eu	1464	Extinct		.	.
6	Santorini	Greece	Eu	367	Active		.	.
7	Vesuvius	Italy	Eu	1281	Active	Rome	6	$985

Completing the tutorial To complete the tutorial, add a note describing the project. Click the words **Process Flow** in the Project Tree. Then select **File ▶ New ▶ Note** from the menu bar. Enter a brief description of the project in the Note window in the workspace.

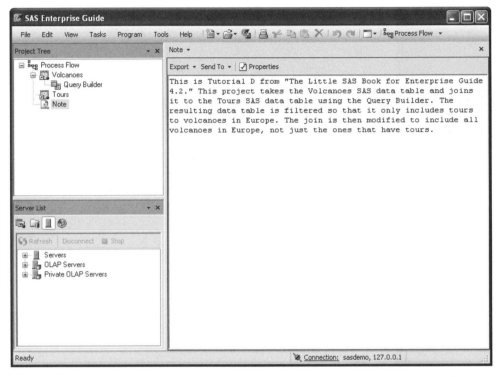

Now save the project and exit SAS Enterprise Guide. Select **File ▶ Save Project As** from the menu bar. Navigate to the location where you want to save the project, give the project the name **TutorialD**, and click **Save**. Then select **File ▶ Exit** from the menu bar to close SAS Enterprise Guide.

Tutorial D

REFERENCE SECTION

1

"Every tradition begins as an innovation, and every innovation is built on the traditions before it."

JOE CRAVEN

From Joe Craven, award-winning multi-instrumentalist, musical archaeologist, and educator, www.joecraven.com. Reprinted by permission of the author.

CHAPTER 1

SAS Enterprise Guide Basics

1.1 ▶ SAS Enterprise Guide Windows

SAS Enterprise Guide has many windows. You can customize the appearance of SAS Enterprise Guide—closing some windows, opening others, and resizing them all—until it looks just the way you want. Then SAS Enterprise Guide will remember those settings so the next time you open it, everything will be just where you left it.

Here is SAS Enterprise Guide with its windows in their default positions.

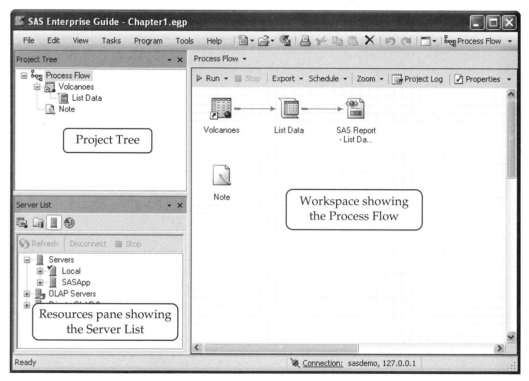

Some windows are open by default while some are closed or hidden behind other windows. You can open or unhide the major windows using the **View** menu.

Docked windows   Some of the windows in SAS Enterprise Guide are docked. Most of the docked windows can appear on the left or right side of the application. To change a window from one side to the other, click the down arrow (▼) in the upper-right corner of the window and select **Dock Left** or **Dock Right** from the pop-up menu. From this menu, you can also select **Auto Hide**. If you hide a window, it will be reduced to a tab along the side. To view a hidden window, position your cursor over the window's tab. When you move the cursor out of the window, it will be reduced to a tab again. To unhide a window, click its tab or select it from the **View** menu. These windows are docked:

 Project Tree   The Project Tree window displays the items in a project in a hierarchical tree diagram. This window is open by default.

Server List The Server List window lists available SAS servers, and the files and SAS data libraries on those servers. A SAS server is any computer on which SAS software is installed. The computer on which you run SAS Enterprise Guide may or may not be a SAS server. This window appears in the Resources pane, and is open by default.

Task List The Task List window lists all available tasks and task templates. Using the drop-down list at the top of this window, you can choose to display tasks by category, tasks by name, or task templates. You can open a task by double-clicking its name in this window. This window appears in the Resources pane, and is closed by default. To open this window, click its icon in the Resources pane.

SAS Folders The SAS Folders window lists any folders that have been defined in metadata. This window appears in the Resources pane, and is closed by default. To open this window, click its icon in the Resources pane.

Prompt Manager The Prompt Manager window lists any prompts defined for the current project. This window appears in the Resources pane, and is closed by default. To open this window, click its icon in the Resources pane.

Task Status The Task Status window displays notes about tasks that are currently running. This window is different from other docked windows because it is docked to the bottom of the application, and you cannot move it or reduce it to a tab. This window is closed by default. To open the Task Status window, select it from the **View** menu.

Workspace The workspace is not itself a window, but it is very important. This is where the Process Flow and document windows appear. The workspace is always there and cannot be closed. However, you can open and close individual items inside the workspace.

Process Flow The Process Flow window displays the items in a project and their relationship using a process flow diagram. You can open only one project at a time, but you can create as many process flows as you wish inside a single project. You can open the Process Flow by selecting it from the **View** menu, by double-clicking its name in the Project Tree, by selecting it from the drop-down list at the top of the workspace, by selecting the ⬚ Process Flow ▾ drop-down list on the menu bar, or by pressing **F4**.

Document windows The document windows display your data, results, programs, logs, and notes. There is a different type of icon for every kind of document. This icon represents a SAS data table.

Menus and tools The menus and tools across the top of SAS Enterprise Guide (also called the menu bar) are always the same. However, the menus and tools inside the workspace (also called the workspace toolbar) change. For example, the options above a Process Flow are different from the options above a data table. You can also right-click many objects to open a pop-up menu for that object. So you can see that there are often several ways to do the same thing. This book cannot list all the ways to do every action, but with a little exploration you can find them.

Restoring windows Once you have rearranged your windows, you may decide you want them back where they started. To restore them to their original locations, select **Tools ▶ Options** from the menu bar. Then in the General page of the Options window, click **Restore Window Layout**.

1.2 Splitting the Resources Pane and Workspace

The Resources pane and the workspace are busy places. The Resources pane is home to four windows, while the workspace accommodates even more. By default, you can see only one item at a time, but you can see more if you split the Resources pane or workspace.

Splitting the Resources pane To split the Resources pane, click the down-arrow (▼) at the top of the pane, and select **Show Multiple** from the pull-down list. At first, you will only see one window because only one window is open.

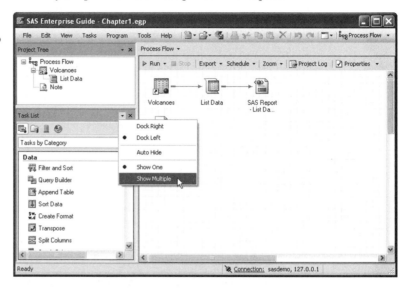

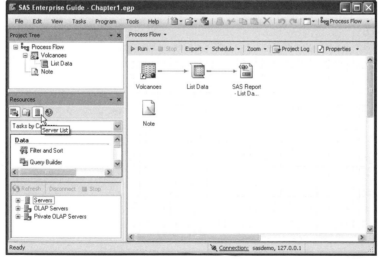

To open other windows, click their icons: Task List , SAS Folders , Server List , or Prompt Manager . You can open all four windows at once in the Resources pane if you wish. In this example, two windows are open, the Task List and the Server List.

To return the Resources pane to normal, click the down-arrow and select **Show One**.

Maximizing the workspace It may be helpful to make the workspace as large as possible before you split it. To do this, select **View ▶ Maximize Workspace** from the menu bar. When you maximize the workspace, the Project Tree and Resources pane become tabs pinned to the edge of SAS Enterprise Guide. You can temporarily expand those windows by moving the cursor over a tab. When you move the cursor away, the window will be reduced to a tab again. To return the workspace to its normal size, select **View ▶ Maximize Workspace** again.

Splitting the workspace You can split the workspace into two pieces. First, open any items you wish to view. Then click the Workspace Layout icon on the menu bar ⬜, and select either **Stacked** or **Side By Side** from the pull-down list. You can also do this by selecting **View ▶ Workspace Layout** from the menu bar.

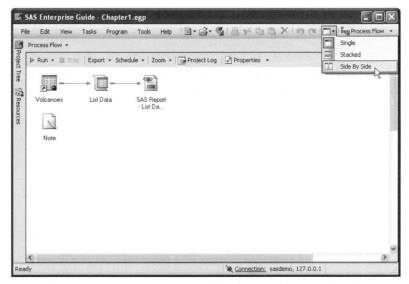

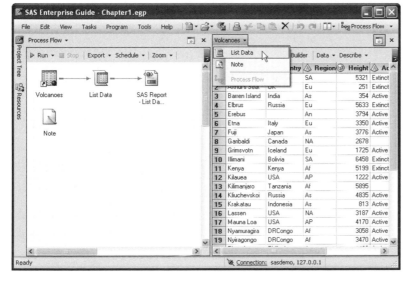

You can click the down-arrow at the top of the workspace to view a drop-down list of all items that are currently open. To display an item, select it from the list.

To unsplit the workspace, click the Workspace Layout icon again, and select **Single** from the pull-down list. You can also click one of the Xs in the upper-right corners to close that section of the workspace.

Chapter 1

1.3 ▶ Projects

In SAS Enterprise Guide, all the work you do is organized into projects. A project is a collection of related data, tasks, results, programs, and notes. Projects help you by keeping track of everything, even if your data are scattered in many directories or on more than one computer. That way, when you come back to an old project six months or a year later, you won't be left wondering which data sets you used or what reports you ran.

You can have as many projects as you like, and you can use a data set over and over again in different projects, so there is a lot of flexibility. However, you can have only one project open at a time. Also, if you share a project file with someone else, that person must have access to your data files and any other items you reference.

To create a new project, select **File ▶ New ▶ Project** from the menu bar. To open an existing project, select **File ▶ Open ▶ Project** and navigate to your project.

Project Tree and Process Flow   The Project Tree window displays projects in a hierarchical tree diagram, while the Process Flow window displays projects using a process flow diagram. In either window, the items in your project are represented by icons, and connected to show the relationship between items. Here are examples of a Project Tree and a Process Flow showing the same project. This project contains several types of items: data, tasks, results, a program, and a note.

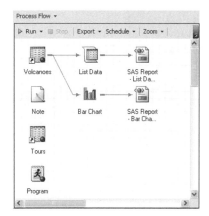

 Data   Data files in a project may be SAS data tables, raw data files, or files from other databases or applications, such as Microsoft Excel spreadsheets. Projects contain shortcuts to data files, not the actual data. If you delete a project, your data files will still exist. This icon represents a SAS data table.

 Tasks   Tasks are specific analyses or reports that you run, such as List Data or Bar Chart. Every time you run a task, SAS Enterprise Guide adds an icon representing that task. This icon represents the Bar Chart task.

 Results   Results are the reports or graphs produced by tasks you run. Results are represented by icons labeled with the type of output (SAS Report, HTML, PDF, RTF, or text) and the name of the task. This icon represents output in SAS Report format.

Notes Notes are optional text files you can use to document your work, or record comments or instructions for later use. To create a note, select **File ▶ New ▶ Note** from the menu bar. A text window will open, allowing you to type whatever you wish.

 Programs Programs are files that contain SAS code. You can open existing programs in SAS Enterprise Guide, or you can write new programs.

Showing properties and opening items You can display the properties for any item by right-clicking its icon in the Project Tree or Process Flow and selecting **Properties** from the pop-up menu. You can open any item by double-clicking its icon, or by right-clicking its icon and selecting **Open** from the pop-up menu.

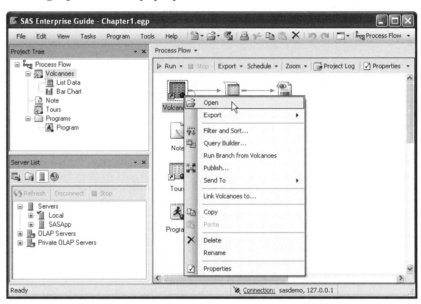

Renaming and deleting items You can rename most items by right-clicking the item and selecting **Rename** from the pop-up menu. You can delete an item in a project by right-clicking and selecting **Delete**. Note that if you delete data from a project, only the shortcut to that data is deleted, not the actual data file.

Saving a project To save a project, select **File ▶ Save** *project-name* or **File ▶ Save** *project-name* **As** from the menu bar. Each project is saved as a single file and has a file extension of .egp. You can save data, programs, and results in separate files by right-clicking the icon for that item and selecting **Export** from the pop-up menu.

1.4 Managing Process Flows

In SAS Enterprise Guide, you can have only one project open at a time. However, you can have an unlimited number of process flows within a single project. So, if you have a complex project, you may want to divide it into several process flows.

Adding new process flows To add a new process flow to a project, select **File ▶ New ▶ Process Flow** from the menu bar, or right-click the current process flow and select **New ▶ Process Flow** from the pop-up menu. No matter how many process flows you create, the Project Tree will show all of them in a single tree diagram.

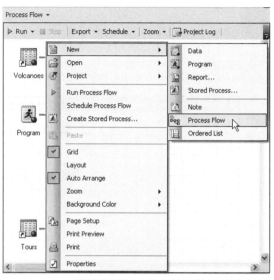

When you right-click a process flow, the pop-up menu displays options for customizing the appearance of that process flow. Options include Grid, Layout, Auto Arrange, Zoom, and Background Color.

To view a process flow, double-click its name in the Project Tree, or click the down-arrow (▼) above the workspace to open a pull-down list.

When you add a new process flow, it is named Process Flow *n*. To give a process flow a more descriptive name, right-click its name in the Project Tree and select **Rename** from the pop-up menu. To delete a process flow, right-click its name in the Project Tree and select **Delete** from the pop-up menu.

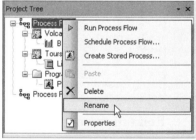

Moving and copying items To move items from one process flow to another, hold down the control key (CTRL), and click all the items you want to move. Then right-click, and select **Move to ▶** *process-flow-name* from the pop-up menu. In this example, three items are being moved to the process flow named TourReports.

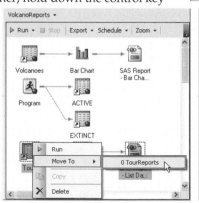

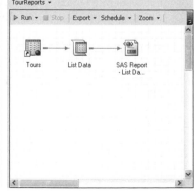

Copying items is similar to moving items except that you cannot copy results. Select the items to be copied using control-click. Then right-click the items and select **Copy** from the pop-up menu, and right-click the target process flow and select **Paste**.

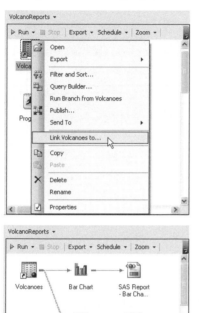

Linking items When you run a process flow, items are executed from top left to bottom right, following the branches created by links between items. You can add links between items to show relationships that may not be clear, or to force items to run in a particular order. For example, if you create a format that is used by a task, you might want to add a link indicating that the task follows the format. To add a link, right-click the initial item and select **Link** *item-name* **to** from the pop-up menu. A Link window will open

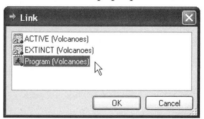

showing all the other items to which you can link. Select the item to which you want to link, and click **OK**.

In this process flow, the Volcanoes data icon has been linked to a program icon to show that this program uses the Volcanoes data table. Notice that when you add links they use a dashed line instead of a solid line.

To delete a link that you previously added, right-click the icon for that link ➡ in the Project Tree and select **Delete** from the pop-up menu.

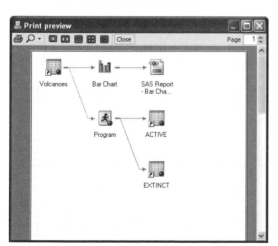

Printing process flows You can print a copy of your process flow. To control page size and orientation, click the process flow and select **File ▶ Page setup for Process Flow** from the menu bar. To preview a printout, select **File ▶ Print preview for Process Flow**. To print the process flow, select **File ▶ Print Process Flow**. Here is the Print preview window for the VolcanoReports process flow.

Chapter 1

1.5 ▶ Running and Rerunning Tasks

Running tasks is, of course, what SAS Enterprise Guide is all about. Regardless of which task you choose to run, the basic steps are the same: open the task, select the data, and then run the task.

Opening a task To open a task, select it from the **Tasks** menu, or click its name in the Task List window, or open a Data Grid and then select the task from the workspace toolbar. The window for that task will open. In this example, the List Data task is being selected in the Task List window.

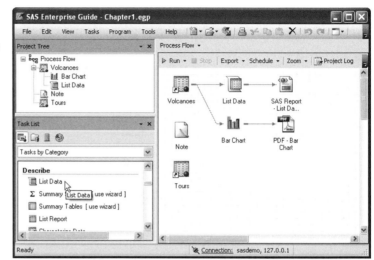

Selecting the data table When you open a task, it will use the data table that is currently active. If a Data Grid is open, then that data table will be active. You can also make a data table active by simply clicking its icon in the Project Tree or Process Flow before you open a task.

After you open a task, you can change the data table by clicking the **Edit** button in the Data page of the task window. The Edit Data and Filter window (not shown) will open where you can choose an alternate data table for the task. See section 5.1 for details about the Edit Data and Filter window.

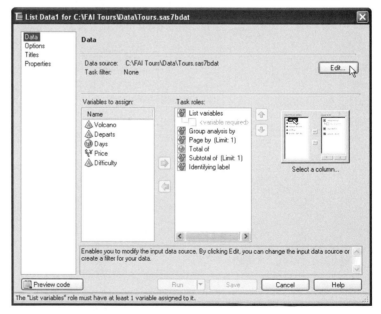

Running a task Every task includes a Data page where you assign variables to task roles. Using the selection pane on the left, you can open other pages. The preceding image shows the List Data task, which has four pages: Data, Options, Titles, and Properties. When you are satisfied with all the settings, click the **Run** button. If you have more than one SAS server, your task will run on the same server where the data table is stored. If you decide you want to stop a

task while it's running, select **Program ▶ Stop** from the menu bar, or click the **Stop** button ■ on the workspace toolbar above the Process Flow. When the task has finished running, the results will be displayed in the workspace.

Rerunning a task

To make changes to a task and run it again, first reopen the task window. You can do this by clicking **Modify Task** on the workspace toolbar for the Results tab. You can also reopen a task by right-clicking the task icon in the Project Tree or Process Flow, and selecting **Modify** *task-name* from the pop-up menu.

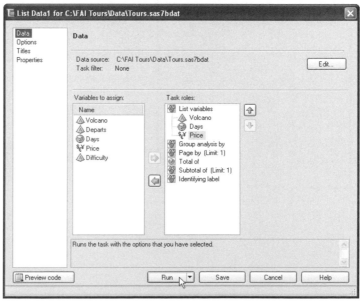

Once the task window is open, you can make changes. Then click the **Run** button to rerun the task.

If you just want to rerun a task without reopening the task window, click **Refresh** on the workspace toolbar for the Results tab. You can also right-click the task icon in the Project Tree or Process Flow, and select **Run** from the pop-up menu.

1.6 ▶ Creating and Exporting Task Templates

Even with the simplest tasks, there are many ways to customize your results. Once you have spent a lot of time changing titles, choosing options, and specifying a style; you might wish you could save all those settings and use them to create new results. With task templates, you can.

Task templates allow you to save tasks in a form that is independent of data. In other words, task templates save all your settings except the assignment of variables to task roles and certain data-dependent options. Most tasks can create templates, but a few of the more data-driven tasks (including Summary Tables and Append Table) cannot. SAS programmers will be interested to know that task templates are unrelated to the various kinds of templates created by the Output Delivery System.

Creating a task template To create a task template from a task that you have already run, select **Tasks ▶ Task Templates ▶ Task Template Manager** from the menu bar. This opens the Task Template Manager. Click **New** to open the New Task Template window.

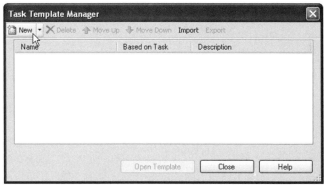

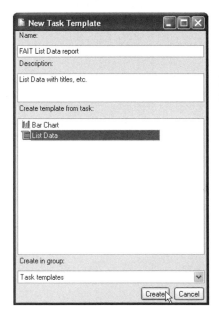

In the New Task Template window, type a name for the new template in the **Name** box. You can type an optional description in the **Description** box if you wish. The area labeled **Create template from task** lists all the tasks currently in the project. Choose a task by clicking its name. Then click **Create**. The new task template will be listed in the Task Template Manager. Click **Close**.

You can also create task templates directly from tasks. If the task window is open, then you can click the down-arrow (▼) on the **Run** button, and select **Create Template** from the pull-down list.

To delete a task template, simply open the Task Template Manager, click the task template name, and click **Delete**.

Using a task template Once you create a task template, unless you delete it, it will be available to you every time you open SAS Enterprise Guide. There are two ways to open a task template. You can select **Tasks ▶ Task Templates ▶** *task-template-name* from the menu bar, or you can open the Task List window, select **Task Templates** from the drop-down list, and click the name of your task template.

By default, when you open a task template, it uses the active data table. After you open a task template, you can choose a different data table by clicking the **Edit** button in the Data page.

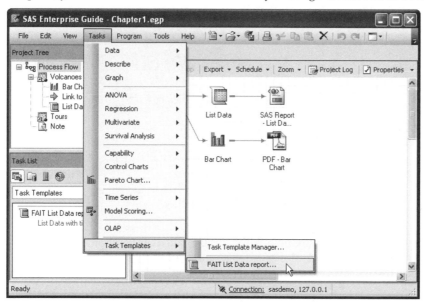

Exporting a task template When you create a task template, it will be saved in a default location. This location is associated with your Windows user account. To share task templates with other people (including anyone who uses the same computer, but a different Windows account), you must export the templates. To do this, open the Task Template Manager, and click **Export**. SAS Enterprise Guide will prompt you to select the templates you wish to export, and to specify a location for saving them.

To import task templates, open the Task Template Manager and click **Import**. Then navigate to the location of the task templates you wish to import.

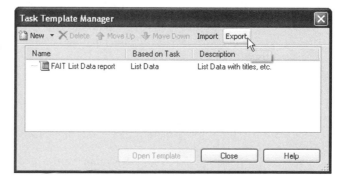

1.7 SAS Data Tables

SAS Enterprise Guide can read and write many kinds of data files (see Chapter 2 for more on this topic), but for most purposes, you will want to have your data in a special form called a SAS data table. When you open a SAS data table, it is displayed in the workspace in a Data Grid. The following Data Grid shows the Tours data table that was created in Tutorial A. A new tour has been added for the volcano Lassen.

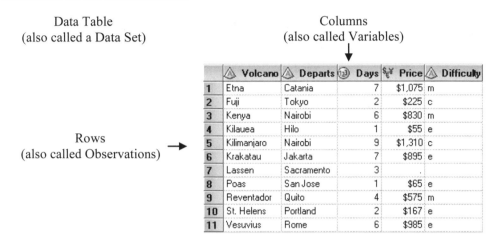

Data Table
(also called a Data Set)

Columns
(also called Variables)

Rows
(also called Observations)

Terminology In SAS Enterprise Guide, rows are also called observations, columns are also called variables, and data tables are also called data sets. SAS Enterprise Guide uses all these terms. Some tasks use the term columns and others refer to variables, depending on the context.

Data types and data groups In SAS Enterprise Guide, there are two basic types of data: numeric and character. Numeric data are divided into four data groups: numeric, currency, time, and date. For each of these, SAS Enterprise Guide has special tools: informats for reading that type of data, functions for manipulating that type of data, and formats for displaying that type of data. SAS Enterprise Guide uses a different icon to identify each kind of data.

 Character data may contain numerals, letters, or special characters (such as $ and !) and can be up to 32,767 characters long. Character data are represented by a red pyramid with the letter A on it.

 Currency data are numeric values for money and are represented by a picture of the dollar, euro, and yen symbols.

 Date data are numeric values equal to the number of days since January 1, 1960. The table below lists four dates, and their corresponding SAS date and formatted values:

Date	SAS date value	MMDDYY10. formatted value
January 1, 1959	-365	01/01/1959
January 1, 1960	0	01/01/1960
January 1, 1961	366	01/01/1961
January 1, 2010	18263	01/01/2010

You will rarely see unformatted SAS date values in SAS Enterprise Guide. However, because dates are numeric, you can use them in arithmetic expressions to find, for example, the number of days between two dates. Datetime values are included in this data group, and are the number of seconds since January 1, 1960. Date data are represented by a picture of a calendar.

 Time data are numeric values equal to the number of seconds since midnight. Time data are represented by a picture of a clock.

 Other numeric data, that are not dates, times, or currency, are simply called numeric. They may contain numerals, decimal places (.), plus signs (+), minus signs (-), and E for scientific notation. Numeric data are represented by a blue ball with the numbers 1, 2, and 3 on it.

Numeric versus character If the values of a column contain letters or special characters, they must be character data. However, if the values contain only numerals, then they may be either numeric or character. You should base your decision on how you will use the data. Sometimes data that consist solely of numerals make more sense as character data than as numeric. Zip codes, for example, are made up of numerals, but it just doesn't make sense to add or subtract zip codes. Such values work better as character data.

Column names Column names in SAS Enterprise Guide may be up to 32 characters in length, and can begin with or contain any character, including blanks.

Moving data between SAS Enterprise Guide and Base SAS Any data created in SAS Enterprise Guide can be used in Base SAS, but the default rules for naming variables are different. Base SAS uses the VALIDVARNAME=V7 SAS system option, while SAS Enterprise Guide uses VALIDVARNAME=ANY. For the sake of compatibility, you may want to follow these rules when naming columns: choose column names that are 32 characters or fewer in length, start with a letter or underscore, and contain only letters, numerals, and underscores.

Missing data Sometimes, despite your best efforts, your data may be incomplete. The value of a particular column may be missing for some rows. In those cases, missing character data are represented by blanks, and missing numeric data are represented by a single period (.). In the preceding Data Grid, the value of Price is missing for the tour of Lassen, and its place is marked by a period. The value of Difficulty is missing for the same tour and is left blank.

Documentation stored in SAS data tables In addition to your actual data, SAS data tables contain information about the data table, such as its name, the date that you created it, and the version of SAS you used to create it. SAS also stores information about each column in the data table, including its name, type, and length. This information is sometimes called the descriptor portion of the data table, and it makes SAS data tables self-documenting. This information is what you see in the Properties windows for data tables and columns. These Properties windows are described in more detail in the next two sections.

1.8 Properties of Data Tables

Someday you may be given a SAS Enterprise Guide project that was created by someone else. If you are unsure what the project does, then it would be a good idea to start by checking the properties of the data tables.

Opening the Properties window To display information about a data table, first open it in a Data Grid by double-clicking the data icon in the Project Tree or Process Flow. Then click the Properties icon ☑ on the workspace toolbar to open the table Properties window.

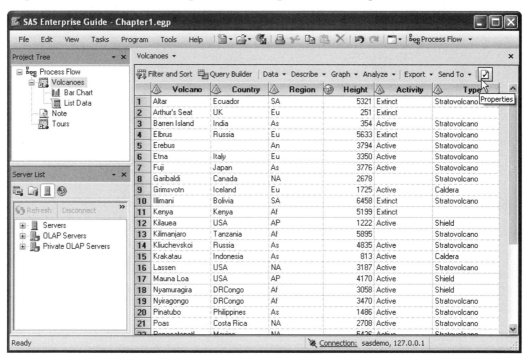

You can also right-click a data icon in the Project Tree or Process Flow, and select Properties from the pop-up menu.

General page

When the table Properties window opens, it displays the General page. The General page lists basic information about the table: its name, when it was created and last modified, and whether it is a SAS data table or some other type of file.

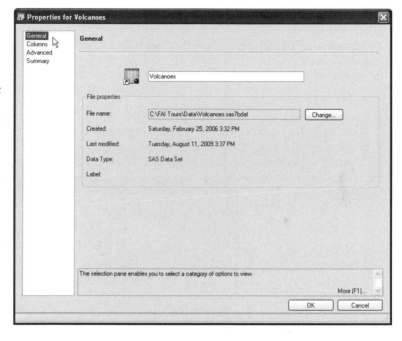

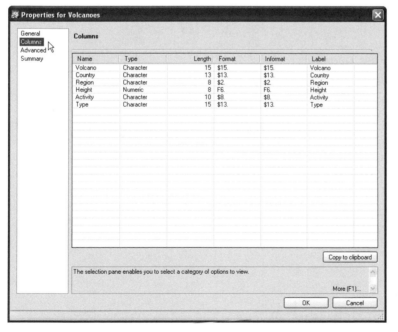

Columns page

If you click **Columns** in the selection pane on the left, the Columns page will open. Here, SAS Enterprise Guide displays information about each column: its name, type, length, format, informat, and label. You cannot change the properties of columns in the Properties window for a data table. To make changes, use the Properties window for an individual column as described in the next section.

1.9 ▶ Properties of Columns

The column Properties window displays properties for an individual column. You can use this window inside a task to change labels and display formats, but those changes will apply only to the results of that task rather than the original data table. However, if you open the column Properties window inside a Data Grid, then any changes you make will be saved with the data table.

Setting the update mode   The Data Grid opens in read-only mode. In this mode you cannot edit the data, and you cannot change column properties. To switch to update mode, select **Edit ▶ Protect Data** from the menu bar. This toggles the data table from read-only to update

mode. To return to read-only mode, select **Edit ▶ Protect Data** again.

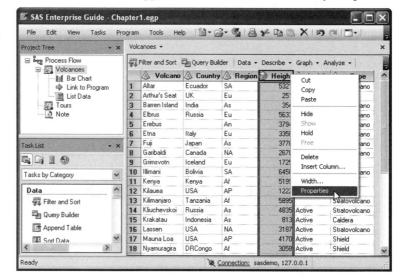

Opening the Properties window
To open the column Properties window, right-click the header of a column and select **Properties** from the pop-up menu. In this Data Grid, Properties is being selected for the column Height.

General page   The Properties window has several pages. If there is no selection pane on the left, then the data table is in read-only mode and you need to switch to update mode.

The General page displays basic information for the column: its name, label, type, group, and length. You can change any of these properties. In this example, the column name has been changed to **HeightMeters**, and the label to **Height in Meters**. This column is **numeric** and has a length of **8**.

Informats page Click **Informats** in the selection pane on the left to open the Informats page. Informats (also called input formats or read-in formats) tell SAS Enterprise Guide how to interpret input data. There are different informats for character, numeric, date, time, and currency data. In this example, the column uses the default numeric informat, *w.d*, with a width of **6** and no decimal places. This informat can be written as 6.0. See the next section for a table of commonly used informats.

In SAS Enterprise Guide 4.2, you can use informats when you import data files, and when you write SAS programs. However, informats are not used when you type data values into a Data Grid. Instead, the Data Grid uses the data type and data group that you specify to determine how to interpret any data values you enter.

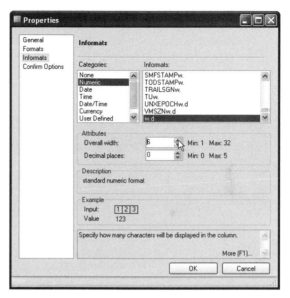

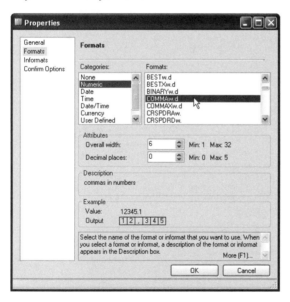

Formats page Click **Formats** in the selection pane on the left to open the Formats page. Formats (also called display formats) tell SAS Enterprise Guide how data should look in Data Grids or reports. There are different formats for character, numeric, date, time, and currency data. In this example, the format **COMMA*w.d*** with a width of **6** and no decimal places has been selected. This format can be written as COMMA6.0. See section 1.11 for a table of commonly used formats.

	Volcano	Country	Region	HeightMeters	Activity	Type
1	Altar	Ecuador	SA	5,321	Extinct	Stratovolcano
2	Arthur's Seat	UK	Eu	251	Extinct	
3	Barren Island	India	As	354	Active	Stratovolcano
4	Elbrus	Russia	Eu	5,633	Extinct	Stratovolcano
5	Erebus		An	3,794	Active	Stratovolcano
6	Etna	Italy	Eu	3,350	Active	Stratovolcano

Results Here is the Data Grid showing the new name, HeightMeters, and the format with commas.

1.10 Selected Informats

SAS informats (also called input formats or read-in formats) tell SAS Enterprise Guide how to interpret input data. You can specify informats when you import data, in a SAS program, or in a Data Grid. However, in SAS Enterprise Guide 4.2, informats are not used to interpret data that you type into a Data Grid. Here are a few of the many informats available in SAS Enterprise Guide.

Informat	Definition	Width range	Default width
Character			
$w.	Reads character data—trims leading blanks	1–32,767	none
$UPCASEw.	Converts character data to uppercase	1–32,767	8
Date, Time, and Datetime[1]			
ANYDTDTEw.	Reads dates in any form—when dates are ambiguous, uses the DATESTYLE system option to determine	5–32	9
DATEw.	Reads dates in the form: *ddmonyy* or *ddmonyyyy*	7–32	7
DATETIMEw.	Reads datetime values in the form: *ddmonyy hh:mm:ss.ss*	13–40	18
DDMMYYw.	Reads dates in the form: *ddmmyy* or *ddmmyyyy*	6–32	6
JULIANw.	Reads Julian dates in the form: *yyddd* or *yyyyddd*	5–32	5
MMDDYYw.	Reads dates in the form: *mmddyy* or *mmddyyyy*	6–32	6
TIMEw.	Reads time in the form: *hh:mm:ss.ss* (hours:minutes:seconds—24-hour clock)	5–32	8
Numeric			
w.d	Reads standard numeric data	1–32	none
COMMAw.d	Removes embedded commas and $, converts left parentheses to minus sign	1–32	1
PERCENTw.	Converts percentages to proportions	1–32	6

---

[1] SAS date values are the number of days since January 1, 1960. Time values are the number of seconds past midnight, and datetime values are the number of seconds past midnight on January 1, 1960.

The examples below show input data and resulting data values for each informat. The results shown are unformatted data values. See sections 3.1 and 3.2 for information about assigning display formats.

Informat	Input data	Results	Input data	Results
Character				
$10.	Lassen	Lassen	St. Helens	St. Helens
$UPCASE10.	Lassen	LASSEN	St. Helens	ST. HELENS
Date, Time, and Datetime				
ANYDTDTE10.	01jan1961 1961001	366 366	31.01.1961 01/31/61	396 396
DATE9.	1jan1961	366	31 jan 61	396
DATETIME14.	1jan1960 10:30	37800	1jan1961 10:30	31660200
DDMMYY10.	01.01.1961	366	31/01/61	396
JULIAN7.	1961001	366	61031	396
MMDDYY10.	01-01-1961	366	01/31/61	396
TIME8.	10:30	37800	10:30:15	37815
Numeric				
5.1	1234	123.4	-12.3	-12.3
COMMA10.0	$1,000,001	1000001	(1,234)	-1234
PERCENT5.	5%	0.05	(20%)	-0.2

1.11 Selected Standard Formats

SAS formats (also called display formats) tell SAS Enterprise Guide how to display or print data. You can apply formats in a column Properties window in a Data Grid, a task, or a query. Here are a few of the many formats available in SAS Enterprise Guide.

Format	Definition	Width range	Default width
Character			
$UPCASE*w*.	Converts character data to uppercase	1–32767	Length of variable or 8
$*w*.	Writes standard character data—default for character data	1–32767	Length of variable or 1
Date, Time, and Datetime[1]			
DATE*w*.	Writes SAS date values in form *ddmonyy* or *ddmonyyyy*	5–11	7
DATETIME*w.d*	Writes SAS datetime values in form *ddmmmyy:hh:mm:ss.ss*	7–40	16
DTDATE*w*.	Writes SAS datetime values in form *ddmonyy* or *ddmonyyyy*	5–9	7
EURDFDD*w*.	Writes SAS date values in form *dd.mm.yy* or *dd.mm.yyyy*	2–10	8
JULIAN*w*.	Writes SAS date values in Julian date form *yyddd* or *yyyyddd*	5–7	5
MMDDYY*w*.	Writes SAS date values in form *mm/dd/yy* or *mm/dd/yyyy*—default for dates	2–10	8
TIME*w.d*	Writes SAS time values in form *hh:mm:ss.ss*—default for times	2–20	8
WEEKDATE*w*.	Writes SAS date values in form *day-of-week, month-name dd, yy* or *yyyy*	3–37	29
WORDDATE*w*.	Writes SAS date values in form *month-name dd, yyyy*	3–32	18
Numeric			
BEST*w*.	SAS System chooses best format—default format for numeric data	1–32	12
COMMA*w.d*	Writes numbers with commas	2–32	6
DOLLAR*w.d*	Writes numbers with a leading $ and commas separating every three digits—default for currency	2–32	6
E*w*.	Writes numbers in scientific notation	7–32	12
EUROX*w.d*	Writes numbers with a leading € and periods separating every three digits	2–32	6
PERCENT*w.d*	Writes numeric data as percentages	4–32	6
w.d	Writes standard numeric data	1–32	none

[1] SAS date values are the number of days since January 1, 1960. Time values are the number of seconds past midnight, and datetime values are the number of seconds past midnight on January 1, 1960.

The examples below show unformatted data values and formatted results for each display format.

Format	Data value	Results	Data value	Results
Character				
$UPCASE10.	Lassen	LASSEN	St. Helens	ST. HELENS
$6.	Lassen	Lassen	St. Helens	St. He
Date, Time, and Datetime				
DATE9.	366	01JAN1961	396	31JAN1961
DATETIME16.	37800	01JAN60:10:30	2629800	31JAN60:10:30
DTDATE9.	37800	01JAN1960	2629800	31JAN1960
EURDFDD10.	366	01.01.1961	396	31.01.1961
JULIAN7.	366	1961001	396	1961031
MMDDYY10.	366	01/01/1961	396	01/31/1961
TIME8.	37800	10:30:00	37815	10:30:15
WEEKDATE15.	366	Sun, Jan 1, 61	396	Tue, Jan 31, 61
WORDDATE12.	366	Jan 1, 1961	396	Jan 31, 1961
Numeric				
BEST10.	1000001	1000001	-12.34	-12.34
BEST6.	1000001	1E6	100001	100001
COMMA12.2	1000001	1,000,001.00	-12.34	-12.34
DOLLAR13.2	1000001	$1,000,001.00	-12.34	$-12.34
E10.	1000001	1.000E+06	-12.34	-1.234E+01
EUROX13.2	1000001	€1.000.001,00	-12.34	€-12,34
PERCENT9.2	0.05	5.00%	-1.20	(120.00%)
10.2	1000001	1000001.00	-12.34	-12.34

1.12 Scheduling Projects to Run at Specific Times

Sometimes you may want to create a project now, but run it later. For example, if you have data files that are updated on a regular basis, you might want to automatically rerun the project once a week using the new data. Or, if your data files are very large, you might want to run your projects at night so that SAS Enterprise Guide is not using valuable resources during work hours.

Opening the Schedule window You can schedule a complete project or just a process flow. To schedule a project, select **File ▶ Schedule** *project-name* from the menu bar. To schedule a process flow, right-click the name of the process flow in the Project Tree and select **Schedule** *process-flow-name* from the pop-up menu. This opens the Microsoft Windows Task Scheduler with the Task tab on top. When you schedule a project, SAS Enterprise Guide creates a script that is saved in a file on your computer. The name and path of this script is displayed in the **Run** box. The **Start in** box displays the folder in which the script will run. Your computer and user name are displayed in the **Run as** box.

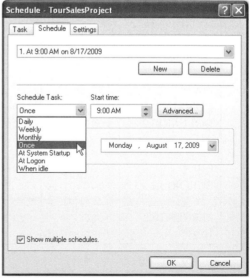

If you will not be logged on at the time the project runs, then make sure the box next to **Run only if logged on** is unchecked, and click the **Set password** button to open the Set Password window. Enter the password for your user name (the same password you use when you log on to your computer), and click **OK**.

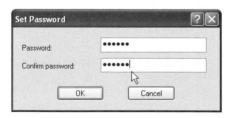

Setting the run frequency To tell SAS Enterprise Guide when to run the project, click the **Schedule** tab. Click the **New** button. Then select the frequency to run the project from the drop-down list under **Schedule Task**. You can schedule your project to run just once at a specified time as shown here, or you can schedule your project to run on a regular basis.

Setting the date and time To set the time the project will start running, click the up and down arrows on the **Start time** box, or simply click the time and type a new value. To choose a date other than today, click the down-arrow in the **Run on** box and select a date from the pull-down calendar.

Other settings If you click the **Settings** tab, you will see other options, including the maximum length of time a project will be allowed to run, and whether it will run if your computer has gone into sleep mode.

When you are satisfied with all the settings, click **OK** to schedule the project.

Running the project The project will not run if it is open or if the computer is turned off at the time the project is scheduled to run. However, if you have a different project open, the scheduled project will still run.

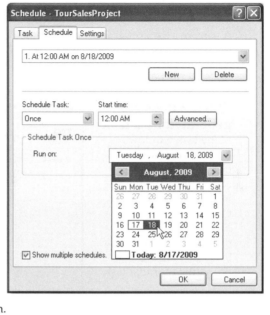

Viewing the results To see the results of your scheduled run, open the project after it has completed running. If you are not sure whether a project ran, you can confirm this by opening the Properties window for that project. To open the Properties window for a project, select **File ▶ Project Properties** from the menu bar. The **Last modified** field shows the date and time that the project last ran.

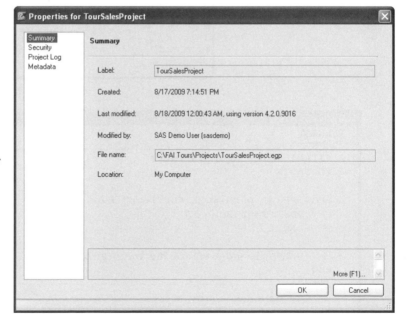

1.13 Editing SAS Programs Generated by a Task

If you are a SAS programmer, you may want to make a few changes to the programs generated by SAS Enterprise Guide. There is more than one way to do this. You can insert your own SAS code into the program associated with a task, or you can save the code generated by a task in a separate file which you can then edit and run.

Previewing code generated by a task

Many task windows have a **Preview code** button in the lower-left corner. If you click this button, SAS Enterprise Guide will open a Code Preview window displaying the code that SAS Enterprise Guide has written for that task.

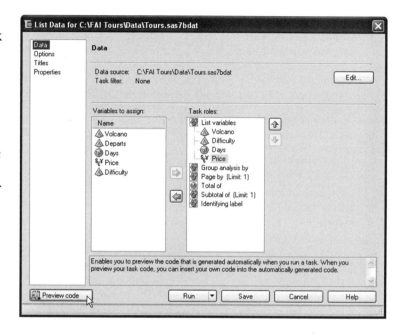

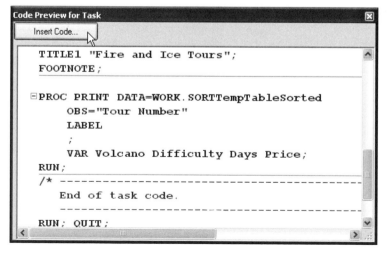

Inserting code in a task

Here is a Code Preview window for a List Data task. You can see that it uses PROC PRINT. If you want to add code to the task, click the **Insert Code** button. This opens a User Code window. You cannot edit the existing code generated by a task, but the User Code window allows you to add code at specific points in the program.

In the User Code window, double-click **<double-click to insert code>** at the point where you wish to add your own custom code. An Enter User Code window will open. Type the custom code you wish to add. When you are done, click **OK**. Your new code will appear in the User Code window. Click **OK** in the User Code window. When you run the task, SAS Enterprise Guide will run the code you inserted along with the code generated by the task.

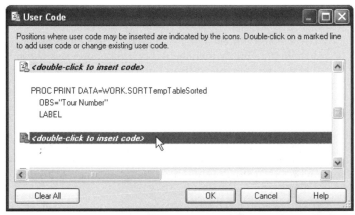

Editing code generated by a task If you want to be able to edit the entire program generated by a task, or code from tasks that do not have a Preview code button, you can make a copy of the program, and then edit it. To do this, run the task, and then right-click the task icon in the Project Tree or Process Flow, and select **Add As Code Template**. SAS Enterprise Guide will open a Program window containing the code generated by the task.

You can edit this code in any way you wish. Because this code is a copy of the code generated by the task, any changes you make here will not affect the task, nor will any changes you make to the task be reflected in this code.

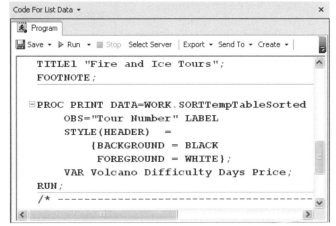

When you have made all the changes you wish and are ready to run the program, click **Run** on the workspace toolbar for the Program window. Your program will run on the server that has been set as your default. To choose a different server, click **Select Server.** If you decide you want to stop a program while it's running, click the Stop

button ■ on the workspace toolbar for the Program window. You can also use the Program menu on the menu bar to control execution of your program.

Programs created in this way are embedded in your project, and are not saved as separate files. For more information on embedding programs, see the next section.

1.14 Writing and Running Custom SAS Programs

You can accomplish a lot using tasks in SAS Enterprise Guide, but sometimes you may need to do something for which there is no predefined task. At those times, you can run a SAS program that was written outside SAS Enterprise Guide, or you can write a new one.

Writing a new SAS program To create a new SAS program, open an empty Program window by selecting **File ▶ New ▶ Program** from the menu bar. A Program window will open in the workspace. The program editor in SAS Enterprise Guide is syntax-sensitive, which means that SAS keywords are displayed in blue, comments are green, quoted strings are magenta, and so forth.

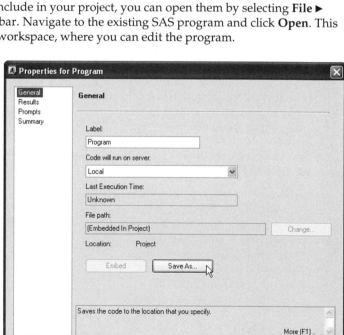

Opening an existing SAS program If you have existing SAS programs that you want to include in your project, you can open them by selecting **File ▶ Open ▶ Program** from the menu bar. Navigate to the existing SAS program and click **Open**. This opens a Program window in the workspace, where you can edit the program.

Saving a program in a file Any new programs you write are automatically embedded in your project. This means that the program's code does not exist in a file outside of the project. To save a SAS program outside its project, click **Save** on the workspace toolbar for the Program window, or right-click the program icon in the Project Tree or Process Flow and select **Save** *program-name* **As** from the pop-up menu. You can also save a program from the Properties for *program-name* window. To view the properties of a program, click **Properties** on the workspace toolbar for the Program window, or right-click the program icon in the Project Tree or Process Flow and select **Properties** from the pop-up menu. Then in the General page, click **Save As**. If you save the program in a file, then it is not embedded, and any changes you make to it in SAS Enterprise Guide will be saved in the file rather than as part of your project. The icon for a program saved in a file includes a little arrow indicating that the project contains a shortcut to the program rather than the actual program .

Embedding a program in a project
When you open a SAS program that has been saved in a separate file, it is not automatically embedded in your project. If you want to embed the program in your project, then open the Properties window for the program and click **Embed**. After you embed the program, any changes you make to it in SAS Enterprise Guide will be saved as part of your project rather than in the separate file. The icon for embedded code looks like this.

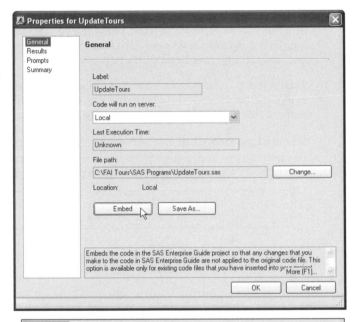

Running your program
When you are ready to run your program, click **Run** on the workspace toolbar for the Program window. Your program will run on the server that has been set as your default. To choose a different server, click **Select Server**. If you decide you want to stop a program while it's running, click the **Stop** button on the workspace toolbar for the Program window. You can also use the Program menu on the main menu bar to control your program.

1.15 Viewing Program and Project Logs

A SAS log is a record of what SAS did. Just about everything you do in SAS Enterprise Guide generates a SAS log. Logs contain the actual code that SAS ran, plus any error messages, warnings, or notes.

Different types of logs A program log is the log that is generated when you run a SAS program. Tasks generate logs too, but when you run tasks, you have little need to view the task log. That is because tasks rarely produce errors or warnings. Every time you rerun a program or task, the old log is replaced with a new one.

The Project Log, on the other hand, is a single cumulative record of everything that has been run in a particular project. By default, the Project Log is turned off. Once you turn the Project Log on, nothing disappears from it unless you clear the log.

Viewing a program log After a program runs, the results are displayed in the workspace. To open the program log, click the tab labeled **Log**. Here is a portion of the program log generated by the SAS program in the preceding section.

```
Program  | Log | Output Data (2) | Results
Export ▾ Send To ▾ Create ▾ | Project Log | Properties

23          DATA NewTours;
24              UPDATE 'C:\FAI Tours\Data\Tours' NewData;
25              BY Volcano;

NOTE: There were 10 observations read from the data set C:\FAI Tours\Data\Tours.
NOTE: There were 2 observations read from the data set WORK.NEWDATA.
NOTE: The data set WORK.NEWTOURS has 11 observations and 5 variables.
NOTE: DATA statement used (Total process time):
      real time            0.14 seconds
      cpu time             0.04 seconds

26          PROC PRINT DATA = NewTours;
```

One of the first things you will notice when you look at a log is that it contains more lines of SAS code than were in your original program. That is because SAS Enterprise Guide adds housekeeping statements to the beginning and end of your program to make sure that it runs properly when it is passed to your SAS server.

If your program contains any errors, its icon will include a red X ▨. Programs that contain warnings (but no errors) have icons with yellow triangles ▨. Even if there are no errors or warnings, it is a good habit to check the program log when you write your own SAS programs. Just because a program runs without errors or warnings does not mean that it produced the correct results.

Viewing the Project Log To turn on the Project Log, first open it by clicking **Project Log** on the workspace toolbar for the Process Flow or selecting **View ▶ Project Log** from the menu bar. Then on the workspace toolbar for the Project Log, click **Turn On**. Once the Project Log is turned on, it will keep a continuous history of everything that runs in that project.

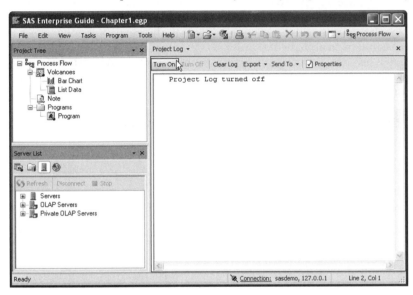

The Project Log includes the date and time when each action occurred. Click the plus sign (+) to expand a section, or the minus sign (-) to collapse it. You can also split the Project Log into two pieces by clicking and dragging the top border (the line just below the workspace toolbar) of the Project Log window.

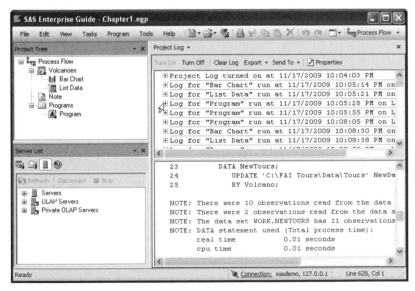

To clear the Project Log, click **Clear Log** on the workspace toolbar for the Project Log. To turn it off, click **Turn Off**.

1.16 Using the Options Window

The Options window allows you to change many default behaviors in SAS Enterprise Guide. To open the Options window, select **Tools ▶ Options** from the menu bar.

Changing the way data are handled To see options for data, click **Data General** in the selection pane on the left. If you have large data tables, columns might be easier to find if they are arranged in alphabetical order. To list columns alphabetically in task windows, check the box in front of **Display columns in alphabetical order**. By default, the Data Grid uses column names, not labels, for column headers. To change this, check the box in front of **Use labels for column names**. If you have large data tables on remote servers, you may be able to improve performance by unchecking **Automatically open data when added to project**.

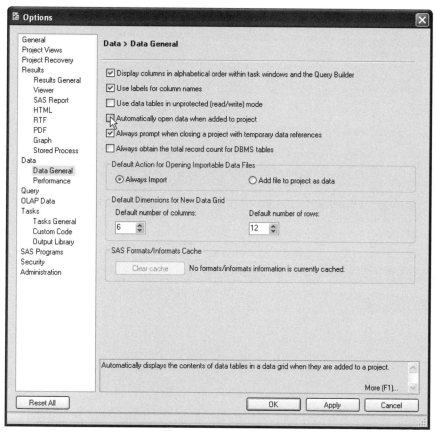

Changing the default titles and footnotes To change the default titles and footnotes, click **Tasks General** in the selection pane on the left. In this page, you can specify new default titles and footnotes, or set them to blank. Some tasks include in the results the name of the SAS procedure used by that task. In these results you will see titles like "The FREQ Procedure" or "The ANOVA Procedure." You can eliminate these titles by unchecking the box labeled **Include SAS procedure titles in results**.

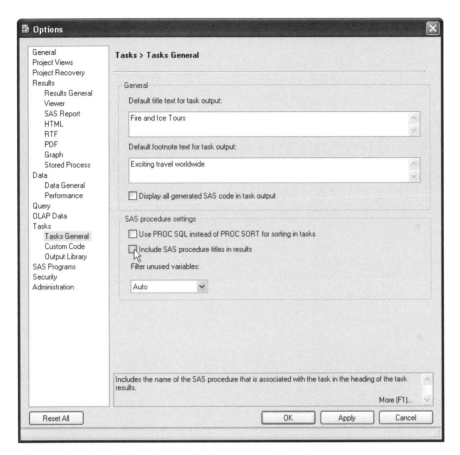

Changing the default result format and style To change the default format for results, click **Results General** in the selection pane on the left to open the Results General page (not shown). Then check all the formats you want to use: **SAS Report**, **HTML**, **PDF**, **RTF**, or **text output**. To change the default style for results, click the name of the format (such as **PDF**) in the selection pane on the left to open a page for that format (not shown), and then select a style. See Tutorial B or Chapter 11 for more about changing result formats and styles.

Running code automatically If you have SAS code that you would like to run automatically, click **SAS Programs** in the selection pane on the left to open the SAS Programs page (not shown). Select an option under the heading **Additional SAS code**. Then click **Edit**, type your code in the Edit window, and click **Save**. The option **Submit SAS code when server is connected** is particularly useful for submitting LIBNAME statements. You can also click **Custom Code** in the selection pane on the left, and specify code to be run before or after tasks.

Restoring the window layout To restore windows to their default layout, click **General** in the selection pane on the left to open the General page (not shown). Then click the **Restore Window Layout** button.

Saving and resetting options To close the Options window and save the changes you have made, click **OK**. Once you set options, they stay in effect for future SAS Enterprise Guide sessions. If at a later time, you decide you want to restore everything in the Options window to the default settings, simply click the **Reset All** button in the lower left corner.

2

" **There is no knowledge that is not power.** "

RALPH WALDO EMERSON

From the essay "Old Age" in *The Atlantic*, 1862.

CHAPTER 2

Bringing Data into a Project

2.1 ▶ Sources of Data

Before you can analyze your data, before you can run a report, before you can do anything with your data, SAS Enterprise Guide must be able to read your data. Your data might be in a data warehouse on a mainframe, or on a piece of paper sitting on your desk. Whatever form your data take, there is a way to get your data into SAS Enterprise Guide.

 New SAS data tables If you have a small amount of data, or if you've collected the data yourself, then you may find the easiest way to get your data into SAS Enterprise Guide is to type them directly into a Data Grid. To do this, just open an empty Data Grid like the one below, set the properties for the columns, and enter your data. SAS Enterprise Guide makes a SAS data table (also called a SAS data set) from the data you type into a Data Grid. Sections 2.4 to 2.6 describe Data Grids in more detail.

	A	B	C	D	E	F
1						
2						
3						
4						
5						
6						
7						
8						
9						
10						
11						
12						

 Existing SAS data tables You may have SAS data tables that were created in SAS or in another project in SAS Enterprise Guide. To open a SAS data table in SAS Enterprise Guide, select **File ▶ Open ▶ Data** from the menu bar. In the Open Data window, navigate to the location of the SAS data table. Once you have found the data table you want, click **Open**. SAS Enterprise Guide will immediately add the SAS data table to your project and display it in a Data Grid.

	Volcano	Departs	Days	Price	Difficulty
1	Etna	Catania	7	$1,075	m
2	Fuji	Tokyo	2	$225	c
3	Kenya	Nairobi	6	$830	m
4	Kilauea	Hilo	1	$55	e
5	Kilimanjaro	Nairobi	9	$1,310	c
6	Krakatau	Jakarta	7	$895	e
7	Poas	San Jose	1	$65	e
8	Reventador	Quito	4	$575	m
9	St. Helens	Portland	2	$167	e
10	Vesuvius	Rome	6	$985	e

 Raw data files Raw data files are files that contain no special formatting. They are sometimes called text, ASCII, sequential, or flat files and can be viewed using a simple text editor, such as Microsoft Notepad. SAS data tables and Microsoft Excel files are not raw data files. If you open a spreadsheet or SAS data table in Microsoft Notepad, you'll see lots of strange characters that Microsoft Notepad simply can't interpret.

SAS Enterprise Guide can read just about any type of raw data file including delimited data files and fixed-column data files. In delimited data files, a delimiter separates the data values. CSV (comma-separated values) files use commas as delimiters. Other files may use a different delimiter such as a tab, semicolon, or space. Fixed-column data files are similar to delimited data files, but instead of having a delimiter separating the data values, the data values are lined up in tidy vertical columns. Reading raw data files is described in more detail in sections 2.8 and 2.9.

 Other software files SAS Enterprise Guide can read files produced by many other types of software. When you install SAS Enterprise Guide, you get everything you need to read most PC data files. You do not need to install any additional software to read data in these formats:

- dBASE files
- HTML files
- IBM Lotus 1-2-3 files
- Microsoft Access files
- Microsoft Excel files
- Microsoft Exchange files
- Paradox files

However, if you have large PC data files, you may be able to improve performance by using SAS/ACCESS software. To read files this way, you must have SAS/ACCESS (either SAS/ACCESS Interface to PC Files or SAS/ACCESS Interface to ODBC, depending on the type of data files you are reading), and it must be installed on the same computer where SAS is installed. Then you select the option **Import the data using SAS/ACCESS Interface to PC Files whenever possible** in the Import wizard. Section 2.7 shows an example of reading a Microsoft Excel file.

 If you have SAS/ACCESS Interface to PC Files software, you can also read data in these formats:

- JMP files
- SPSS save files in Microsoft Windows format (with a .sav extension)
- Stata files in Microsoft Windows format (with a .dta extension)

To read these files, select **Tasks ▶ Data ▶ Import** *data-type* **file** from the menu bar. A task icon will be added to your project, and the imported table will be saved in your WORK library. The WORK library is erased when you exit SAS Enterprise Guide. To recreate the table at a later time, just rerun the task.

SAS Enterprise Guide can read many other kinds of database files, including Oracle and DB2. To read these other database files, you must have the corresponding SAS/ACCESS product (such as SAS/ACCESS Interface to Oracle or SAS/ACCESS Interface to DB2) installed on the same computer where SAS is installed. Then you define a SAS data library on that computer using the corresponding SAS/ACCESS engine. The SAS data library tells SAS Enterprise Guide where to find the data file and how to read it.

2.2 ▶ Locations for Data

Before you can read a data file, you must tell SAS Enterprise Guide where to find it. For any particular file, there may be several ways to do this.

Server List window

Most types of files can be brought into a project using the Server List window. This window appears in the Resources pane. To view the Server List window, select **View ▶ Server List** from the menu bar, or click the Server List icon ▦ in the Resources pane.

A SAS server is any computer running SAS software. The Server List window lists all the SAS servers that are available to you, and the files and

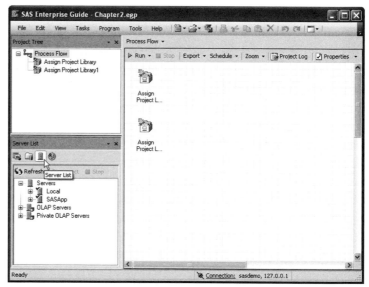

SAS data libraries on those servers. To see more detail for any part of the list (such as **Libraries** or **Files**) click the plus signs (+).

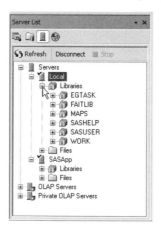

Libraries A SAS data library is a set of SAS files residing in a particular location. Instead of referring to the location by its full path, you identify it by a short name, called a libref. Here are some libraries you are likely to see:

WORK is a special library for temporary data tables. The WORK library is erased when you exit SAS Enterprise Guide.

SASUSER is the default library for output data tables and is permanent on most systems, so your data tables will not be erased by SAS Enterprise Guide. However, on z/OS and some UNIX systems, SASUSER may be temporary. In some environments, SASUSER may be read-only. If you have more than one SAS server, then you may have a SASUSER library on each server.

EGTASK is another special library. If a library with this name has been defined on your system, then SAS Enterprise Guide will use it as the default for output data sets instead of SASUSER.

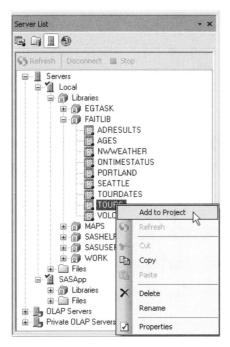

You may have other libraries that have been defined for your use. This Server List window shows that a library named FAITLIB has been defined.

If you want to define your own libraries, there are several ways to do that. These include using the Assign Project Library task (see the next section), using the SAS Enterprise Guide Explorer, and submitting a LIBNAME statement from a Program window or via the Options window (see section 1.16).

To view the data sets in a SAS data library, click the plus sign (+) next to the library's name. You can add a data set to your project by clicking its name and dragging it into the Process Flow, or by right-clicking its name and selecting **Add to Project** from the pop-up menu. In this window, the Tours data set is being added to the project.

Files If you click **Files** in the Server List window, SAS Enterprise Guide will list the folders or directories on that SAS server. From there, you can navigate through the server's directory system to find the file you want. These files may be SAS data tables or other types of files such as Excel spreadsheets. The file extension for a standard SAS data table in Windows is .sas7bdat.

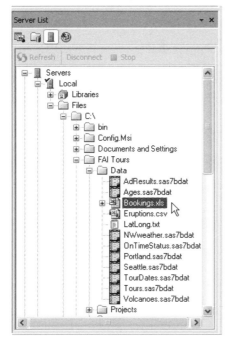

You can add a file to your project by clicking its name and dragging it into the Process Flow, or by right-clicking its name and selecting **Add to Project** from the pop-up menu.

Notice that the SAS data tables in the library FAITLIB are also listed under Files. That is because the FAITLIB data library points to that Windows subdirectory. If you add a SAS data table from Files, SAS Enterprise Guide will automatically define a library for you and give it a name like ECLIB000.

Other ways to bring data into a project

Most types of files can be brought into a project by selecting either **File ▶ Open ▶ Data**, or **File ▶ Import Data** from the menu bar. For some types of files, opening the data produces the same result as importing it. For other types of files, importing produces a different result. See sections 2.7 to 2.9 for more information about importing Microsoft Excel and raw data files.

To bring JMP, SPSS, or Stata data files into a project, you must import them. See the preceding section for a description of how to do this.

2.3 Assigning Libraries with the Assign Project Library Task

A SAS data library is a set of SAS files stored in a particular location. You use SAS data libraries to tell SAS Enterprise Guide where to find existing data tables, and where to save new ones. This section describes how to define SAS data libraries using the Assign Project Library task.

Assign Project Library wizard To define a project library, select **Tools ▶ Assign Project Library** from the menu bar. The Assign Project Library wizard will open. This wizard has four windows.

In the first window, type a name for your new library. The library name cannot be longer than eight characters; must start with a letter or underscore; and can contain only letters, numerals, and underscores. This name is called a libref, and it is like a nickname for your library. Next select the server where your data are stored. In this example, a library named FAITLIB is being created, and it will reside on the Local server. Click **Next** when you are done.

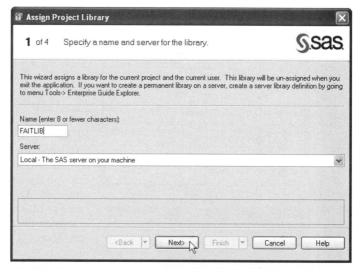

In the second window, you specify the engine. The SAS data engine determines the type of data that will reside in this library. Click the down-arrow on the box labeled **Engine type** to select the general type of engine, and then click the down-arrow on the box labeled **Engine** to select the engine. Depending on the engine type you choose, other options may appear in the lower portion of the window. For ordinary SAS data tables, use an engine type of **File System**, and the **BASE** engine. In the box labeled **Path**, type the path for your library, or click the **Browse** button to navigate to the location of your data. Click **Next** when you are done.

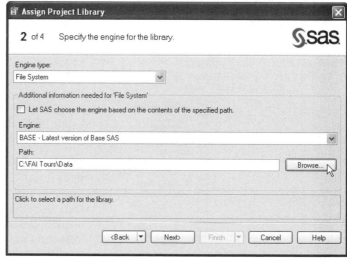

In the third window (not shown), you can specify options for your library.

In the fourth window, you can test your new library by clicking **Test Library**. Click **Finish** to close the wizard and create your library.

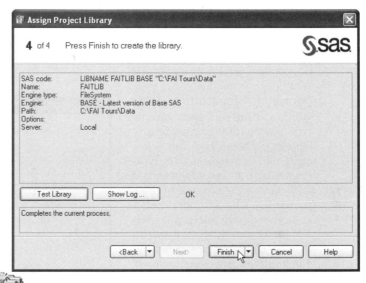

An Assign Project Library icon 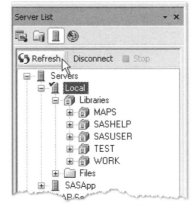 will be added to your Project Tree and Process Flow windows. However, the new project library may not automatically appear in the Server List window. If not, then click the server (such as Local), and click **Refresh**.

Rerunning the Assign Project Library task

When you open SAS Enterprise Guide, project libraries are not automatically assigned. Before you can use project libraries (and any data accessed via them), you must rerun any Assign Project Library tasks.

You can rerun an Assign Project Library task by right-clicking its icon in the Project Tree or Process Flow and selecting **Run** from the pop-up menu, or by clicking its icon and selecting **Run ▶ Run Assign Project Library** on the workspace toolbar above the Process Flow.

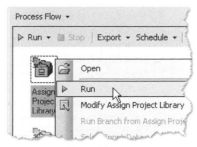

Alternatively, you can rerun your entire process flow. Click **Run** on the workspace toolbar above the Process Flow, or right-click the name of the process flow in the Project Tree and select **Run** *process-flow-name* from the pop-up menu. Just be sure that your Assign Project Library icons appear before any tasks that use those libraries. Since projects run from top left to bottom right, you may want to move any Assign Project Library icons to the upper-left corner of the Process Flow.

2.4 ► Creating New SAS Data Tables in a Data Grid

Using the Data Grid, you can browse and edit existing SAS data tables, or create new ones. To open an empty Data Grid, select **File ► New ► Data** from the menu bar. This opens the New Data wizard, which has two windows.

Name and location In the first window of the New Data wizard, type a name for your new data table in the **Name** box. This is a name that you make up. The name must follow the rules for standard SAS names (32 characters or fewer; start with a letter or underscore; and contain only letters, numerals, and underscores). Next choose a location where the new data table will be stored. This location must be a SAS data library. If a suitable library is not listed, then cancel the New Data wizard and define a new library before starting over (see section 2.3). In this example, the name Seattle has been typed in the Name box and the FAITLIB library has been selected. When you are satisfied, click **Next**.

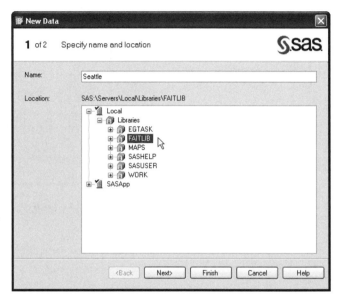

Column properties In the second window of the New Data wizard, specify the properties for each column in your new data table. At first the columns are named A, B, C, and so on. To display the properties of a particular column, click its name in the list on the left under the heading **Columns**. To change a column property, click its value in the list on the right under the heading **Column Properties**. You can type a name for the column and an optional label. Then specify the data type and data group by clicking the word **Type** or **Group** and selecting from the pull-down list. In the Seattle data table, the fourth column has the name

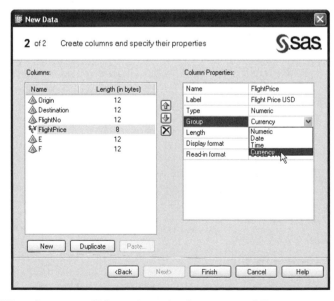

FlightPrice, a label of Flight Price USD, a data type of Numeric, and a data group of Currency.

To change a read-in format (also called an informat) or a display format (also called a format), click its value under Column

Properties. The ellipsis button will appear 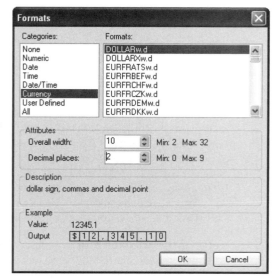. Click the ellipsis button to open a Formats window. The Formats window that opens looks the same regardless of whether you are modifying an informat or a format. See sections 1.10 and 1.11 for tables of commonly used informats and formats.

The Formats window shown here is for the format for FlightPrice. The format is set to DOLLAR*w.d* with a width of 10 and 2 decimal places. This format can be written as DOLLAR10.2. When you are satisfied, click **OK** to return to the second window of the New Data wizard.

You can also open a window for the informat, and any informats you specify will be saved with the column properties. However, in SAS Enterprise Guide 4.2, Data Grids do not use informats to interpret input data. Instead, Data Grids use the data type and data group that you specify to determine how to interpret any data values you enter.

In the second window of the New Data wizard, you can add more columns by clicking **New**. You can delete columns by clicking the name of that column and then clicking the delete button

. When you are satisfied with your columns and their properties, click **Finish** to close the wizard and create an empty data table.

Entering data Once you have created the data table, you can begin typing data into it. Any value you enter must fit the data type and data group you specified. You can copy and paste values. To move the cursor, click a cell, or use the tab and arrow keys.

Here is the Seattle data table with column attributes defined, and three rows of data entered.

	Origin	Destination	FlightNo	FlightPrice
1	Seattle	Catania	BA48	$802.00
2	Seattle	Hilo	HA21	$677.00
3	Seattle	Jakarta	AA119	1815
4				.
5				.
6				.
7				.
8				.
9				.
10				.
11				.
12				.

2.5 ▶ Editing SAS Data Tables in a Data Grid

Editing SAS data tables is easy—whether you need to add new rows or columns, fix errors, or update values—but there are a few points to keep in mind.

Copying a SAS data table When you edit a SAS data table in a Data Grid, any changes you make are permanent, even if you don't save the project. Therefore, unless you are absolutely sure about the changes you make, you should make a copy of the data table before editing. To make a copy, right-click the data icon in the Project Tree or Process Flow window and select **Export ▶ Export** *table-name* from the pop-up menu. Choose a location for the new data table and give it a name. Or, open the table in a Data Grid, and select **Export ▶ Export** *table-name* from the workspace toolbar. When you export a data table, your new copy does not appear in your project, so after you export the data table, you must open it in your project.

Setting the update mode Unless you are creating a new SAS data table, any data tables you open in SAS Enterprise Guide will initially be set to read-only mode. This prevents you from accidentally changing the data. To edit SAS data tables, you must change to update mode. Click the data icon in the Project Tree or Process Flow to make it active, and select **Edit ▶ Protect Data** from the menu bar. To switch back to read-only mode, select **Edit ▶ Protect Data** again.

Editing data values To change a value in a Data Grid, simply click the cell and start typing. You can also copy and paste values. In SAS Enterprise Guide 4.2, the Data Grid does not use informats to interpret input data. Instead, data values you enter will be interpreted based on the data type and data group for that column. After you enter a value, it will be displayed using the format for that column. If you are not sure which data type, data group, and format a column uses, you can find out by displaying the column properties. To do this, right-click the column header in the Data Grid, and select **Properties** from the pop-up menu.

Adding or removing a column To add a column to a data table, right-click a column header next to the place where you want to add a column, and select **Insert Column** from the pop-up menu. The Insert window will open.

	Origin	Des			FlightPrice
1	Seattle	Catania	Cut		$1,045.00
2	Seattle	Hilo	Copy		$677.00
3	Seattle	Jakarta	Paste		$1,815.00
4	Seattle	Nairobi	Hide		$1,761.00
5	Seattle	Quito	Show		$833.00
6	Seattle	Rome	Hold		$596.00
7	Seattle	Sacrame	Free		$352.00
8	Seattle	San Jose	Delete		$480.00
9	Seattle	Tokyo	Insert Column...		$721.00
			Width...		
			Properties		

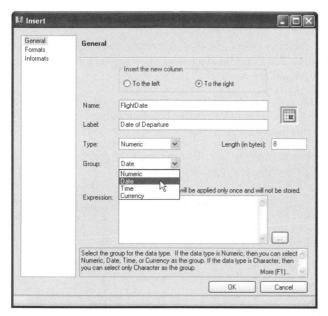

In the General page of the Insert window, indicate whether you want the new column to be inserted to the left or the right. Then type a name and optional label for the column, and select the length, data type, and group. If you click **Formats** or **Informats** in the selection pane on the left, then you can specify display or read-in formats for the new column. In this case, the column will be named FlightDate, and will have a label of Date of Departure. Its type will be Numeric. It will be in the Date group, and will use the default format for dates, MMDDYY10.

To delete a column, right-click the column you want to delete and select **Delete** from the pop-up menu.

Adding or removing rows   To add rows to a data table, right-click the row number at the point where you want to add rows, and select **Insert rows** from the pop-up menu. The Insert Rows window will open. Specify the number of rows you want to insert, and whether you want them to be inserted above or below. Then click **OK**.

You can also right-click a row and select **Append a row** to add a row at the bottom of the table. To delete rows, click the row you want to delete (or use shift-click to select more than one row). Then right-click, and select **Delete rows**.

In this data table, a new row has been added for a flight to Sacramento, and a new column has been added for FlightDate.

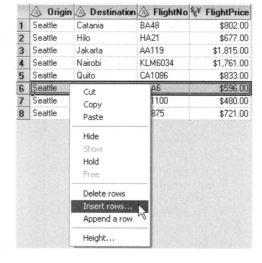

	Origin	Destination	FlightNo	FlightPrice
1	Seattle	Catania	BA48	$802.00
2	Seattle	Hilo	HA21	$677.00
3	Seattle	Jakarta	AA119	$1,815.00
4	Seattle	Nairobi	KLM6034	$1,761.00
5	Seattle	Quito	CA1086	$833.00
6	Seattle	A6		$596.00
7	Seattle	100		$480.00
8	Seattle	875		$721.00

	Origin	Destination	FlightDate	FlightNo	FlightPrice
1	Seattle	Catania	08/14/2011	BA48	$802.00
2	Seattle	Hilo	07/14/11	HA21	$677.00
3	Seattle	Jakarta	.	AA119	$1,815.00
4	Seattle	Nairobi	.	KLM6034	$1,761.00
5	Seattle	Quito	.	CA1086	$833.00
6	Seattle	Rome	.	USA6	$596.00
7	Seattle	Sacramento	.	SW345	$352.00
8	Seattle	San Jose	.	CA1100	$480.00
9	Seattle	Tokyo	.	UA875	$721.00

2.6 Inserting Computed Columns in a Data Grid

In addition to entering and editing data, the Data Grid also allows you to compute new columns based on the value of existing columns. For example, if a teacher had scores for five exams, she could add a new column that would equal the mean of all the scores.

When you add a computed column to a data table, all the same caveats apply as when editing data tables. You'll probably want to save a copy of your table before making changes, and you must switch to update mode. For a discussion of these topics, see the previous section.

The Fire and Ice Tours company hopes to increase sales by offering a ten percent discount off the price of tours. To compute the new prices, insert a new column.

Inserting the column To add a computed column to a data table, you start the same way you would to insert an empty column. First right-click a column header next to the place where you want to add a column, and select **Insert Column** from the pop-up menu. The Insert window will open.

	Volcano	Departs	Days	Pric		
1	Etna	Catania	7	$1,07	Cut	
2	Fuji	Tokyo	2	$22	Copy	
3	Kenya	Nairobi	6	$83	Paste	
4	Kilauea	Hilo	1	$5	Hide	
5	Kilimanjaro	Nairobi	9	$1,31	Show	
6	Krakatau	Jakarta	7	$89	Hold	
7	Poas	San Jose	1	$6	Free	
8	Reventador	Quito	4	$57	Delete	
9	St. Helens	Portland	2	$16	Insert Column...	
10	Vesuvius	Rome	6	$98	Width...	
					Properties	

In the General page of the Insert window, indicate whether you want the new column to be inserted to the left or the right. Then type a name and optional label for the column, and select the length, data type, and group. In this example, the new column will have the name FallPromo, a label of Tour Price with 10% Discount, a type of Numeric, a group of Currency, and a length of 8.

If you want to specify the read-in or display format, click **Informats** or **Formats** in the selection pane on the left. This example uses the default format and informat.

Insert

General | Formats | Informats

General

Insert the new column
○ To the left   ● To the right

Name: FallPromo

Label: Tour Price with 10% Discount

Type: Numeric   Length (in bytes): 8

Group: Currency

Note: The expression will be applied only once and will not be stored.

Expression: Price * 0.9

More (F1)...

OK   Cancel

At the bottom of the Insert window is a box labeled **Expression**. You can type an expression in this box and SAS Enterprise Guide will use that expression to compute the values of the new column. In this example, you can see that the expression **Price * 0.9** has been entered so the values of the new column will equal the value of the Price column multiplied by 0.9. When you are satisfied, click **OK**, and the new column will be added to the Data Grid.

Here is the Data Grid showing the new column FallPromo.

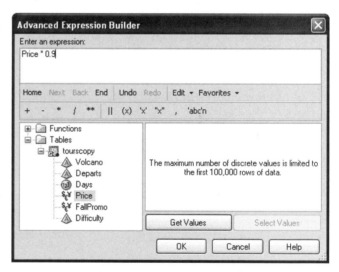

	Volcano	Departs	Days	Price	FallPromo	Difficulty
1	Etna	Catania	7	$1,075	$968	m
2	Fuji	Tokyo	2	$225	$203	c
3	Kenya	Nairobi	6	$830	$747	m
4	Kilauea	Hilo	1	$55	$50	e
5	Kilimanjaro	Nairobi	9	$1,310	$1,179	c
6	Krakatau	Jakarta	7	$895	$806	e
7	Poas	San Jose	1	$65	$59	e
8	Reventador	Quito	4	$575	$518	m
9	St. Helens	Portland	2	$167	$150	e
10	Vesuvius	Rome	6	$985	$887	e

Building the expression In this example, the expression was simple so it was easy to type it in the Expression box. However, if the syntax of your expression were more complicated, you might want some help. To get help building your expression, click the ellipsis button [...] next to the box labeled **Expression** in the Insert window. The Advanced Expression Builder will open.

At the top of the Advanced Expression Builder is a box labeled **Enter an expression**. You can type in this box, or you can use the buttons and lists below to construct an expression.

The Advanced Expression Builder is similar to the expression builder available in the Query Builder. See Tutorial C or sections 4.3 and 4.4 for examples of building expressions.

Computing columns in a Data Grid versus in a query You can add a computed column to a data table in a Data Grid or in the Query Builder, but there is an important difference. When you compute a column in a Data Grid, the expression is applied only once, and is not saved. You cannot change an expression after it has been applied. So, if you wanted to see tour prices with a 20 percent discount, you would have to insert a completely new column. On the other hand, if you compute a column in a query, then you can re-open the query, make changes, and rerun it as many times as you wish.

2.7 Importing Microsoft Excel Spreadsheets

When you open or import a Microsoft Excel spreadsheet, SAS Enterprise Guide converts it to a SAS data set.

Input data This example uses a Microsoft Excel spreadsheet named Bookings.xls, which contains six columns: the office that booked the tour, the customer identification number, the tour identification number, the number of travelers, the money deposited, and the date the deposit was made. Notice that the first row contains the column names.

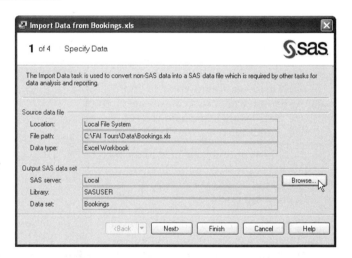

Import Data wizard There are several ways to open a Microsoft Excel file. You can select **File ▶ Open ▶ Data** or **File ▶ Import Data** from the menu bar, or drag the file from the Server List window to the Process Flow. The Import Data wizard will open.

The Import Data wizard has four windows. In the first window under the heading **Output SAS data set**, appears the SAS server, SAS data library, and data set name for the data set you are creating. To change any of these, click **Browse**. When you are satisfied, click **Next**.

In the second window under the heading **Select range**, you specify either a sheet, a specific range of cells, or a named range. You can also check the option **First row of range contains field names** to use values from the first row of the spreadsheet for column names. You can check the option **Rename columns to comply with SAS naming conventions** to tell SAS Enterprise Guide to automatically rename columns according to traditional rules for SAS names.

(See section 1.7 for a discussion of column names, and moving data between SAS Enterprise Guide and Base SAS.) For the Bookings data, import Sheet1 and use the first row as column names, and click **Next**.

In the third window, you see the column properties that SAS Enterprise Guide suggests for your data. To make changes, highlight the column you wish to change, and then click **Modify**. The Field Attributes window will open allowing you to change any column attribute. No changes are needed for this example. Click **Next**.

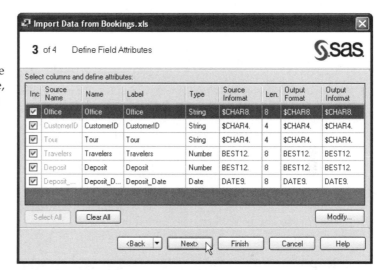

In the fourth window, you can choose options including **Import the data using SAS/ACCESS Interface to PC Files whenever possible**. If you have SAS/ACCESS Interface to PC Files software and you have large spreadsheets, using this option may be faster than the default.

When you are satisfied with the settings, click **Finish**.

Results The new data set will appear in a Data Grid. The data set opens in read-only mode, but because the data are now in a SAS data set, you can change to update mode to edit the data. Any changes you make will not be applied to the original Microsoft Excel spreadsheet.

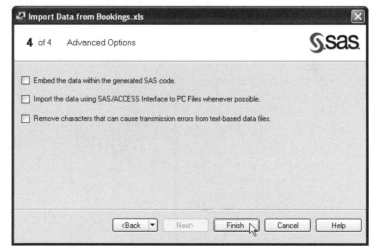

2.8 Importing Delimited Raw Data

Delimited raw data files have a special character separating the data values. That character is often a comma (as in CSV or comma-separated values files), but it can also be a tab, semicolon, space, or some other character.

Input data This example uses data from a file named Eruptions.csv. There are four variables: the volcano name, followed by the date an eruption started, the date that eruption ended, and the Volcanic Explosivity Index (VEI). Notice that this file has commas between the data values, and the first line contains the column names.

```
Volcano, StartDate, EndDate, VEI
Barren Island, 12/20/1795, 12/21/1795, 2
Barren Island, 12/20/1994, 06/05/1995, 2
Erebus, 12/12/1912, . , 2
Erebus, 01/03/1972, . , 1
Etna, 02/06/1610, 08/15/1610, 2
Etna, 06/04/1787, 08/11/1787, 4
Etna, 01/30/1865, 06/28/1865, 2
```

Opening a delimited data file You can open a raw data file by selecting **File ▶ Open ▶ Data** from the menu bar. When you do this, SAS Enterprise Guide opens the file in a simple text editor. Using this editor, you can view the data, and you can edit the data, but you cannot use the data in any task when it is opened this way. In order to use raw data in a task, you must import it.

Import Data wizard
To import a raw data file, select **File ▶ Import Data** from the menu bar. The Open window will appear. Navigate to the file you wish to import, and click **Open**. The Import Data wizard will open.

The Import Data wizard has four windows. In the first window under the heading **Output SAS data set**, appears the SAS server, SAS data library, and data set name for the data set you are creating.

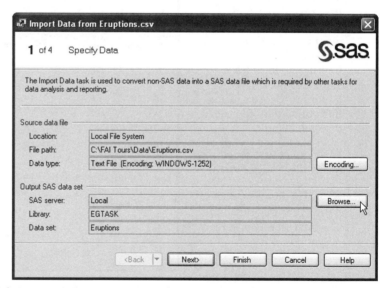

To change any of these, click **Browse**. When you are satisfied, click **Next**.

In the second window, select **Delimited fields**. To specify the delimiter for your file, click the down-arrow on the box and either select a delimiter (such as **Comma** or **Tab**) from the pull-down list, or select **Other** and type the delimiter into the box on the right. You can also check the option **File contains field names on record number**, and type a number in the corresponding box to use values in that row as column names. You can check the option **Rename columns to**

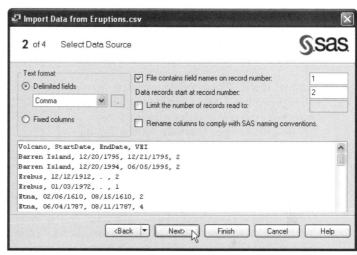

comply with SAS naming conventions to tell SAS Enterprise Guide to automatically rename columns according to traditional rules for SAS names. (See section 1.7 for a discussion of column names, and moving data between SAS Enterprise Guide and Base SAS.) For the Eruptions data, select **Comma** as the delimiter, and use the first record for column names. Click **Next**.

In the third window, you see the column properties that SAS Enterprise Guide suggests for your data. To make changes, highlight the column you wish to change, and then click **Modify**. The Field Attributes window will open allowing you to change any column attribute. No changes are needed for this example. Click **Next**.

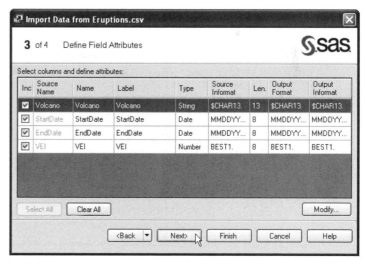

In the fourth window (not shown), you can specify options for embedding data and removing characters that may produce errors. When you are satisfied with the settings, click **Finish**.

Results The data set will appear in a Data Grid. The data set opens in read-only mode, but because the data are now in a SAS data set, you can change to update mode to edit the data. Any changes you make will not be applied to the original data file.

	Volcano	StartDate	EndDate	VEI
1	Barren Island	12/20/1795	12/21/1795	2
2	Barren Island	12/20/1994	06/05/1995	2
3	Erebus	12/12/1912		2
4	Erebus	01/03/1972		1
5	Etna	02/06/1610	08/15/1610	2
6	Etna	06/04/1787	08/11/1787	4
7	Etna	01/30/1865	06/28/1865	2

2.9 Importing Fixed-Column Raw Data

Fixed-column raw data files are similar to delimited raw data files, but instead of having a delimiter separating the data values, the data values are lined up in tidy vertical columns.

Input data This example uses data from a file named LatLong.txt, which contains three variables: the name of the volcano, followed by its latitude and longitude. Notice that the column names appear in the first row, and the data values are vertically aligned.

Volcano	Latitude	Longitude
Altar	-1.67	-78.42
Barren Island	12.28	93.52
Elbrus	43.33	42.45
Erebus	-77.53	167.17
Etna	37.73	15.00
Fuji	35.35	138.73
Garibaldi	49.85	-123.00

Opening a fixed-column data file You can open a raw data file by selecting **File ▶ Open ▶ Data** from the menu bar. When you do this, SAS Enterprise Guide opens the file in a simple text editor. Using this editor, you can view the data, and you can edit the data, but you cannot use the data in any task when it is opened this way. In order to use raw data in a task, you must import it.

Import Data wizard To import a raw data file, select **File ▶ Import Data** from the menu bar. The Open window will appear. Navigate to the file you wish to import, and click **Open**. The Import Data wizard will open.

The Import Data wizard has four windows. In the first window under the heading **Output SAS data set**, appears the SAS server, SAS data library, and data set name for the data set you are creating. To change any of these, click **Browse**. When you are satisfied, click **Next**.

> **Import Data from LatLong.txt**
>
> **1** of 4   Specify Data   §.sas.
>
> The Import Data task is used to convert non-SAS data into a SAS data file which is required by other tasks for data analysis and reporting.
>
> **Source data file**
> Location: Local File System
> File path: C:\FAI Tours\Data\LatLong.txt
> Data type: Text File (Encoding: WINDOWS-1252)   [Encoding...]
>
> **Output SAS data set**
> SAS server: Local   [Browse...]
> Library: EGTASK
> Data set: LatLong
>
> [<Back |▼] [Next>] [Finish] [Cancel] [Help]

In the second window, select **Fixed columns**. At the bottom of this window is a box displaying the data file. Click the ruler above the data to tell SAS Enterprise Guide where each variable begins. For the LatLong data, the volcano name starts at 1, latitude starts at 15, and longitude starts at 24. You can also check the option **File contains field names on record number**, and type a number in the corresponding box to use values in that row as column names. You can check the option **Rename columns to comply with SAS naming conventions** to tell SAS Enterprise Guide to automatically rename columns according to traditional

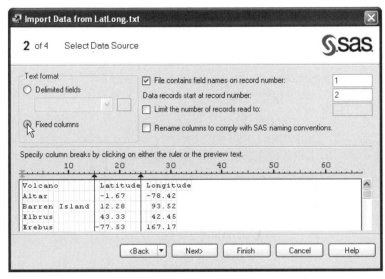

rules for SAS names. (See section 1.7 for a discussion of column names, and moving data between SAS Enterprise Guide and Base SAS.) For the LatLong data, use the first record as column names, and click **Next**.

In the third window, you see the column properties that SAS Enterprise Guide suggests for your data. To make changes, highlight the column you wish to change, and then click **Modify**. The Field Attributes window will open allowing you to change any column attribute. No changes are needed for this example. Click **Next**.

In the fourth window (not shown), you can specify options for embedding data and removing characters that may produce errors. When you are satisfied with the settings, click **Finish**.

Results The data set will appear in a Data Grid. The data set opens in read-only mode, but because the data are now in a SAS data set, you can change to update mode to edit the data. Any changes you make will not be applied to the original data file.

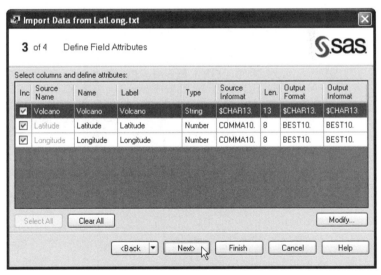

2.10 Exporting Data

After you have read your data into SAS Enterprise Guide and worked with it, you may want to access it in some other form. SAS Enterprise Guide can write data in these formats:

- Comma-separated values (CSV) files
- dBASE files
- HTML files
- IBM Lotus 1-2-3 files
- Microsoft Access 2002-2003 files
- Microsoft Excel 97-2003 files
- Paradox files
- SAS data tables
- Space-delimited text files
- Tab-delimited text files

Here is a Data Grid showing the Tours data table, which will be exported as a Microsoft Excel file.

	Volcano	Departs	Days	Price	Difficulty
1	Etna	Catania	7	$1,075	m
2	Fuji	Tokyo	2	$225	c
3	Kenya	Nairobi	6	$830	m
4	Kilauea	Hilo	1	$55	e
5	Kilimanjaro	Nairobi	9	$1,310	c
6	Krakatau	Jakarta	7	$895	e
7	Poas	San Jose	1	$65	e

To export data from SAS Enterprise Guide, click **Export** on the workspace toolbar for the Data Grid and select **Export** *data-table-name* or **Export** *data-table-name* **As A Step In Project**. You can also export data by right-clicking the data icon in the Project Tree or Process Flow, and selecting **File ► Export ► Export** *data-table-name* or **File ► Export ► Export** *data-table-name* **As A Step In Project** from the pop-up menu.

Exporting If you select **Export** *data-table-name*, then an Export window will open. Navigate to the location where you want to save the new file, specify a name for the file, select the type of file you want to create, and click **Save**. When you export data, no icon will appear in the Project Tree or Process Flow.

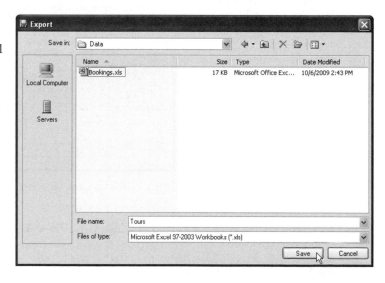

Exporting as a step in a project

If you select **Export As A Step In Project**, the Export wizard will open. The number of windows in the wizard depends on the type of file you are creating. For an Excel file, there are five windows.

In the first window, select the data table you wish to export, and click **Next**.

In the second window, select the type of file you wish to create, and click **Next**.

In the third window (not shown), indicate whether you want to use labels for column names, and click **Next.**

In the fourth window (not shown), choose either **Local Computer** or **SAS Servers**, and then click the **Browse** button to navigate to the location where you want the table to be saved. You can only export a SAS data table to a computer that has SAS installed on it. In this window, you can also choose whether to **Overwrite existing output**. When you are satisfied, click **Next.**

In the fifth window (not shown), confirm your settings by clicking **Finish**.

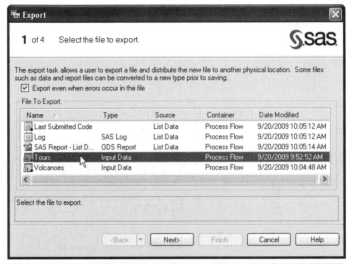

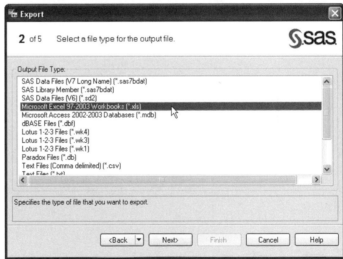

An Export File task icon 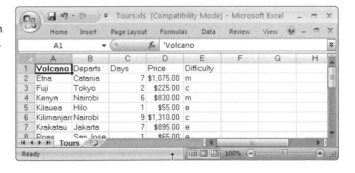 will be added to your project, along with an icon for the newly exported data. Every time you run your project, your data file will be automatically re-exported. Here is the Tours data table after being exported as a spreadsheet and opened in Microsoft Excel.

3

" Knowledge is of two kinds. We know a subject ourselves or we know where we can find information upon it. "

SAMUEL JOHNSON

From Boswell's *Life of Johnson*, 1775. As quoted in *The Cyclopedia of Practical Quotations: English, Latin, and Modern Foreign Languages* by Jehiel Keeler Hoyt, 1896.

CHAPTER 3

Changing the Way Data Values Are Displayed

3.2 Applying Standard Formats in a Task

Every time you run a task that produces a report, SAS Enterprise Guide decides how the data should be displayed. That's good, but sometimes the way that SAS Enterprise Guide displays data may not be exactly what you want. You can change the way data are displayed by applying a format in a Data Grid or query, but then the format will be saved with the data set. If you don't want the format to be saved with the data, then you can apply the format directly in a task.

	Volcano	StartDate	EndDate	VEI
1	Barren Island	12/20/1795	12/21/1795	2
2	Barren Island	12/20/1994	06/05/1995	2
3	Erebus	12/12/1912	.	2
4	Erebus	01/03/1972	.	1
5	Etna	02/06/1610	08/15/1610	2
6	Etna	06/04/1787	08/11/1787	4
7	Etna	01/30/1865	06/28/1865	2
8	Etna	12/16/2005	12/22/2005	1
9	Fuji	12/16/1707	02/24/1708	5
10	Grimsvotn	10/31/1603	11/01/1603	2

Here is the Eruptions data set. The previous section showed how to apply the format WEEKDATE*w.d* to the variable StartDate in a Data Grid. This example uses the List Data task to show how you can apply the same format in a task.

To open the task, click the data icon in the Project Tree or Process Flow and select **Tasks ▶ Describe ▶ List Data** from the menu bar. The List Data window will open, displaying the Data page.

Opening the Properties window To open a Properties window for a variable, right-click the name of the variable you want to modify (in either the **Variables to assign** area or the **Task roles** area), and select **Properties** from the pop-up menu. In this example, the variables Volcano, StartDate, and VEI have been assigned to the **List variables** role, and **Properties** is being selected for StartDate.

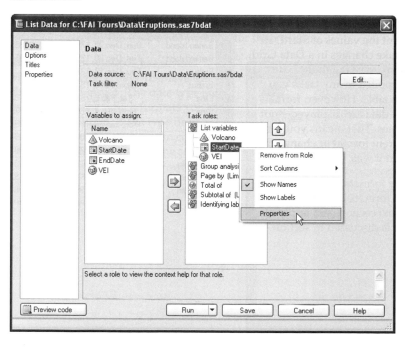

Here is the Properties window for the variable StartDate. You cannot change a variable's data type or group using the Properties window inside a task. To make that change, use the Properties window inside a Data Grid, as described in the preceding section.

Click **Change** to open the Formats window.

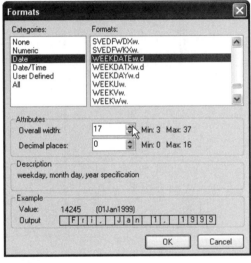

Selecting formats In the Formats window, choose the category of formats you want to see, and then click the name of the format you want to use. In the area labeled **Attributes**, specify the overall width (the longest number of characters or digits that will be allowed for this variable). For numeric variables, you may also specify the number of decimal places. The area labeled **Example** shows a sample of how this format will look. See section 1.11 for a list of commonly used formats.

In this Formats window, the category Date has been selected, along with the format WEEKDATE*w.d*, an overall width of 17, and no decimal places. This format can be written as WEEKDATE17.0.

When you are satisfied with the format, click **OK**. Then click **OK** in the Properties window, and click **Run** in the task window.

Report Listing			
Row number	Volcano	StartDate	VEI
1	Barren Island	Sun, Dec 20, 1795	2
2	Barren Island	Tue, Dec 20, 1994	2
3	Erebus	Thu, Dec 12, 1912	2
4	Erebus	Mon, Jan 3, 1972	1
5	Etna	Sat, Feb 6, 1610	2
6	Etna	Mon, Jun 4, 1787	4
7	Etna	Mon, Jan 30, 1865	2
8	Etna	Fri, Dec 16, 2005	1
9	Fuji	Fri, Dec 16, 1707	5
10	Grimsvotn	Fri, Oct 31, 1603	2

Results Here is the beginning of the report using the new format for StartDate. Any formats you apply in a task are not saved in the original data set and will not be used in other tasks.

3.3 Defining Your Own Character Formats

Even with all the standard formats provided by SAS Enterprise Guide, there are times when you need something different. In those cases, you can create a user-defined format. Basically, user-defined formats allow you to specify a set of labels that will be substituted for specific values or ranges of values in your data. To do this, open the Create Format window by selecting **Tasks ▶ Data ▶ Create Format** from the menu bar.

Create Format options To create a format for a character variable, select a **Format type** of **Character**. Then type a name for the new format in the **Format name** box. This name must be 31 characters or fewer in length; cannot start or end with a numeral; and can contain only letters, numerals, or underscores. This example shows a character format named RegionName being created.

Any formats stored in the WORK library (the default) will be deleted when you exit SAS Enterprise Guide. To save your format, choose a different library. If you have more than one SAS server, be sure to save your format on the same server where you run tasks. If you choose to leave your format in the WORK library, you can always regenerate it later by rerunning the Create Format task. When you are satisfied, click **Define formats** in the selection pane on the left.

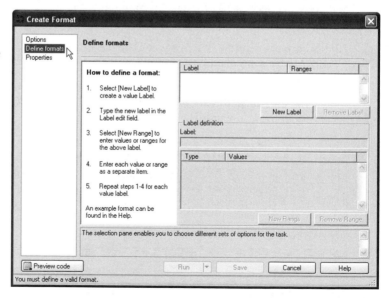

Defining formats You define formats in a stepwise fashion. First, click **New Label** and type a label in the **Label** box. Then click **New Range,** and under **Values** type the data value that corresponds to that label. Data values are case-sensitive, so "yes" is not the same as "Yes." Repeat these steps until you have created all the labels you wish. In this example, you can see that the label Africa is being applied to the data value Af. Repeat the process to apply Antarctica to An, Australia/Pacific to AP, Asia to As, Europe to Eu, North America to NA, and South America to SA.

To specify a range of data values (such as A–D) rather than a discrete value, click the down-arrow (▼) under **Type** and select **Range** from the pull-down list. When you do that, a second box will appear under Values so that you can type in the two end points for your range.

You can specify a label to be used for missing values or for all other values by clicking the down-arrow in the box labeled **Values.** In this window, you can see that the label Error will be applied to all other data values. When you are satisfied with the format labels and ranges, click **Run** to create the format.

All character format names begin with a dollar sign, and end with a period, so this format will be named $RegionName. A more detailed example of creating a character format appears in Tutorial B.

Using custom formats You can apply a user-defined format to a variable in the same ways you apply standard formats: in a Data Grid, a task, or a query. Section 3.5 shows the $RegionName. format being used in a List Data task.

3.4 ► Defining Your Own Numeric Formats

The previous section showed how to create a user-defined format for a character variable. Creating a user-defined format for a numeric variable is similar, but you have a few more options. Start by selecting **Tasks ► Data ► Create Format** from the menu bar to open the Create Format window.

Create Format options Select a **Format type** of **Numeric**. Then type a name for the new format in the **Format name** box. This name must be 32 characters or fewer in length; cannot start or end with a numeral; and can contain only letters, numerals, or underscores. This example shows a numeric format named HeightGroup being created.

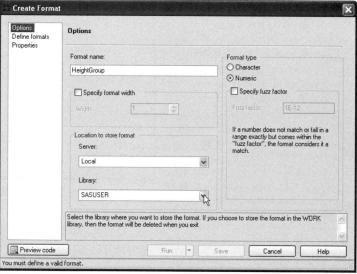

Any formats stored in the WORK library (the default) will be deleted when you exit SAS Enterprise Guide. To save your format, choose a different library. If you have more than one SAS server, be sure to save your format on the same server where you run tasks. If you choose to leave your format in the WORK library, you can always regenerate it later by rerunning the Create Format task. When you are satisfied, click **Define formats** in the selection pane on the left.

Defining formats You define formats in a stepwise fashion. First, click **New Label** and type a label in the **Label** box. Then click **New Range** and enter the data values corresponding to that label. Repeat these steps for the second label, and so on, until you have created all the labels you wish.

When you specify the data values, you have some choices. Under **Type**, click the down-arrow (▼) to open the pull-down list and select either **Discrete** (if you have a single value) or **Range**. In this example, you can see the label Pip-squeak will be substituted for a range of values up to 500.

You can make ranges inclusive or exclusive. In this example, the label Middling maps to values from 500 up to (but excluding) 4000. If you see a red X over ranges at the top of the window, it means that your ranges are overlapping and you will probably want to make one of them exclusive.

You can specify a label to be used for special values by clicking the arrow in the box labeled **Values**. For discrete values, you can select **All Other Values** or **Missing Values**. For ranges, you can select **Low** (the lowest possible value) and **High** (the highest). In this window, the label Stupendous has been mapped to data values from 4000 to High. When you are satisfied with the format labels and ranges, click **Run** to create the format.

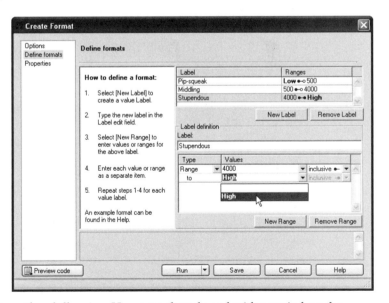

Unlike character formats, numeric formats do not begin with a dollar sign. However, they do end with a period, so the name of this format will be HeightGroup.

Using custom formats You can apply a user-defined format to a variable in the same ways you apply standard formats: in a Data Grid, a task, or a query. The next section shows the HeightGroup. format being applied in a List Data task.

3.5 Applying User-Defined Formats

You apply user-defined formats in exactly the same ways you apply standard formats: in a Data Grid, a task, or a query. The example in this section applies two user-defined formats, $RegionName. and HeightGroup. (from sections 3.3 and 3.4), in a List Data task.

Here is a simple report from a List Data task using the Volcanoes data set. The variables Volcano, Region, and Height have been assigned to serve in the List variables role. Notice that the data values are unformatted.

Report Listing

Row number	Volcano	Region	Height
1	Altar	SA	5321
2	Arthur's Seat	Eu	251
3	Barren Island	As	354
4	Elbrus	Eu	5633
5	Erebus	An	3794
6	Etna	Eu	3350
7	Fuji	As	3776
8	Garibaldi	NA	2678
9	Grimsvotn	Eu	1725
10	Illimani	SA	6458

You can apply a format when you first run a task or you can add it later. To change an existing report, re-open the task window by right-clicking the task icon in the Project Tree or Process Flow and selecting **Modify** *task-name* from the pop-up menu.

Opening the Properties window

To apply a format in a task, right-click the name of the variable you want to change in the Data page (in either the **Variables to assign** area or the **Task roles** area), and select **Properties** from the pop-up menu. In this example, **Properties** is being selected for the variable Region.

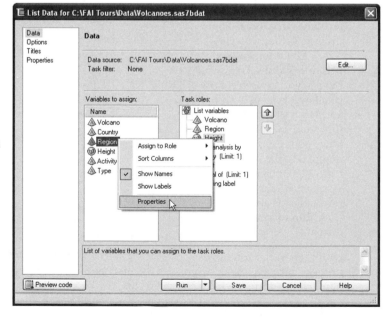

Using custom formats In the Properties window, click **Change** to open the Formats window for that variable.

Then in the Formats window, select the category **User Defined**. All the formats you have created will be listed. Here is the Formats window for the variable Region. Because Region is character, only character formats are listed. In this case, $REGIONNAME. is being selected.

Once you have selected the correct format, click **OK** in the Formats window and click **OK** in the Properties window.

From the Data page of the task window, you can open the Properties window for other variables. Once you have applied all the formats you want, click **Run** in the task window.

Results Here is the new report with user-defined formats applied. You can see that the values of Region are now displayed using the $RegionName. format that was created in section 3.3. In addition, the values of Height are now displayed using the HeightGroup. format created in section 3.4.

In this example, the user-defined formats were applied to list variables. The result was that the

Report Listing

Row number	Volcano	Region	Height
1	Altar	South America	Stupendous
2	Arthur's Seat	Europe	Pip-squeak
3	Barren Island	Asia	Pip-squeak
4	Elbrus	Europe	Stupendous
5	Erebus	Antarctica	Middling
6	Etna	Europe	Middling
7	Fuji	Asia	Middling
8	Garibaldi	North America	Middling
9	Grimsvotn	Europe	Middling
10	Illimani	South America	Stupendous

formats simply replaced one value with another. However, if you apply a user-defined format to a variable assigned to a task role that groups the data, then it changes the structure of the report. See section 7.9 for an example of creating a grouped report with a user-defined format.

4

" The power to question is the basis of all human progress. "

INDIRA GANDHI

Attributed to Indira Gandhi (1917-1984), prime minister of India.

CHAPTER 4

Modifying Data Using the Query Builder

Introducing the Query Builder

The Query Builder is a tool for manipulating your data. The Query Builder takes a table (or tables), performs some type of data manipulation, and produces a new table. The set of data manipulation instructions defined in the Query Builder is called a query. There are several types of data manipulation you can perform in the Query Builder including:

- Creating new columns based on values of existing columns
- Summarizing data
- Sorting data
- Creating a subset of your data
- Joining data tables

Opening the Query Builder There are several ways to open the Query Builder. Perhaps the easiest way is to first open the data table that you want to use for your query, then click the **Query Builder** button on the workspace toolbar.

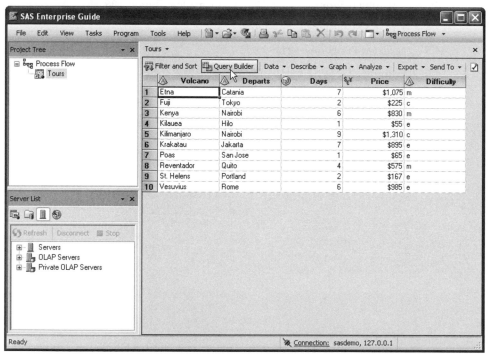

You can also open the Query Builder by clicking the data icon in the Project Tree or Process Flow to make it active, and selecting **Tasks ▶ Data ▶ Query Builder** from the menu bar. Alternatively, you can right-click the data icon in the Project Tree or Process flow and select **Query Builder** from the pop-up menu.

Giving the query a name Queries created in the Query Builder have names that are used to label the query icon in the Process Flow and Project Tree. By default, the first query in your project is named "Query Builder." Any additional queries will be named "Query Builder 1," "Query Builder 2," and so forth. To change the name, enter the new name in the box labeled **Query name** located at the top left. In this example, the query name is "Add Price in Euros."

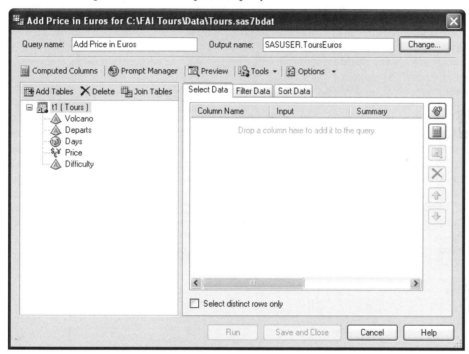

Changing the output table name Data tables produced by the Query Builder are stored in a default location and given a name starting with the letters QUERY. To change either the storage location or the table name, click the **Change** button located next to the Output name. This opens a Save File window where you can navigate to the desired storage location and give the table an appropriate name. In this example, the data table will be stored in the SASUSER library and will have the name ToursEuros.

Results The result of a query can be a data table (the default), a data view, or a report. Data views do not contain data. Instead, views contain the instructions needed to create a data table. Data tables and data views produced by the Query Builder can be used in tasks just like any other data table. Reports are for viewing or printing only and cannot be used in tasks. Changing the query result type is discussed in section 4.10.

In order to run the query, you must select the columns you want in your result (discussed in the next section), and you will probably want to perform some other data manipulations. After making the desired selections in the Query Builder and clicking **Run**, a new data table (view or report) will be added to your project. Here is what the Process Flow looks like after running the Query Builder. In this example, the Tours data table is the input to a query named "Add Price in Euros" and the result is a data table named ToursEuros.

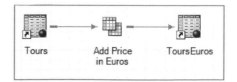

4.2 Selecting Columns in a Query

To run a query, you must tell SAS Enterprise Guide which columns to include in the result. You select columns on the **Select Data** tab of the Query Builder where you can also set properties for columns.

Open the Query Builder by clicking the data icon in the Project Tree or Process Flow to make it active, and selecting **Tasks ▶ Data ▶ Query Builder** from the menu bar. Here is a sample of the Volcanoes data table used in this example.

	Volcano	Country	Region	Height	Activity	Type
1	Altar	Ecuador	SA	5321	Extinct	Stratovolcano
2	Arthur's Seat	UK	Eu	251	Extinct	
3	Barren Island	India	As	354	Active	Stratovolcano
4	Elbrus	Russia	Eu	5633	Extinct	Stratovolcano
5	Erebus		An	3794	Active	Stratovolcano
6	Etna	Italy	Eu	3350	Active	Stratovolcano
7	Fuji	Japan	As	3776	Active	Stratovolcano
8	Garibaldi	Canada	NA	2678		Stratovolcano
9	Grimsvotn	Iceland	Eu	1725	Active	Caldera
10	Illimani	Bolivia	SA	6458	Extinct	Stratovolcano

Selecting the data   When you open the Query Builder window, the **Select Data** tab is on top, and no columns are selected. To select a column for the query, click the column name in the box on the left and drag it to the **Select Data** tab on the right. You can also right-click the column and choose **Select Column** from the pop-up menu. To add more than one column at a time, hold down the control (CTRL) key (or Shift if you want to select a whole group) when you click the column names. You can also add all the columns in a table to the query, by clicking the table name and dragging it to the **Select Data** tab. In this example, the columns Volcano, Country, Region, and Height have been selected but not yet dragged to the Select Data tab.

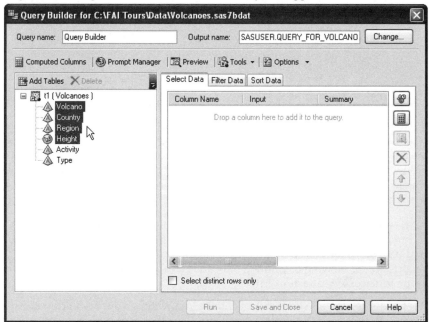

If you want to remove a column from the **Select Data** tab, click the column name on the **Select Data** tab and click the delete button ⊠ on the right side of the window. You can also change the order of the columns using the up and down arrow buttons ⬆ ⬇.

Setting properties for columns You can change the properties of a column in a query by clicking the column name on the **Select Data** tab and clicking the

Properties button 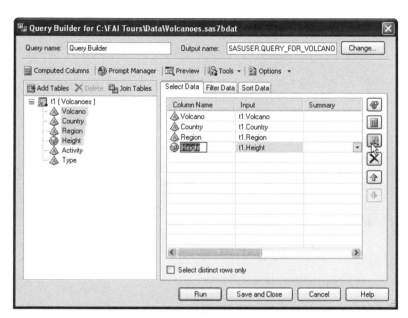 located on the right side of the window.

This opens the Properties window for the column. If you want the column name for the output data table to be different than the input data table, then enter the new name in the Alias field. To change the format associated with the column, click the **Change** button. This opens the Formats window where you can choose the desired format. You can also specify a label and length for the column. Here the **Height** column is given the alias **Meters** and label **Height in Meters**. Click **OK** to return to the Query Builder window. After selecting columns and setting properties, click **Run** in the Query Builder window.

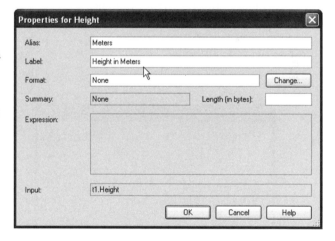

Results Here is the data table created by the query. In this result, notice that the column that was named Height in the original table is now named Meters in the output table. Also, the Activity and Type columns from the original table are not included here.

	Volcano	Country	Region	Meters
1	Altar	Ecuador	SA	5321
2	Arthur's Seat	UK	Eu	251
3	Barren Island	India	As	354
4	Elbrus	Russia	Eu	5633
5	Erebus		An	3794
6	Etna	Italy	Eu	3350
7	Fuji	Japan	As	3776
8	Garibaldi	Canada	NA	2678
9	Grimsvotn	Iceland	Eu	1725
10	Illimani	Bolivia	SA	6458

4.3 Creating Columns Using Mathematical Operators

Sometimes you need to create a new column based on data values in other columns. You could do this in a Data Grid, but then if you add new rows, they will not automatically have the computed values. If you use the Query Builder, then every time you run the query it will recompute the new column for all rows including any new ones.

Here is a portion of the Eruptions data table that is used for this example. Open the Query Builder by clicking the data icon in the Project Tree or Process Flow to make it active, and selecting **Tasks ▸ Data ▸ Query Builder** from the menu bar.

	Volcano	StartDate	EndDate	VEI
1	Barren Island	12/20/1795	12/21/1795	2
2	Barren Island	12/20/1994	06/05/1995	2
3	Erebus	12/12/1912	.	2
4	Erebus	01/03/1972		1
5	Etna	02/06/1610	08/15/1610	2
6	Etna	06/04/1787	08/11/1787	4
7	Etna	01/30/1865	06/28/1865	2
8	Etna	12/16/2005	12/22/2005	1
9	Fuji	12/16/1707	02/24/1708	5
10	Grimsvotn	10/31/1603	11/01/1603	2

The Query Builder opens with the **Select Data** tab on top. Select the columns for the query. For this example, the Volcano, StartDate, and EndDate columns are selected.

Creating a new column

To create a new column, click the **Computed Columns** button located near the top of the window. This opens the Computed Columns window.

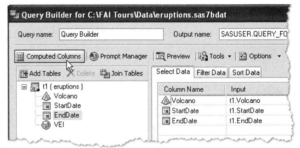

Click **New** to open the New Computed Column wizard.

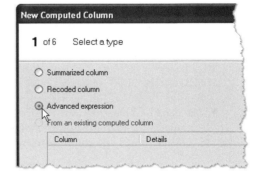

The New Computed Column wizard has up to six windows depending on which type of column you are creating. In the first window, choose **Advanced Expression**, and click **Next**.

Building the expression

At the top of the second window is a box where you can type your expression. If you like, you can let SAS Enterprise Guide help you build the expression. The bottom left part of the window shows nodes for **Functions**, **Tables,** and **Selected Columns**. To add columns to the expression, expand either the **Tables** or **Selected Columns** node to locate the desired column. Then double-click the column and it will be added to the expression text box. You can use the various operator buttons that appear below the

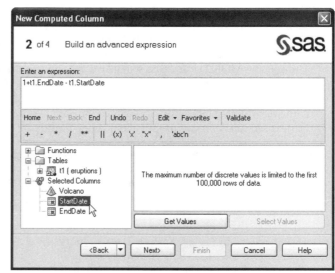

expression text box to build your expression. In this example, the length of the eruption is computed in days. Because the StartDate and EndDate are both SAS date values (the number of

days since January 1, 1960), you can simply subtract the start date from the end date and add one. When you are finished building the expression, click **Next**.

In the third window you can set the properties of the new column. In this example the column is given a meaningful name and alias. At this point, you can click **Next** to see a summary of your new column in the fourth window (not shown), or click **Finish**. Click **Close** in the Computed Columns window and then click **Run** in the Query Builder.

Results Here are the results of the query including the new column Duration. Notice that the values for Duration are missing for rows where the values for EndDate are missing. If you have missing values for columns that are part of the expression, then the results will be missing.

	Volcano	StartDate	EndDate	Duration
1	Barren Island	12/20/1795	12/21/1795	2
2	Barren Island	12/20/1994	06/05/1995	168
3	Erebus	12/12/1912	.	.
4	Erebus	01/03/1972	.	.
5	Etna	02/06/1610	08/15/1610	191
6	Etna	06/04/1787	08/11/1787	69
7	Etna	01/30/1865	06/28/1865	150
8	Etna	12/16/2005	12/22/2005	7
9	Fuji	12/16/1707	02/24/1708	71
10	Grimsvotn	10/31/1603	11/01/1603	2

4.4 ► Creating Columns Using Functions

SAS Enterprise Guide has many built-in functions you can use to build expressions when creating new columns. A function takes a value and turns it into another related value. For example, the MONTH function will take a date and return just the month. The LOG function will return the natural log of a number. There are many functions to choose from in over 20 different categories including character, date and time, descriptive statistics, financial, mathematical, trigonometric, and truncation. Some of the commonly used functions are listed in the next section. You can use functions when you create new columns in the Query Builder.

Here is a portion of the data table that contains data on individual tours including the departure date. To create a column that has the day of month the tour departs, you can use the Day function. To open the Query Builder, click the data icon in the Project Tree or Process Flow to make it active, and select **Tasks ► Data ► Query Builder** from the menu bar. The Query Builder opens with the **Select Data** tab on top. Select the

	Tour	Volcano	DepartureDate	Guide
1	PS27	Poas	08/05/2011	Carlos
2	SH40	St. Helens	06/19/2011	Casey
3	SH41	St. Helens	07/05/2011	Casey
4	SH42	St. Helens	07/23/2011	Casey
5	SH43	St. Helens	08/15/2011	Kelly
6	FJ12	Fuji	09/12/2011	Cooper
7	ET01	Etna	08/05/2011	Cooper
8	KE05	Kenya	05/31/2011	Kelly

columns for the query. In this example Tour, Volcano, and DepartureDate are selected.

Creating a new column   As discussed in the previous section, to create a new column, click the **Computed Columns** button in the Query Builder window. This opens the Computed Columns window. Click **New**, select **Advanced Expression** in the first window of the New Computed Column wizard, and click **Next**.

Choosing a function   In the second window, expand the **Functions** node located in the lower left portion of the window to list all available functions. The functions are listed alphabetically and also grouped by category. Expand the **Categories** node to show all the categories of functions. Then expand the node for the desired function category. For this example, choose the **Date and Time** category and scroll down to locate the **DAY** function. Clicking the function name will display information about the function in the lower right portion of the window. Double-clicking the function name will add it to the expression text box located at the top of the window.

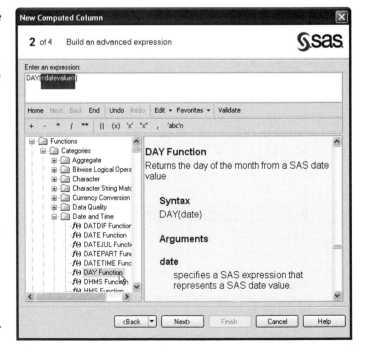

Defining arguments for functions Most functions take some sort of argument. When the function is inserted into the expression, a placeholder for the argument appears in the expression. You must replace the placeholder in the function with a valid argument. If the function calls for a character value, that value can be a character column or a character string enclosed in quotation marks. If the function calls for a numeric value, that value can be a numeric column or a number. The DAY function requires a SAS date value that is numeric.

Collapse the Functions node to display the available tables and selected columns. After adding a function to the expression, the placeholder for the function— <DateValue> for this example— will be highlighted. Double- click the desired column name, and the placeholder will be replaced by the column you selected, in this case the DepartureDate column from the TourDates table (t1). If you want to use a constant value in the function instead of a column, you can either type the value directly in the expression box in the appropriate location, or use the **Get Values** button to

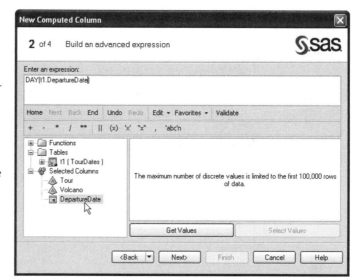

list discrete values for particular columns. Note that it may take a long time to get all the values if your data table is large or if there are many possible values for the column. After listing discrete values, either double-click the value to enter it into the expression, or highlight the value and click **Select Values**.

After you define your expression, you can check it by clicking **Validate**. The Validate window will open telling you whether your expression is valid. Close the Validate window, make any necessary changes, and click **Next.** In the third window of the wizard (not shown), you can give the new column a meaningful name and alias, and also assign the column a format if desired. For this example, the new column is named Day. Click **Next** to display a summary of your new computed column in the fourth window (not shown), then click **Finish** to return to the Computed Columns window. Click **Close** in the Computed Columns window, and then click **Run** in the Query Builder.

	Tour	Volcano	DepartureDate	Day
1	PS27	Poas	08/05/2011	5
2	SH40	St. Helens	06/19/2011	19
3	SH41	St. Helens	07/05/2011	5
4	SH42	St. Helens	07/23/2011	23
5	SH43	St. Helens	08/15/2011	15
6	FJ12	Fuji	09/12/2011	12
7	ET01	Etna	08/05/2011	5
8	KE05	Kenya	05/31/2011	31

Results Here are the query results, which now include the new column Day. Day is the day of the month the tour departs.

4.5 Selected Functions

The following table lists the definition and form of commonly used functions.

Function name	Form of function	Definition
Mathematical		
LOG	LOG(numValue)	Natural logarithm
LOG10	LOG10(numValue)	Logarithm to the base 10
Descriptive Statistics		
MAX	MAX(numValue,numValue,…)	Largest non-missing value
MEAN	MEAN(numValue,numValue,…)	Arithmetic mean of non-missing values
MIN	MIN(numValue,numValue,…)	Smallest non-missing value
SUM	SUM(numValue,numValue,…)	Sum of non-missing values
Character		
LENGTH	LENGTH(charValue)	Returns the position of the last non-blank character (missing values have a length of 1)
SUBSTR{Extract}	SUBSTR(charValue,position,n)	Extracts a substring from a character value starting at 'position' for 'n' characters or until end if no 'n'
TRANSLATE	TRANSLATE(charValue,to-1, from-1,…to-n,from-n)	Replaces 'from' characters in character value with 'to' characters (one-to-one replacement only—you cannot replace one character with two, for example)
UPCASE	UPCASE(charValue)	Converts all letters in character value to uppercase
Date and Datetime[1]		
DATEPART	DATEPART(SAS-datetime-value)	Converts a datetime to a SAS date value
DAY	DAY(SAS-date-value)	Returns the day of the month from a SAS date value
MDY	MDY(month,day,year)	Returns a SAS date value from month, day, and year values
MONTH	MONTH(SAS-date-value)	Returns the month (1–12) from a SAS date value
QTR	QTR(SAS-date-value)	Returns the yearly quarter (1–4) from a SAS date value
TODAY	TODAY()	Returns the current date as a SAS date value

---

[1] A SAS date value is the number of days since January 1, 1960. A SAS datetime is the number of seconds since midnight January 1, 1960.

Here are examples using the selected functions.

Function name	Example	Result	Example	Result
Mathematical				
LOG	LOG(1)	0.0	LOG(10)	2.30259
LOG10	LOG10(1)	0.0	LOG10(10)	1.0
Descriptive Statistics				
MAX	MAX(9.3,8,7.5)	9.3	MAX(–3,.,5)	5
MEAN	MEAN(1,4,7,2)	3.5	MEAN(2,.,3)	2.5
MIN	MIN(9.3,8,7.5)	7.5	MIN(–3,.,5)	–3
SUM	SUM(3,5,1)	9.0	SUM(4,7,.)	11
Character				
LENGTH	LENGTH('hot lava')	8	LENGTH('eruption')	8
SUBSTR{Extract}	SUBSTR('(916)734-6281',2,3)	'916'	SUBSTR('Tour12',5)	'12'
TRANSLATE	TRANSLATE ('6/16/2004','-','/')	'6-16-2004'	TRANSLATE ('hot lava', 'j','l')	'hot java'
UPCASE	UPCASE('St. Helens')	'ST. HELENS'	UPCASE('Fuji')	'FUJI'
Date and Datetime				
DATEPART	DATEPART(86400)	1	DATEPART(31536000)	365
DAY	DAY(0)	1	DAY(290)	17
MDY	MDY(1,1,1960)	0	MDY(10,17,1960)	290
MONTH	MONTH(0)	1	MONTH(290)	10
QTR	QTR(0)	1	QTR(290)	4
TODAY	TODAY()	*today's date*	TODAY()–1	*yesterday's date*

4.6 ▶ Adding a Grand Total to a Data Table

Using the Query Builder, you can create columns that contain summary statistics for existing columns. For example, you may want to calculate a grand total over all the rows of data and put the result in a new column. Then you could, for example, compute the percent of the total for each row because the one grand total value is repeated for each row in the data.

Here is a sample of the AdResults data, which contains the amounts spent on advertising for the Fire and Ice Tours company for both its Seattle and Portland offices. This example creates a new column that has the total amount spent for both offices for the time period. To open the Query Builder, click the data icon in the Project Tree or Process Flow to make it active, and select **Tasks ▶ Data ▶ Query Builder** from the menu bar.

	City	Month	AdDollars	Bookings
8	Seattle	8	250	17
9	Seattle	9	250	22
10	Seattle	10	325	20
11	Seattle	11	400	25
12	Seattle	12	500	31
13	Portland	1	325	25
14	Portland	2	290	19
15	Portland	3	250	17
16	Portland	4	300	18

Summarizing the data First select the columns for the query, in this case all the columns in the AdResults table. Initially no summary statistics are listed for the columns on the **Select Data** tab. To summarize data in a column, click the column name on the **Select Data** tab, then click the down arrow in the Summary cell. Choose the summary statistic you want to use from the drop-down list. For this example, choose **SUM**.

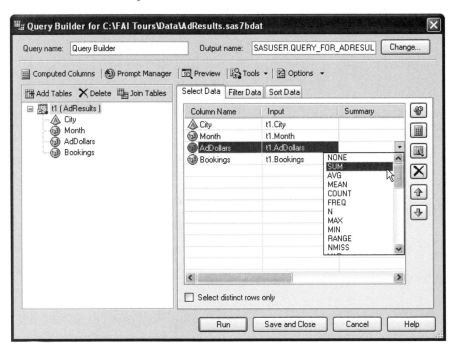

Selecting summary groups After you choose a summary statistic, the original column will be replaced by the newly summarized column. By default, all selected columns are used for the summary groups. To create a grand total, you don't want any summary groups. Uncheck **Automatically select groups** in the Summary Groups section of the Query Builder so that no groups are selected.

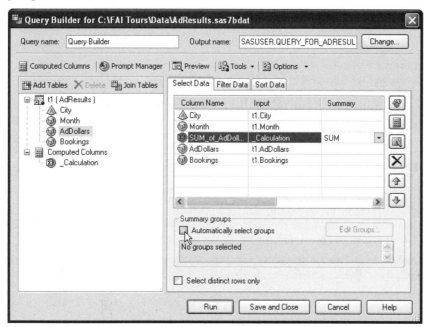

Setting properties for the new column The alias for the new column combines the summary statistic and the old column name. The alias will become the column name in the SAS data table generated by the query. If you don't like the alias, you can change it in the Properties window. Click the column name, then click the Properties button on the right side of the Query Builder window to open the Properties window.

Adding back the original column Because the newly computed column replaces the original column, the original column will not be in the output data table unless you add it back. If you want to keep the original column, as well as the newly computed column, then click the original column name in the box on the left and drag it to the **Select Data** tab. Use the up- or down-arrow buttons on the right side of the window to position the original column where you want. In this example, the original column, AdDollars, has been added back in the query and positioned above the Bookings column. When you are satisfied, click **Run**.

Results Here are the results of the query including the new column SUM_OF_AdDollars. Notice that the new column has the same value for all rows.

	City	Month	SUM_of_AdDollars	AdDollars	Bookings
8	Seattle	8	7845	250	17
9	Seattle	9	7845	250	22
10	Seattle	10	7845	325	20
11	Seattle	11	7845	400	25
12	Seattle	12	7845	500	31
13	Portland	1	7845	325	25
14	Portland	2	7845	290	19
15	Portland	3	7845	250	17
16	Portland	4	7845	300	18

4.7 Adding Subtotals to a Data Table

The previous section showed how you can create new columns that summarize all the rows in a data table. This section shows how to summarize all the rows that belong to a group. The steps are the same as adding a grand total, with the additional step of selecting a group column.

Here is a sample of the results from the previous section where the SUM_OF_AdDollars column contains the grand total of the AdDollars column. In this example, the total amount spent by each city's office will be calculated instead of the grand total. Re-open the query by clicking the **Modify**

	City	Month	SUM_of_AdDollars	AdDollars	Bookings
8	Seattle	8	7845	250	17
9	Seattle	9	7845	250	22
10	Seattle	10	7845	325	20
11	Seattle	11	7845	400	25
12	Seattle	12	7845	500	31
13	Portland	1	7845	325	25
14	Portland	2	7845	290	19
15	Portland	3	7845	250	17
16	Portland	4	7845	300	18

Task button on the workspace toolbar for the query result. This opens the Query Builder window.

Summarizing the data   Here is the query from the previous section that contains all the columns from the AdResults table and the SUM_OF_AdDollars column, which is the grand total for the AdDollars column. To change the SUM_OF_AdDollars column to a sub-total by City, click the **Edit Groups** button. This opens the Edit Groups window.

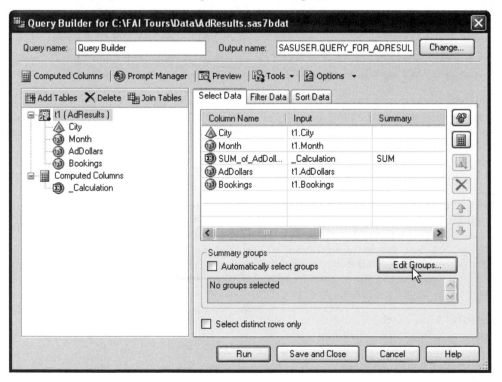

Selecting groups In the Edit Groups window, select the column or columns to use for the groups. Click the column name, City for this example, in the **Available columns** list and click the plus arrow ⮕ to add it to the **Group by** list. Click **OK** to return to the Query Builder window.

Notice that the name for the summarized column, in this case SUM_OF_AdDollars, does not change. But now the grouping column, City from the AdResults table (t1), appears in the area labeled **Summary Groups** near the bottom of the window. Click **Run** to run the query.

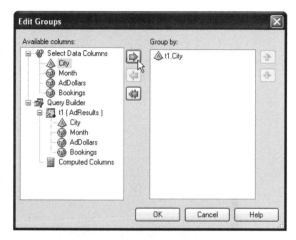

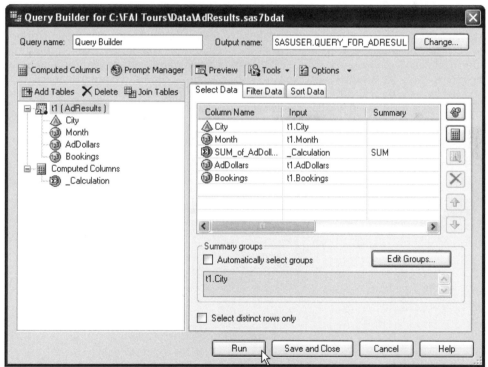

Results Here are the results of the query. Notice that the rows for Seattle have a different value for SUM_OF_AdDollars than the rows for Portland. Also the resulting data table is now sorted by the grouping column.

	City	Month	SUM_of_AdDollars	AdDollars	Bookings
8	Portland	3	3665	250	17
9	Portland	1	3665	325	25
10	Portland	10	3665	350	24
11	Portland	12	3665	400	33
12	Portland	4	3665	300	18
13	Seattle	7	4180	150	17
14	Seattle	3	4180	525	32
15	Seattle	6	4180	325	18
16	Seattle	12	4180	500	31

4.8 Creating Summary Data Tables in a Query

The previous section showed how you can create new columns that summarize all the rows belonging to a group. The summarized values were repeated for each row that belonged to the group. But if you want only one row for each group showing just the summarized values, you can do this in a query by eliminating all columns that are not either grouped or summarized.

Here is a sample of the AdResults data that contains the amounts spent on advertising for the Fire and Ice Tours company for its Seattle and Portland offices. This example creates a new table with two rows showing the total number of bookings and amount spent by each office. To open the Query Builder, click the data icon in the Project Tree or Process Flow to make it active, and select **Tasks ▶ Data ▶ Query Builder** from the menu bar.

	City	Month	AdDollars	Bookings
8	Seattle	8	250	17
9	Seattle	9	250	22
10	Seattle	10	325	20
11	Seattle	11	400	25
12	Seattle	12	500	31
13	Portland	1	325	25
14	Portland	2	290	19
15	Portland	3	250	17
16	Portland	4	300	18

Select the summary and group columns   To create a summary data table, select just the columns that will be either summarized or grouped. Choose the type of summarization from the drop-down list that appears when you click the Summary cell for the selected column on the **Select Data** tab. In this example, the AdDollars and the Bookings columns are summed. Because **Automatically select groups** is checked by default, all the columns that are not summarized are included in the group. For this example, City is the grouping column because it is the only column selected for the query that is not summarized.

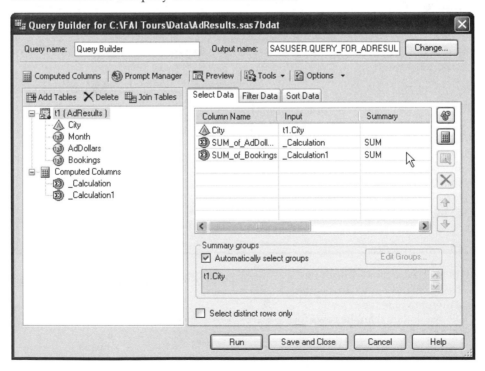

Setting properties for the new columns SAS Enterprise Guide assigns aliases to the summarized columns combining the summary statistic and the old column names. For example, the alias for the sum of the column AdDollars would be SUM_of_AdDollars. The alias will become the column name in the SAS data table generated by the query. If you don't like the alias, you can change it in the Properties window for the column. Click the column name on the **Select Data** tab of the Query Builder, then click the Properties button 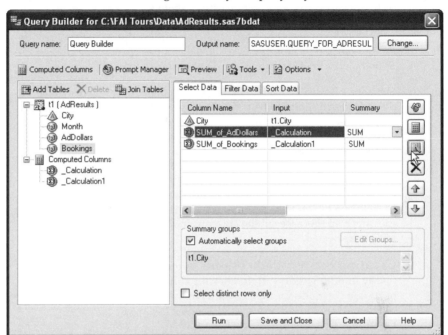 on the right side of the Query Builder to open the Properties window.

In the Properties window for the column, you can specify a new alias, give the column a label, and change the format for the column. After making the desired changes to the properties, click **OK.** Then click **Run** in the Query Builder to produce the result. For this example, the alias for the summarized column SUM_of_AdDollars is changed to Total_Dollars_Spent.

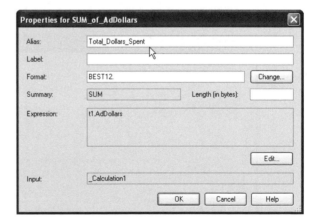

Results Here is the SAS data table created containing the summarized data. Notice that the new table contains only one row for each value of the grouping column, City.

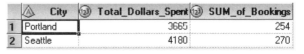

	City	Total_Dollars_Spent	SUM_of_Bookings
1	Portland	3665	254
2	Seattle	4180	270

4.9 ▶ Recoding Values in a Query

If you want to group data together based on a set of values in a column, you can do this by recoding a column in the Query Builder. For example, if you have sales offices from several different cities, you may want to group them by region. If region is not already defined in the data, then you can define it using the Query Builder. Recoding a column is similar to creating and applying user-defined formats to a column. But, when you recode a column, you create a newly computed column where the data values are actually changed. When you use formats, only the way the data values are displayed is changed.

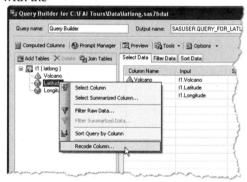

Here are a few rows from the Latlong data table, which gives the latitude and longitude of volcanoes from around the world. Using the recode feature of the Query Builder you can group the volcanoes by zone, according to the value of the column Latitude. To open the Query Builder, click the data icon in the Project Tree or Process Flow to make it active, and select **Tasks ▶ Data ▶ Query Builder** from the menu bar. This opens the Query Builder window with the **Select Data** tab on top. Select the columns for the query. In this case, all the columns in the table are selected.

Creating the recoded column In the Query Builder window, right-click the column to recode (Latitude for this example) in the list of columns on the left and select **Recode Column**. This opens the New Computed Column wizard.

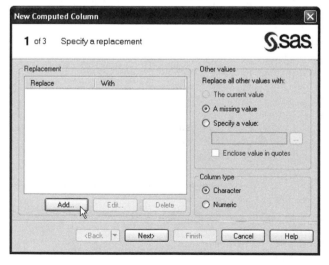

In the first window, specify the type of column to be created (either character or numeric) in the area labeled **Column Type**. For this example, choose **Character**. Then click **Add** to open the Specify a Replacement window.

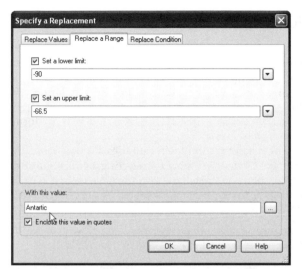

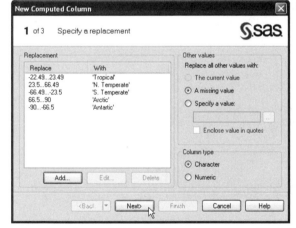

Defining the replacements In the Specify a Replacement window, there are three tabs: **Replace Values**, **Replace a Range**, and **Replace Condition**. Use Replace Values for one-to-one replacements. It probably makes the most sense to use the Replace a Range feature for numeric data, but it can be used for character data if you want to replace a set of values that fall into a consecutive range alphabetically. Use the Replace Condition feature when you want to use a conditional operator such as "Less Than" or "In a List" to specify your replacements. For this example, click the **Replace a Range** tab. Enter the lower and upper limits of the range of values to replace in the appropriate boxes. If you want to see what the current values are, then click the down-arrow to the right of the box and a window will open showing all the values. In the box labeled **With this value**, type the new value that you want to replace the old range of values. When you are satisfied, click **OK**.

The replacement logic you defined will appear in the first window of the wizard. Click **Add** again to add another replacement and repeat this procedure for all the replacements you want to make. You can also choose what to do with values that do not fall into the ranges you specified. For this example, replacing other values with **A missing value** is fine. When you are finished, click **Next**.

In the second window (not shown), give the new column a meaningful name and alias and also specify the length and format. For this example, the column name and alias is Zone and the format is None. At this point, you can click **Next** to see a summary in the third window (not shown), or click **Finish**. Then click **Run** in the Query Builder window to run the query.

	Volcano	Latitude	Longitude	Zone
1	Altar	-1.67	-78.42	Tropical
2	Barren Island	12.28	93.52	Tropical
3	Elbrus	43.33	42.45	N. Temperate
4	Erebus	-77.53	167.17	Antartic
5	Etna	37.73	15	N. Temperate
6	Fuji	35.35	138.73	N. Temperate
7	Garibaldi	49.85	-123	N. Temperate
8	Grimsvotn	64.42	-17.33	N. Temperate
9	Illimani	-16.39	-67.47	Tropical
10	Kenua	-0.09	37.18	Tropical

Results Here is a sample of the query result. Notice that both the Latitude column and the new column, Zone, are part of the query result.

4.10 Changing the Result Type of Queries

When you run a query using the Query Builder, you have a choice about the type of result the query produces. A query can produce a SAS data table, a SAS data view, or a report. A SAS data view is similar to a SAS data table, except that it does not contain any data. Instead, SAS data views contain the instructions required to create a new data table. Data tables and views generated by the Query Builder can be used as a source of data for tasks. Reports are for viewing or printing only.

Setting the default result type The default result type for queries is a data table, but you can change the default. To do this, open the Options window by selecting **Tools ▶ Options** from the menu bar. Click **Query** in the selection pane on the left to open the Query page. Near the bottom of this page is a drop-down list under **Save query result set as**. Select the desired result type. All subsequent queries you build will use this as the default result type.

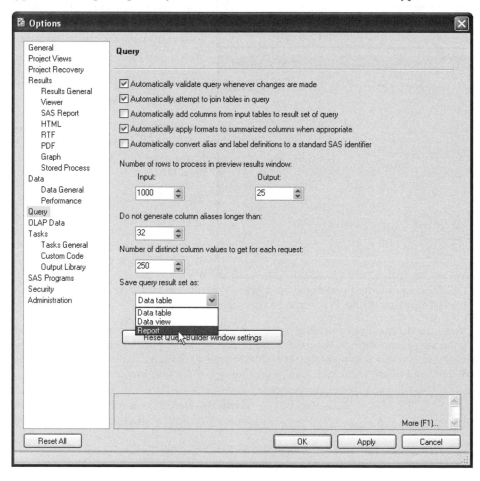

Setting the result type for a query If you want to change the result type of an individual query, you can do this in the Results page of the Query Options window for the query. Click the **Options** button in the Query Builder window and select **Options for This Query**. Note that you can also select **Defaults for All Queries** to open the Options window shown on the previous page.

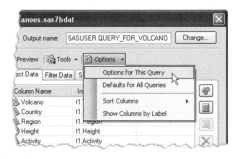

In the Results page of the Query Options window, check **Override the corresponding default settings in Tools -> Options**, and then select the type of result you want for the query. You can choose a data table, data view, or report. Changes made in the Query Options window affect only the results of the current query.

If you choose the Report type, you may also want to give your report a title or footnote. You can assign titles and footnotes in the Titles page of the Query Options window.

Query report All the query examples so far in this book have shown the result as a data table. Here is a partial view of a report generated from a query of the Volcanoes data table with the title Volcanoes Report. Note that in query reports, the column labels are used instead of the column names.

Volcanoes Report

Volcano	Country	Region	Height in Meters
Altar	Ecuador	SA	5321
Arthur's Seat	UK	Eu	251
Barren Island	India	As	354
Elbrus	Russia	Eu	5633
Erebus		An	3794
Etna	Italy	Eu	3350
Fuji	Japan	As	3776
Garibaldi	Canada	NA	2678
Grimsvotn	Iceland	Eu	1725

5

"I find that a great part of the information I have was acquired by looking up something and finding something else along the way."

FRANKLIN P. ADAMS

Attributed to Franklin P. Adams (1881-1960), newspaper columnist, satirist, and poet.

CHAPTER 5

Sorting and Filtering Data

5.1 Filtering Data in a Task

Sometimes you don't want to use all the rows in a data table. There are several ways to subset or filter data in SAS Enterprise Guide. If you want to create a new data table, then use the Filter and Sort task or the Query Builder as shown later in this chapter. However, if you simply want to run a task and do not need to create a new data table, then you can filter data directly in the task.

Here is the TourDates data table. This example uses the List Data task to demonstrate how to filter data in a task. To open the List Data task, click the data icon in the Project Tree or Process Flow to make it active. Then select **Tasks ▶ Describe ▶ List Data** from the menu bar. The List Data window will open, displaying the Data page. For this example, all the columns in the table are assigned to the List variables role.

	Tour	Volcano	DepartureDate	Guide
1	PS27	Poas	08/05/2011	Carlos
2	SH40	St. Helens	06/19/2011	Casey
3	SH41	St. Helens	07/05/2011	Casey
4	SH42	St. Helens	07/23/2011	Casey
5	SH43	St. Helens	08/15/2011	Kelly
6	FJ12	Fuji	09/12/2011	Cooper
7	ET01	Etna	08/05/2011	Cooper
8	KE05	Kenya	05/31/2011	Kelly
9	KL18	Kilauea	07/08/2011	Malia
10	KL19	Kilauea	07/15/2011	Malia
11	KL20	Kilauea	07/22/2011	Malia
12	RD02	Reventador	07/11/2011	Carlos
13	VS11	Vesuvius	07/21/2011	Cooper
14	VS12	Vesuvius	08/15/2011	Cooper
15	KJ01	Kilimanjaro	06/09/2011	Kelly
16	KK03	Krakatau	07/19/2011	Kelly

Editing the data source The Data source and Task filter are displayed at the top of the Data page in the task window. By default, no filters are applied to data in a task. To make changes to the filter used for the task, click the **Edit** button. This opens the Edit Data and Filter window.

Creating the filter

In the Edit Data and Filter window is an area labeled **Task filter** that contains four empty boxes. Click the down-arrow on the first box, and select the column you want to use for your filter from the drop-down list.

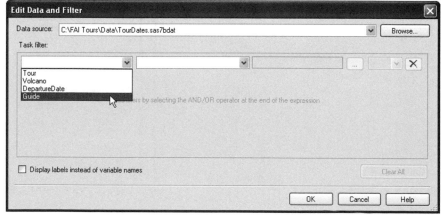

In the second box, select the operator from the drop-down list.

In the third box, either type in a value, or click the ellipsis button 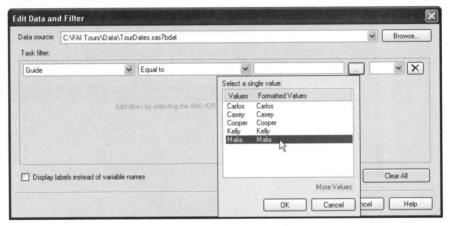 to get a list of values for the selected variable. Select the desired value and click **OK**.

If you want to add another condition to the filter, select AND or OR from the drop-down list in the fourth box. A new row of boxes will appear where you can specify the additional condition. When you are finished specifying the filter conditions, click **OK**.

The filter you defined will appear in the **Task filter** area of the Data page in the task window. Click **Run** to run the task.

Results Here are the results of the List Data task showing only the rows of data that meet the filter condition where Guide is equal to "Malia."

Malia's Tours

Tour	Volcano	DepartureDate	Guide
KL18	Kilauea	07/08/2011	Malia
KL19	Kilauea	07/15/2011	Malia
KL20	Kilauea	07/22/2011	Malia

5.2 Using the Filter and Sort Task

In the Filter and Sort task you can filter or sort your data, or both. The result of the Filter and Sort task is a data table. If you need to join tables or add any computed columns, then use the Query Builder. If you only want to sort the data, then you may choose to use the Sort Data task instead, which offers more sorting options.

Here is a sample of the Eruptions data table, which is sorted by the volcano name and start date of the eruption. To filter and sort the data, click the data icon in the Project Tree or Process Flow to make it active, and select **Tasks ▶ Data ▶ Filter and Sort** from the menu bar. If you have a Data Grid open, you can also open the Filter and Sort task by clicking **Filter and Sort** on the workspace toolbar. The Filter and Sort window will open.

	Volcano	StartDate	EndDate	VEI
1	Barren Island	12/20/1795	12/21/1795	2
2	Barren Island	12/20/1994	06/05/1995	2
3	Erebus	12/12/1912	.	2
4	Erebus	01/03/1972		1
5	Etna	02/06/1610	08/15/1610	2
6	Etna	06/04/1787	08/11/1787	4
7	Etna	01/30/1865	06/28/1865	2
8	Etna	12/16/2005	12/22/2005	1
9	Fuji	12/16/1707	02/24/1708	5
10	Grimsvotn	10/31/1603	11/01/1603	2

Selecting variables The Filter and Sort task has three tabs. On the **Variables** tab, choose the variables you want to keep. Click the desired variable name in the box on the left labeled **Available**. Then click the plus arrow ▷ to move the variable to the area labeled **Selected**. To move all variables at once, click the double plus arrow ▷▷. Unselect variables using the minus arrow ◁ or double minus arrow ◁◁. In this example, all variables are selected except EndDate.

Specifying the filter Click the **Filter** tab. The area labeled **Filter description** contains four boxes. In the first box, choose the variable for the filter. In the second box, choose an operator. Then in the third box, enter the value for the filter. To get a list of all possible values for the selected variable, click the ellipsis button 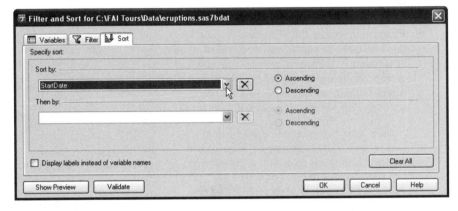. If you want to add another condition to the filter, select AND or OR from the drop-down list in the fourth box. A new row of boxes will appear where you can specify the additional condition. For more complicated filters containing functions or complex logic, click the **Advanced Edit** button to open the Advanced Filter Builder window. In this example the filter selects all eruptions with a volcanic explosivity index (VEI) greater than or equal to 4.

Sorting the data Click the **Sort** tab. Choose a variable from the **Sort by** drop-down list. If you wish, you can choose a second variable from the **Then by** drop-down

list. Each time you choose an additional variable, options will appear allowing you to choose more sorting variables. The default sort order is Ascending. Click **Descending** to reverse the order. In this example, the data will be sorted by StartDate in ascending order. When you are ready to run the task, click **OK**.

	Volcano	StartDate	VEI
1	Vesuvius	12/15/1631	5
2	Santorini	09/27/1650	4
3	Fuji	12/16/1707	5
4	Etna	06/04/1787	4
5	Grimsvotn	01/08/1873	4
6	Vesuvius	12/18/1875	4
7	Krakatau	05/20/1883	6
8	Kliuchevskoi	03/25/1931	4
9	St. Helens	03/27/1980	5
10	Pinatubo	04/02/1991	5
11	Reventador	11/03/2002	4

Results Here is the result of the filter and sort with only the eruptions with VEI greater or equal to 4 and sorted by StartDate. The new data table is given a name starting with the letters FILTER_FOR and is stored in a default location. You cannot change the name or location of data tables created by this task, but you can export the table using any name and location you wish. See section 2.10 for more about exporting data tables.

5.3 Sorting Using the Sort Task

There is little need for you to sort data in SAS Enterprise Guide. If a task requires data to be sorted, SAS Enterprise Guide will usually sort the data automatically. However, there may be times when you want to sort the data yourself. If you have a large data table, for example, you may want to store the data in sorted order. With the data presorted, SAS Enterprise Guide will not have to sort the data and your tasks will run more quickly. At other times, you may want to sort data to make it easier to find values in a Data Grid, or to eliminate duplicate rows.

There are three ways to sort data in SAS Enterprise Guide: the Filter and Sort task, the Sort task, or a query. The Sort task gives you the most control over how the data are sorted, while the Filter and Sort task and a query have other functions in addition to sorting. This section discusses the Sort task.

Here is a portion of the Eruptions data table. To sort the data using the Sort Data task, click the data icon in the Project Tree or Process Flow to make it active, and select **Tasks ▶ Data ▶ Sort Data** from the menu bar. The Sort Data window will open.

	Volcano	StartDate	EndDate	VEI
1	Barren Island	12/20/1795	12/21/1795	2
2	Barren Island	12/20/1994	06/05/1995	2
3	Erebus	12/12/1912	.	2
4	Erebus	01/03/1972	.	1
5	Etna	02/06/1610	08/15/1610	2
6	Etna	06/04/1787	08/11/1787	4
7	Etna	01/30/1865	06/28/1865	2
8	Etna	12/16/2005	12/22/2005	1
9	Fuji	12/16/1707	02/24/1708	5
10	Grimsvotn	10/31/1603	11/01/1603	2
11	Grimsvotn	01/08/1873	08/01/1873	4
12	Grimsvotn	12/18/1998	12/28/1998	3
13	Kilauea	05/30/1840	06/25/1840	0
14	Kilauea	05/24/1969	07/22/1974	0
15	Kliuchevskoi	09/25/1737	11/04/1737	2
16	Kliuchevskoi	03/25/1931	03/27/1931	4
17	Kliuchevskoi	01/20/2005	04/07/2005	2
18	Krakatau	05/20/1883	10/21/1883	6

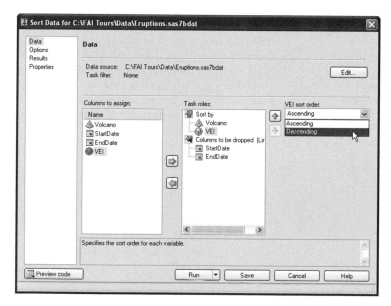

Assigning task roles

Drag the columns you want to sort by to the **Sort by** role. If there is more than one **Sort by** column, SAS Enterprise Guide will sort rows by the first column, then by the second column within values of the first column, and so on. When you assign a column to the Sort by role, a box for the sort order will appear on the right. If you click the down-arrow, you can choose to have the data sorted in ascending (the default) or descending order. If you want to exclude columns from the output, drag those columns to the **Columns to be dropped** role. In this example, the Eruptions data table will be sorted first by Volcano in ascending order, then by VEI in descending order. The StartDate and EndDate columns will be dropped.

Sorting options   To open the Options page, click **Options** in the selection pane on the left. In the Options page, you can select the collating sequence for the sort (such as ASCII, EBCDIC, or Server default). The collating sequence determines the sort order, including whether letters come before numerals or numerals before letters. When SAS Enterprise Guide sorts data, missing values are always lowest in the sort order. In the ASCII collating sequence (the default for Windows computers), uppercase letters come before lowercase letters.

You can also choose options for duplicate records. You can keep all records (the default), keep only the first record for each combination of values of the Sort by columns, or keep only one of each record that is entirely duplicated. Duplicate records must be consecutive to be eliminated, so if you choose the last option, it is a good idea to sort

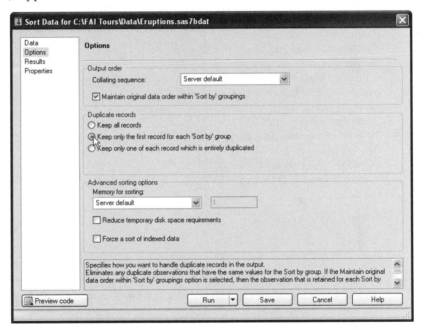

by all the columns in the data table. For this example, **Keep only the first record for each 'Sort by' group** is selected so that the result will have only one record for each Volcano and value of VEI.

Results   The Sort task creates a new SAS data table and displays it in a Data Grid. Notice that this table is sorted first by Volcano, and then by descending values of VEI within Volcano. The resulting data table has fewer rows than the original because it contains only one row for each combination of the two sort columns. SAS Enterprise Guide stores the table with a default name in a default location. To save the data with a different name or location, use the Results page in the Sort Data task. In the Results page, you can also choose to save in a separate table any duplicates that were eliminated by the sort.

	Volcano	VEI
1	Barren Island	2
2	Erebus	2
3	Erebus	1
4	Etna	4
5	Etna	2
6	Etna	1
7	Fuji	5
8	Grimsvotn	4
9	Grimsvotn	3
10	Grimsvotn	2
11	Kilauea	0
12	Kliuchevskoi	4
13	Kliuchevskoi	2
14	Krakatau	6

5.4 Sorting Data in a Query

If all you want to do is create a sorted version of a data table, then you might want to use the Sort Data, or Filter and Sort task. But, if you also want to create new columns or join tables together, then use the Query Builder.

This example uses the Eruptions data table, which is sorted by the name of the volcano. To change the sort order using a query, click the data icon in the Project Tree or Process Flow to make it active, and select **Tasks ▶ Data ▶ Query Builder** from the menu bar. The Query Builder window will open with the **Select Data** tab on top.

Selecting the data   For all queries you need to select the columns that will be in the result. Click and drag to the **Select Data** tab the columns you want. In this example, all columns in the Eruptions table except VEI have been selected, as well as the computed column Duration. (Section 4.3 shows how to create the Duration column.)

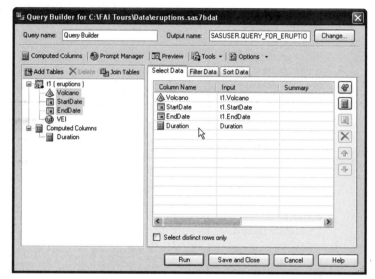

Here is a preview of the data after creating the computed column and before sorting. To preview results, click the **Preview** button in the Query Builder window. Then click the **Results** tab in the Preview window.

Volcano	StartDate	EndDate	Duration
Barren Island	12/20/1795	12/21/1795	2
Barren Island	12/20/1994	06/05/1995	168
Erebus	12/12/1912	.	.
Erebus	01/03/1972	.	.
Etna	02/06/1610	08/15/1610	191
Etna	06/04/1787	08/11/1787	69
Etna	01/30/1865	06/28/1865	150
Etna	12/16/2005	12/22/2005	7
Fuji	12/16/1707	02/24/1708	71
Grimsvotn	10/31/1603	11/01/1603	2

Sorting the data Click the **Sort Data** tab. To sort the data, click the desired column in the list on the left and drag it to the **Sort Data** tab. You can sort by more than one column by dragging multiple columns to the **Sort Data** tab. Notice that even columns not selected for the query (VEI for this example) are listed. You can use columns for sorting even if they don't appear in the result.

If you choose more than one column for sorting, the order of the columns on the **Sort Data** tab will determine how the data are sorted. The data will be sorted by the first column in the list. Then, within unique values of the first column, the data will be sorted by the second column. You can change the sort order by clicking the column name in the **Sort Data** tab and clicking the up- or down-arrow buttons to move the columns. To change the sort direction, click the column name on the **Sort Data** tab. Then click the down-arrow ▼ next to the sort direction for that column, and select either Ascending or Descending from the drop-down list. In this query, the data will be sorted by the computed column Duration in ascending order. Click **Run** in the Query Builder window to create a sorted data table.

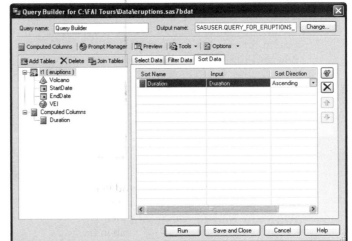

Results Here is a portion of the resulting data table sorted by Duration. Missing values are always lowest in the sort order, so they appear first.

	Volcano	StartDate	EndDate	Duration
1	Erebus	01/03/1972	.	.
2	Erebus	12/12/1912	.	.
3	Villarrica	10/26/2008	.	.
4	Poas	04/08/1996	04/08/1996	1
5	Sabancaya	05/01/1997	05/02/1997	2
6	Reventador	12/12/1856	12/13/1856	2
7	Barren Island	12/20/1795	12/21/1795	2
8	Grimsvotn	10/31/1603	11/01/1603	2
9	Kliuchevskoi	03/25/1931	03/27/1931	3
10	St. Helens	03/26/1847	03/30/1847	5
11	Reventador	02/24/1944	03/01/1944	7
12	Etna	12/16/2005	12/22/2005	7
13	Grimsvotn	12/18/1998	12/28/1998	11

5.5 Filtering Data in a Query

If you want to create a data table that is a subset of another table, you can use the Filter and Sort task or the Query Builder. The Filter and Sort task only filters and sorts data, but the Query Builder can also create computed or summarized columns and join tables together.

Here is a sample of the Volcanoes data table. To filter the data so that only volcanoes in North America and South America appear in the results, click the data icon in the Project Tree or Process Flow and select **Tasks ▶ Data ▶ Query Builder** from the menu bar. This opens the Query Builder window, with the **Select Data** tab on top. Select the columns that you want in the query result (in this example every column except Type). Then click the **Filter Data** tab.

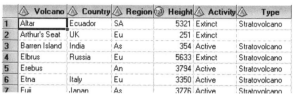

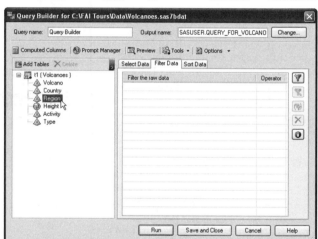

Select the column that you want to use for filtering purposes and drag it to the **Filter Data** tab. If you want to filter based on a summarized column, drag it to the **Filter the summarized data** area of the **Filter Data** tab, which only appears when you have summarized columns in the query. Notice that you can filter by columns that are not even part of the query result. In this example, drag **Region** to the filter area. When you drop the column, the New Filter wizard will open.

Building the filter In the New Filter wizard, you can see the name of the column you dragged to the filter area. Initially, the operator is **Equal to**. To choose a different operator, click the down-arrow to the right of the **Operator** box. In this example, the **In a list** operator is the most useful because it allows you to specify a list of unique values for Region.

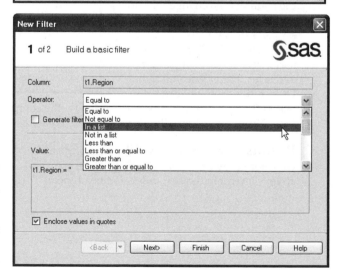

After choosing an operator, choose a value or values for your filter condition. You can type the values in the **Values** box or let SAS Enterprise Guide help you select the values. Click the down-arrow next to the **Values** box. In the window that opens, click **Get Values** and you will see a list of all possible values for the column you selected. Note that if you have large data tables, or lots of possible values, it can take a very long time to retrieve the values. Highlight one or more values by holding down the control (CTRL) key as you select values. In this example, select **NA** and **SA**, and then click **OK**. The values will be inserted into the Values box of the New Filter wizard. If you want to compare the value of the column being filtered to the value in a different column, then you can click the **Columns** tab to get a list of available columns and insert the column into the filter. This is not an option for the **In a list** operator.

Once you have set the filter condition, click **Next** to see a summary of your filter in the second window (not shown), then click **Finish**. The filter will appear on the **Filter Data** tab of the Query Builder window. In this case, the filter selects all rows from the Volcanoes table (t1) where Region has the value of NA or SA. Click **Run** to run the query.

	Volcano	Country	Region	Height	Activity
1	Altar	Ecuador	SA	5321	Extinct
2	Garibaldi	Canada	NA	2678	
3	Illimani	Bolivia	SA	6458	Extinct
4	Lassen	USA	NA	3187	Active
5	Poas	Costa Rica	NA	2708	Active
6	Popocatepetl	Mexico	NA	5426	Active
7	Reventador	Ecuador	SA	3562	Active
8	Sabancaya	Peru	SA	5976	Active
9	Shishaldin	USA	NA	2857	Active
10	St. Helens	USA	NA	2549	Active
11	Villarrica	Chile	SA	2847	Active

Results Here is the data table produced by the query. Only the volcanoes from North and South America are included.

5.6 Creating Compound Filters in a Query

Sometimes you want to base a filter on more than one condition. You can add conditions to a filter using the AND and OR operators. If you use AND, then rows must meet both conditions of the filter to be included in the result. If you use OR, then rows need to meet only one condition or the other. This section shows how to create a compound filter in the Query Builder, but you can create them any place you can create a filter.

In the previous section, the Volcanoes data were filtered so that only the volcanoes in North America and South America appeared in the result. Suppose you also want volcanoes that are in Japan. For this result, you need to select rows where the region is North America or South America, or where the country is Japan. To modify the existing query, click **Modify Task** on the workspace toolbar for the query result. In the Query Builder window, click the **Filter Data** tab.

Adding conditions to a filter To add a condition to an existing filter, drag the column for the new condition from the column list to the **Filter Data** tab. For this example, drag the Country column to the **Filter Data** tab. When you drop the column, the New Filter wizard will open.

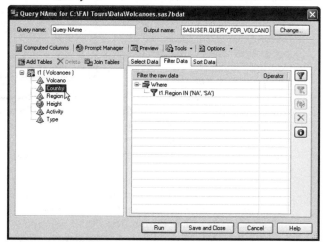

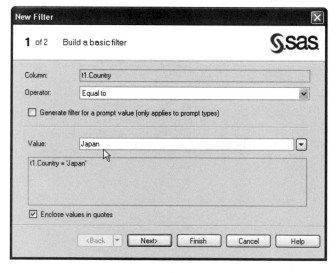

Building the Filter The procedure for specifying the additional condition is the same as if you were creating a single condition filter. First, choose an appropriate operator for your condition, and then either type the desired value in the Value box, or click the down-arrow next to the Value box to get a list of values to choose from. In this example, the filter will choose rows where the Country column from the Volcanoes table (t1) is equal to the value **Japan**. When you are satisfied, click **Next** to see a summary of your filter, then click **Finish**.

Setting the logic

After you create the additional condition, it will be added to the existing filter condition on the **Filter Data** tab. The filter now has two conditions. When you add new conditions to your filter, SAS Enterprise Guide automatically chooses the AND operator. To change to OR, click the down-arrow next to the AND operator and choose OR. For this example, set the operator to **OR**. Click **Run** to run the query.

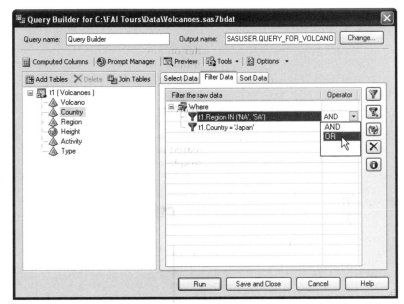

Results Here is the new data table produced after filtering the Volcanoes data table. Now, all the volcanoes from North America and South America are included, as well as all the volcanoes in Japan.

	Volcano	Country	Region	Height	Activity
1	Altar	Ecuador	SA	5321	Extinct
2	Fuji	Japan	As	3776	Active
3	Garibaldi	Canada	NA	2678	
4	Illimani	Bolivia	SA	6458	Extinct
5	Lassen	USA	NA	3187	Active
6	Poas	Costa Rica	NA	2708	Active
7	Popocatepetl	Mexico	NA	5426	Active
8	Reventador	Ecuador	SA	3562	Active
9	Sabancaya	Peru	SA	5976	Active
10	Shishaldin	USA	NA	2857	Active
11	St. Helens	USA	NA	2549	Active
12	Villarrica	Chile	SA	2847	Active

Chapter 5

5.7 Creating a Filter with Advanced Expressions

You can accomplish a lot with basic filters, but sometimes you need more advanced filters containing functions or more complex logic. For these cases, you can create an advanced filter. Advanced filters can be created in the Query Builder or the Filter and Sort task.

Here is a portion of the Bookings data table. This example uses the SUBSTR function in the Query Builder to select rows where the CustomerID starts with the letters "DE." To create a query, click the data icon in the

	Office	CustomerID	Tour	Travelers	Deposit	Deposit_Date
1	Portland	SL28	SH43	10	425	05JUL2011
2	Portland	DE27	PS27	6	75	11JUL2011
3	Portland	SL34	FJ12	4	200	19JUL2011
4	Portland	DI33	SH43	4	150	23JUL2011
5	Portland	BU12	SH43	2	75	23JUL2011
6	Portland	DE31	FJ12	3	175	25JUL2011
7	Portland	WI48	FJ12	2	100	26JUL2011
8	Portland	NG17	PS27	5	65	26JUL2011

Project Tree or Process Flow and select **Tasks ▶ Data ▶ Query Builder** from the menu bar. This opens the Query Builder with the **Select Data** tab on top. Select the columns that you want in the query result. Then click the **Filter Data** tab. For this example, select all columns.

Opening the advanced filter window On the **Filter Data** tab of the Query Builder window, click the New Filter

icon ▼ to open the New Filter wizard.

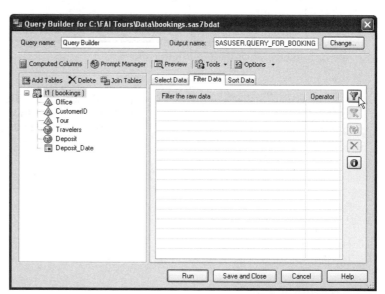

The New Filter wizard has up to five windows depending on which type of filter you select. In the first window, select **Advanced Filter** and click **Next**. (In the Filter and Sort task, click the **Advanced Edit** button on the **Filter** tab.)

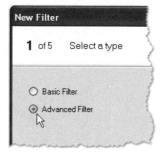

Building the advanced filter

In the second window, type the desired filter expression in the text box labeled **Enter a filter**. If you want to use functions in the expression, you can expand the Functions node in the box on the lower right to view all available functions. All the columns in the table, along with the selected columns for the query, are also listed in this box. In this example, the SUBSTR function is used to select all rows

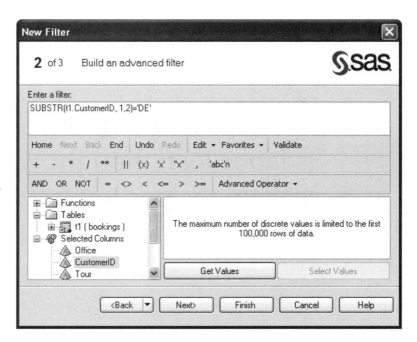

where the first two characters of the CustomerID column from the Bookings data table (t1) are equal to "DE." When you are finished building your filter, click **Next** to see a summary of your filter in the third window (not shown), then click **Finish** to return to the Query Builder window.

Your filter will appear on the **Filter Data** tab of the Query Builder. Click **Run** to run the query and view the results.

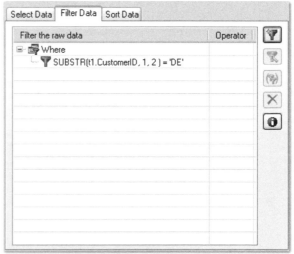

Results Here is the new data table produced after filtering the Bookings data table. Only the rows with a CustomerID that starts with the letters "DE" appear in the result.

	Office	CustomerID	Tour	Travelers	Deposit	Deposit_Date
1	Portland	DE27	PS27	6	75	11JUL2011
2	Portland	DE31	FJ12	3	175	25JUL2011

6

"Learning without thought is labor lost; thought without learning is perilous."

CONFUCIUS

From *Analects* Bk. II, Ch. XV. As quoted in *The Cyclopedia of Practical Quotations: English, Latin, and Modern Foreign Languages* by Jehiel Keeler Hoyt, 1896.

CHAPTER 6

Combining Data Tables

Chapter 6

6.1 Methods for Combining Tables

In SAS Enterprise Guide, there are two basic ways to combine data tables: appending and joining. You append when the tables contain the same (or almost the same) columns. You join when the tables contain the same (or almost the same) rows. This section describes, in general terms, what happens when you combine tables.

Appending tables Appending tables is like stacking them. It only makes sense to append tables if they have columns in common. Appending tables is done with the Append Table task, which is described in the next section.

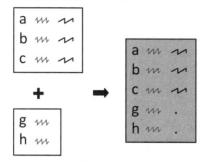

Joining tables To join tables together, the tables need to have a column (or set of columns) that can be used to match rows. You do not need to specify whether the match is one-to-one, one-to-many, or many-to-many—SAS Enterprise Guide determines this automatically. Joining tables is done in the Query Builder, which is described in section 6.3.

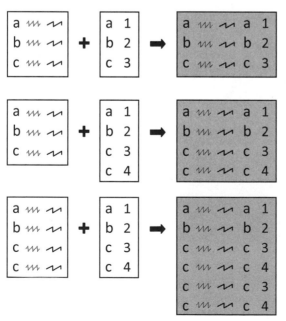

One-to-one match In a one-to-one match, one row from the first table is joined with one row from the second table. The values for the common column are unique in both tables.

One-to-many match In a one-to-many match, one row from the first table is joined with multiple rows from the second table. The values for the common column are unique in only one table.

Many-to-many match In a many-to-many match, the values for the common column are not unique in either table. Each row in the first table is joined with all the matching rows from the second table.

When you join tables together, one table may have rows that do not match any rows contained in the other table. By default, any non-matching rows are deleted. In the Query Builder, you can control which rows end up in the new table based on which table they came from. The Query Builder illustrates this with a join indicator (also known as a Venn diagram). The join indicator consists of two circles representing the two tables. The shaded areas show the parts of the tables that will be kept. You can choose different kinds of joins including inner joins, left joins, right joins, and full outer joins. Controlling the type of join is discussed in section 6.4.

The following graphics all show a one-to-one join, but the join has been modified so that different rows are included in the results.

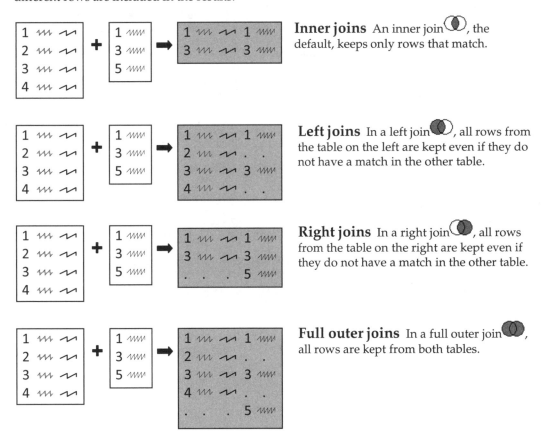

Inner joins An inner join, the default, keeps only rows that match.

Left joins In a left join, all rows from the table on the left are kept even if they do not have a match in the other table.

Right joins In a right join, all rows from the table on the right are kept even if they do not have a match in the other table.

Full outer joins In a full outer join, all rows are kept from both tables.

6.2 Appending Tables

You use the Append Table task to combine tables that contain the same (or almost the same) columns. For example, if you had sales data for January, February, and March in three separate tables, you could append the tables to create one table for the entire quarter.

In this example, a customer living in southern Washington is interested in traveling with the Fire and Ice Tours company. Because this customer lives between Seattle and Portland, she wants to see prices for flights from each city.

Here are two data tables, one showing flights from Portland and the other from Seattle. Looking at these two data tables, you can see they contain the same columns, making them good candidates for appending.

	Origin	Destination	FlightNo	FlightPrice
1	Portland	Catania	L469	$779.00
2	Portland	Hilo	HA25	$703.00
3	Portland	Nairobi	KLM6034	$1,833.00
4	Portland	Rome	D1576	$644.00
5	Portland	San Jose	CA1210	$494.00
6	Portland	Tokyo	UA383	$705.00

To append tables, click one data icon in the Project Tree or Process Flow to make it active, and then select **Tasks ▶ Data ▶ Append Table** from the menu bar. The Append Table window will open.

	Origin	Destination	FlightNo	FlightPrice
1	Seattle	Catania	BA48	$802.00
2	Seattle	Hilo	HA21	$677.00
3	Seattle	Jakarta	AA119	$1,815.00
4	Seattle	Nairobi	KLM6034	$1,761.00
5	Seattle	Quito	CA1086	$833.00
6	Seattle	Rome	USA6	$596.00
7	Seattle	San Jose	CA1100	$480.00
8	Seattle	Tokyo	UA875	$721.00

Adding tables The Append Table window opens showing the active table. To add a table, click **Add Table**, navigate to the table you want to add, and click **OK**. You can append up to 32 tables at once.

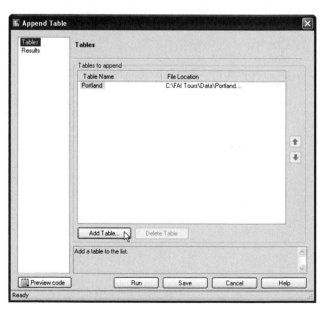

Running the task At this point, you can click **Run** and SAS Enterprise Guide will create the new table, store it in a default location, and give it the name **Append_Table**. (If you have more than one appended table stored in that location, SAS Enterprise Guide will add numbers to the name.) To choose a different name or location, click the **Results** option in the selection pane on the left. Then click **Browse** in the Results page (not shown) to open the Save File window.

In the Save File window, type a name for the new data table in the **File name** box and choose a library. To see the available libraries, click the down arrow in the **Save in** box at the top of the window. In this example, the new data table will be named Port_Sea and will be saved in the SASUSER library. Once you have specified the library and filename, click **Save**.

In the Append Table window, click **Run**. SAS Enterprise Guide will display the results in a Data Grid.

Results Here is the new data table. Notice that SAS Enterprise Guide concatenated the Portland and Seattle tables by matching the columns.

In this case, the two tables contained exactly the same columns. If there had been a column that existed in one table but not the other, then the data values for that column would be set to missing for rows from the other table.

	Origin	Destination	FlightNo	FlightPrice
1	Portland	Catania	L469	$779.00
2	Portland	Hilo	HA25	$703.00
3	Portland	Nairobi	KLM6034	$1,833.00
4	Portland	Rome	D1576	$644.00
5	Portland	San Jose	CA1210	$494.00
6	Portland	Tokyo	UA383	$705.00
7	Seattle	Catania	BA48	$802.00
8	Seattle	Hilo	HA21	$677.00
9	Seattle	Jakarta	AA119	$1,815.00
10	Seattle	Nairobi	KLM6034	$1,761.00
11	Seattle	Quito	CA1086	$833.00
12	Seattle	Rome	USA6	$596.00
13	Seattle	San Jose	CA1100	$480.00
14	Seattle	Tokyo	UA875	$721.00

6.3 Joining Tables

When you append tables, you match columns. But often, instead of matching columns, you need to match rows. For example, a teacher might record grades from homework in one table and grades from tests in another. To compute final grades she would need to match the homework and test scores for each student. This is called joining tables, and you do it with a query.

In the preceding section, two tables were appended to create one table containing all the data about flights. Now the data for each tour can be joined with the matching data for flights. To open the Query Builder, click a data icon in the Project Tree or Process Flow, and select **Tasks ▶ Data ▶ Query Builder** from the menu bar.

	Volcano	Departs	Days	Price	Difficulty
1	Etna	Catania	7	$1,075	m
2	Fuji	Tokyo	2	$225	c
3	Kenya	Nairobi	6	$830	m
4	Kilauea	Hilo	1	$55	e
5	Kilimanjaro	Nairobi	9	$1,310	c
6	Krakatau	Jakarta	7	$895	e
7	Poas	San Jose	1	$65	e
8	Reventador	Quito	4	$575	m
9	St. Helens	Portland	2	$167	e
10	Vesuvius	Rome	6	$985	e

	Origin	Destination	FlightNo	FlightPrice
1	Portland	Catania	L469	$779.00
2	Portland	Hilo	HA25	$703.00
3	Portland	Nairobi	KLM6034	$1,833.00
4	Portland	Rome	D1576	$644.00
5	Portland	San Jose	CA1210	$494.00
6	Portland	Tokyo	UA383	$705.00
7	Seattle	Catania	BA48	$802.00
8	Seattle	Hilo	HA21	$677.00
9	Seattle	Jakarta	AA119	$1,815.00
10	Seattle	Nairobi	KLM6034	$1,761.00
11	Seattle	Quito	CA1086	$833.00
12	Seattle	Rome	USA6	$596.00
13	Seattle	San Jose	CA1100	$480.00
14	Seattle	Tokyo	UA875	$721.00

Adding tables When you open the Query Builder, it will show the active table. To open another table, click the **Add Tables** button, and navigate to the table you want to add. For this example, start with the Tours table, and add the Port_Sea table created in the previous section. You can join up to 32 tables at once.

When you add tables, SAS Enterprise Guide will automatically look for columns with the same name and type. If SAS Enterprise Guide does not find any columns with the same name and type, then a warning message will appear telling you to join the columns manually. Click **OK**.

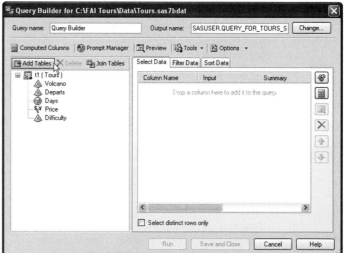

To join two tables manually, click the first table, then right-click the name of one column and select the name of the matching column from the pop-up menu. SAS Enterprise Guide will draw

a line from one column to the other. To correctly match the Tours data table and the Port_Sea table, the destination of a flight must match the city from which a tour departs. To join the tables in this example, click the Tours table, and then right-click the column Departs, and select t2 and Destination from the pop-up menu. A Join Properties window will open (not shown). For this example, accept the default settings by clicking **OK**. In the Tables and Joins window, click **Close**.

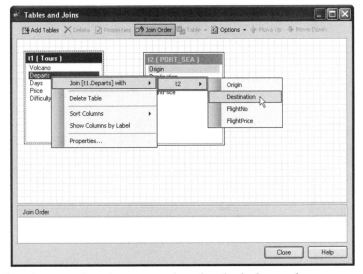

You can use more than one column for matching in a join. For example, a teacher might combine homework and test scores based on both class and student ID number. To specify additional columns for matching, select them manually as described above.

Running the query If you have not already selected the columns to be included in the results, then drag those columns to the **Select Data** tab in the Query Builder. When you are satisfied, click **Run**. SAS Enterprise Guide will display the results in a Data Grid.

Results This Data Grid shows the result of joining the two data tables. Notice that both of the columns used for matching (Departs and Destination) appear in the results. If these columns had the same name (such as City), then a number would have been automatically

	Volcano	Departs	Days	Price	Difficulty	Origin	Destination	FlightNo	FlightPrice
1	Etna	Catania	7	$1,075	m	Portland	Catania	L469	$779.00
2	Etna	Catania	7	$1,075	m	Seattle	Catania	BA48	$802.00
3	Fuji	Tokyo	2	$225	c	Portland	Tokyo	UA383	$705.00
4	Fuji	Tokyo	2	$225	c	Seattle	Tokyo	UA875	$721.00
5	Kenya	Nairobi	6	$830	m	Portland	Nairobi	KLM6034	$1,833.00
6	Kenya	Nairobi	6	$830	m	Seattle	Nairobi	KLM6034	$1,761.00
7	Kilauea	Hilo	1	$55	e	Portland	Hilo	HA25	$703.00
8	Kilauea	Hilo	1	$55	e	Seattle	Hilo	HA21	$677.00
9	Kilimanjaro	Nairobi	9	$1,310	c	Portland	Nairobi	KLM6034	$1,833.00
10	Kilimanjaro	Nairobi	9	$1,310	c	Seattle	Nairobi	KLM6034	$1,761.00
11	Krakatau	Jakarta	7	$895	e	Seattle	Jakarta	AA119	$1,815.00
12	Poas	San Jose	1	$65	e	Portland	San Jose	CA1210	$494.00
13	Poas	San Jose	1	$65	e	Seattle	San Jose	CA1100	$480.00
14	Reventador	Quito	4	$575	m	Seattle	Quito	CA1086	$833.00
15	Vesuvius	Rome	6	$985	e	Portland	Rome	D1576	$644.00
16	Vesuvius	Rome	6	$985	e	Seattle	Rome	USA6	$596.00

added to the name of the second column (resulting in City and City1).

Because there are two tours departing from Nairobi, and two flights with a destination of Nairobi, this is a many-to-many join.

SAS Enterprise Guide kept only the rows that matched. This is an inner join, which is the default type of join. To keep rows that don't match, modify your join as described in the next section.

6.4 Setting the Properties of a Join

By default, when you join tables, SAS Enterprise Guide keeps only rows for which a match is found. Sometimes that may be just what you want, but at other times, you may want to keep all the rows regardless of whether they match, or all the rows from one table, but not the other. To do this, change the properties of the join.

Reopening the Query window To change a query that you have already run, right-click the query icon in the Project Tree or Process Flow and select **Modify Query Builder** from the pop-up menu. The Query Builder will open. Click the **Join Tables** button to open the Tables and Joins window.

To modify a join, right-click the join indicator between the two tables and select **Properties** from the pop-up menu. The Join Properties window will open.

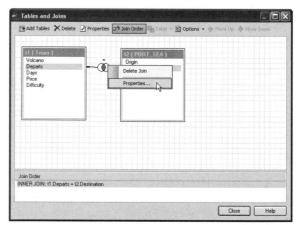

Selecting the type of join In the Join Properties window, you can choose from several types of joins. In this window, **All rows from the left table given a condition** has been selected. Tours is the table on the left, so all rows from Tours will be included regardless of whether there is a matching row in the Port_Sea table. This is called a left join. When you are satisfied with the join condition, click **OK**.

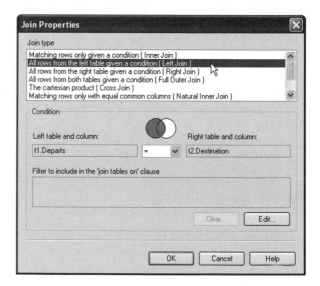

When you return to the Tables and Joins window, you will see that the join indicator between the two tables has changed. In this example, the circle on the left is filled in, indicating that all rows from the Tours data table will be included. When you are satisfied, click **Close**.

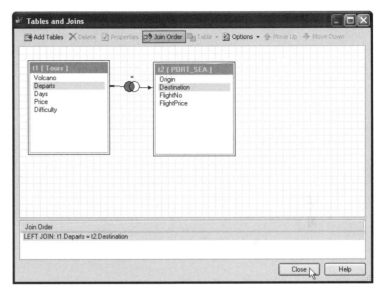

Running the query If you have not already selected the columns to be included in the results, then drag those columns to the **Select Data** tab in the Query Builder. When you are satisfied, click **Run**. SAS Enterprise Guide will display the results in a Data Grid.

Results This Data Grid shows the result of the modified join. This table contains all the tours, including the one for St. Helens. Notice that the values of columns from the Port_Sea table are missing for row 10. That is because there were no flights with a Destination of Portland. Because the customer lives near St. Helens, she doesn't need a flight to go on that tour.

	Volcano	Departs	Days	Price	Difficulty	Origin	Destination	FlightNo	FlightPrice
1	Etna	Catania	7	$1,075	m	Portland	Catania	L469	$779.00
2	Etna	Catania	7	$1,075	m	Seattle	Catania	BA48	$802.00
3	Kilauea	Hilo	1	$55	e	Portland	Hilo	HA25	$703.00
4	Kilauea	Hilo	1	$55	e	Seattle	Hilo	HA21	$677.00
5	Krakatau	Jakarta	7	$895	e	Seattle	Jakarta	AA119	$1,815.00
6	Kenya	Nairobi	6	$830	m	Seattle	Nairobi	KLM6034	$1,761.00
7	Kilimanjaro	Nairobi	9	$1,310	c	Seattle	Nairobi	KLM6034	$1,761.00
8	Kenya	Nairobi	6	$830	m	Portland	Nairobi	KLM6034	$1,833.00
9	Kilimanjaro	Nairobi	9	$1,310	c	Portland	Nairobi	KLM6034	$1,833.00
10	St. Helens	Portland	2	$167	e				.
11	Reventador	Quito	4	$575	m	Seattle	Quito	CA1086	$833.00
12	Vesuvius	Rome	6	$985	e	Seattle	Rome	USA6	$596.00
13	Vesuvius	Rome	6	$985	e	Portland	Rome	D1576	$644.00
14	Poas	San Jose	1	$65	e	Seattle	San Jose	CA1100	$480.00
15	Poas	San Jose	1	$65	e	Portland	San Jose	CA1210	$494.00
16	Fuji	Tokyo	2	$225	c	Seattle	Tokyo	UA875	$721.00
17	Fuji	Tokyo	2	$225	c	Portland	Tokyo	UA383	$705.00

7

" Celui qui a de l'imagination sans érudition a des ailes, et n'a pas de pieds. "

" He who has imagination without learning has wings, but no feet. "

JOSEPH JOUBERT

As quoted in *The Cyclopedia of Practical Quotations: English, Latin, and Modern Foreign Languages* by Jehiel Keeler Hoyt, 1896.

CHAPTER 7

Producing Simple List and Summary Reports

7.1 Creating Simple List Reports

A simple list report has one line for each observation in the data set. It's the kind of report you need when you just want to see your data. You can select some variables and not others, group the data by a particular variable, and insert totals; but as long as you have one line for each observation, it is still a list report. This example creates a list report using the List Data task. You can also use the List Report wizard to create list reports.

Here is a Data Grid showing the Bookings data set used in this example. To open the List Data task, select **Tasks ▶ Describe ▶ List Data** from the menu bar. The List Data window will open, displaying the Data page.

	Office	CustomerID	Tour	Travelers	Deposit	Deposit_Date
1	Portland	SL28	SH43	10	425	05JUL2011
2	Portland	DE27	PS27	6	75	11JUL2011
3	Portland	SL34	FJ12	4	200	19JUL2011
4	Portland	DI33	SH43	4	150	23JUL2011
5	Portland	BU12	SH43	2	75	23JUL2011
6	Portland	DE31	FJ12	3	175	25JUL2011
7	Portland	WI48	FJ12	2	100	26JUL2011
8	Portland	NG17	PS27	5	65	26JUL2011
9	Portland	RA28	PS27	2	30	28JUL2011
10	Portland	ME11	PS27	2	30	28JUL2011
11	Portland	GI08	SH43	8	300	31JUL2011
12	Portland	HI15	SH43	4	150	31JUL2011
13	Portland	MA09	SH43	2	75	31JUL2011

Assigning task roles
You assign variables to roles by clicking the name of a variable and dragging it to the role you want it to have. For the List Data task, you must assign at least one variable to the **List variables** role. In this window, the variables Office, CustomerID, Tour, Travelers, and Deposit have been assigned to serve as list variables.

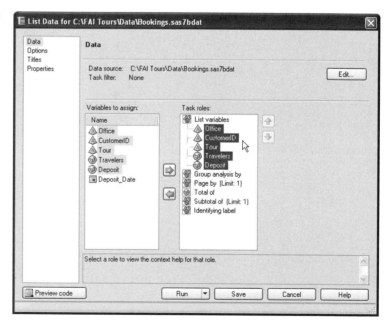

Choosing options To further customize your report, click **Options** in the selection pane on the left. By default, the List Data task will print the row number for each line in the report. If you don't want row numbers, then uncheck **Print the row number**. You can also leave the row number, but change the heading for that particular column. In this example, the heading for the row numbers has been changed to Reservation Number. When you are satisfied with the options, click **Run**.

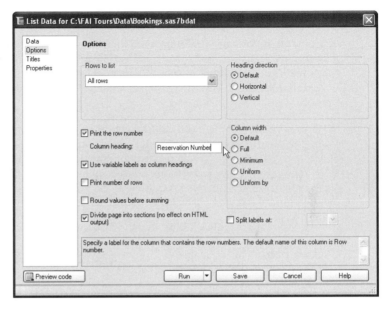

Results Here is the report listing the selected variables for the Bookings data set. Notice that row numbers are included and appear under the heading Reservation Number. This report uses the default title and footnote. The next section shows how to customize titles and footnotes.

Report Listing

Reservation Number	Office	CustomerID	Tour	Travelers	Deposit
1	Portland	SL28	SH43	10	425
2	Portland	DE27	PS27	6	75
3	Portland	SL34	FJ12	4	200
4	Portland	DI33	SH43	4	150
5	Portland	BU12	SH43	2	75
6	Portland	DE31	FJ12	3	175
7	Portland	WI48	FJ12	2	100
8	Portland	NG17	PS27	5	65
9	Portland	RA28	PS27	2	30
10	Portland	ME11	PS27	2	30
11	Portland	GI08	SH43	8	300
12	Portland	HI15	SH43	4	150
13	Portland	MA09	SH43	2	75

Generated by the SAS System ('Local', XP_PRO) on July 23, 2009 at 06:52:53 PM

Chapter 7

7.2 Customizing Titles and Footnotes

By default, reports in SAS Enterprise Guide have titles that describe the type of report, such as "Summary Statistics" or "Analysis of Variance," and footnotes that show the date and time the task was run. That's a good start, but in most cases, you will want titles and footnotes that reflect your unique report. You can easily customize titles and footnotes in any task that produces a report.

You can change the title or footnote when you first run a task, or re-open the task and modify the titles. This example takes the report that was produced in the previous section and gives it a custom title and footnote. To re-open a task, right-click the task icon in the Project Tree or Process Flow and select **Modify List Data** from the pop-up menu. The task window will open.

In the task window, click **Titles** in the selection pane on the left to display the Titles page.

Titles page The area labeled **Section** lists all the titles and footnotes for that particular task. For the List Data task, you can choose **Report Titles** or **Footnote**. Some tasks have additional titles you can change.

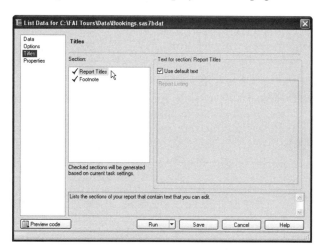

To change a title, click its name in the area labeled **Section**. Then uncheck the **Use default text** option and type up to 10 new titles in the box below. In this example, the title "Report Listing" has been replaced with two titles: "Bookings for Portland" and "July."

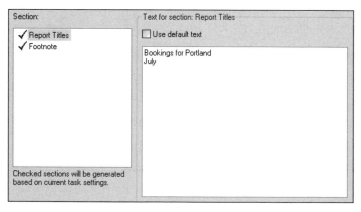

To change a footnote, click **Footnote** in the area labeled **Section**. Then uncheck the **Use default text** option and type up to 10 new footnotes in the box below. In this example, the footnote has simply been deleted.

When you are satisfied with the new titles and footnotes, click **Run** in the task window.

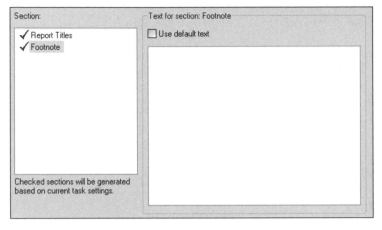

Results Here is the report with the new titles and no footnote.

Reservation Number	Office	CustomerID	Tour	Travelers	Deposit
1	Portland	SL28	SH43	10	425
2	Portland	DE27	PS27	6	75
3	Portland	SL34	FJ12	4	200
4	Portland	DI33	SH43	4	150
5	Portland	BU12	SH43	2	75
6	Portland	DE31	FJ12	3	175
7	Portland	WI48	FJ12	2	100
8	Portland	NG17	PS27	5	65
9	Portland	RA28	PS27	2	30
10	Portland	ME11	PS27	2	30
11	Portland	GI08	SH43	8	300
12	Portland	HI15	SH43	4	150
13	Portland	MA09	SH43	2	75

Bookings for Portland

July

Changing default titles and footnotes If you find yourself changing titles and footnotes a lot, you may want to change the default values. You can do this using the Options window (see section 1.16). To open the Options window, select **Tools ▶ Options** from the menu bar. Then select **Tasks General** from the selection pane on the left. In this page you can specify new titles that will replace the default title for all tasks. You can also set the footnote to blank, or specify new footnotes to replace the default footnote.

7.3 Adding Groups to List Reports

Most tasks that produce reports allow you to assign one or more variables to serve as grouping variables. When you do this, SAS Enterprise Guide divides your data into groups based on the values of the grouping variables, and handles the groups separately. That way, you can get a report for each salesperson, or statistics for each state, or a chart for each quarter.

This example takes the report that was produced in the previous section and adds a grouping variable. To re-open the task, right-click the task icon in the Project Tree or Process Flow and select **Modify List Data** from the pop-up menu. The task window will open.

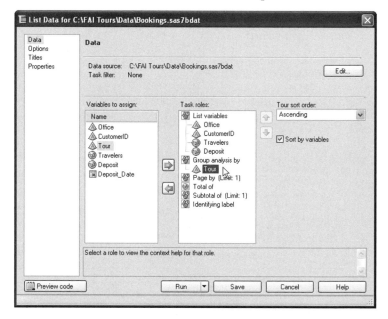

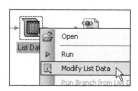

Assigning a variable to the grouping task role To produce a report with observations divided into groups, assign one or more variables to the **Group analysis by** role. Each time you drag a variable name to the Group analysis by role, two items will appear on the right: a pull-down list for the sort order, and a check box labeled **Sort by variables**. You use these options to tell SAS Enterprise Guide whether you want the report to be sorted by that grouping variable and, if so, whether in ascending or descending order. In the List Data window above, the variable Tour is a grouping variable, and the variables Office, CustomerID, Travelers, and Deposit are list variables. When you are satisfied with the variables and their task roles, click **Run**.

Results Here is the report with Tour as a grouping variable. Notice that there is a separate section of the report for each Tour.

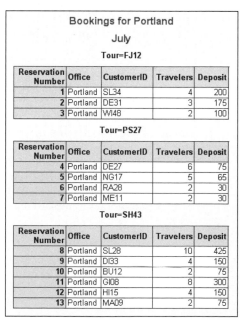

Bookings for Portland

July

Tour=FJ12

Reservation Number	Office	CustomerID	Travelers	Deposit
1	Portland	SL34	4	200
2	Portland	DE31	3	175
3	Portland	WI48	2	100

Tour=PS27

Reservation Number	Office	CustomerID	Travelers	Deposit
4	Portland	DE27	6	75
5	Portland	NG17	5	65
6	Portland	RA28	2	30
7	Portland	ME11	2	30

Tour=SH43

Reservation Number	Office	CustomerID	Travelers	Deposit
8	Portland	SL28	10	425
9	Portland	DI33	4	150
10	Portland	BU12	2	75
11	Portland	GI08	8	300
12	Portland	HI15	4	150
13	Portland	MA09	2	75

Assigning a variable to the identifying label role

When you assign a variable to serve as an identifying label, the values of that variable replace the row numbers in your report. If you assign the same variable to serve as both a grouping variable and an identifying variable, then SAS Enterprise Guide also changes the layout of the report. In this List Data window, the variable Tour has been assigned to both the **Group analysis by** role and the **Identifying label** role. When you are satisfied with the variables and their task roles, click **Run**.

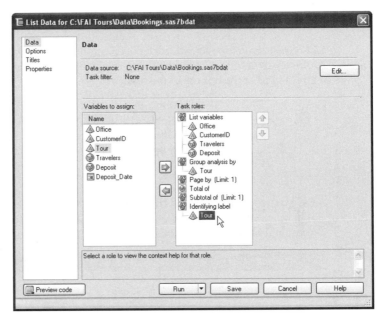

Results Here is the report with Tour serving both as a grouping variable and as an identifying variable. Notice that this report is more compact than the previous one, and that the row numbers have been replaced by the identifying variable.

Bookings for Portland
July

Tour	Office	CustomerID	Travelers	Deposit
FJ12	Portland	SL34	4	200
	Portland	DE31	3	175
	Portland	WI48	2	100
PS27	Portland	DE27	6	75
	Portland	NG17	5	65
	Portland	RA28	2	30
	Portland	ME11	2	30
SH43	Portland	SL28	10	425
	Portland	DI33	4	150
	Portland	BU12	2	75
	Portland	GI08	8	300
	Portland	HI15	4	150
	Portland	MA09	2	75

7.4 ▶ Adding Totals to List Reports

List reports have one line for each observation in a data set, but it is possible to add some summary data to these reports. Using the Total of task role, you can add subtotals for groups and a grand total at the bottom of the report.

This example takes the report that was produced in the previous section and adds totals. To re-open the task, right-click the task icon in the Project Tree or Process Flow and select **Modify List Data** from the pop-up menu. The task window will open.

Assigning a variable to the Total of task role   To produce a list report with totals, assign one or more variables to the Total of task role. To do this, click a variable name and drag it to the **Total of** role. Because this variable will be summed, it must be numeric.

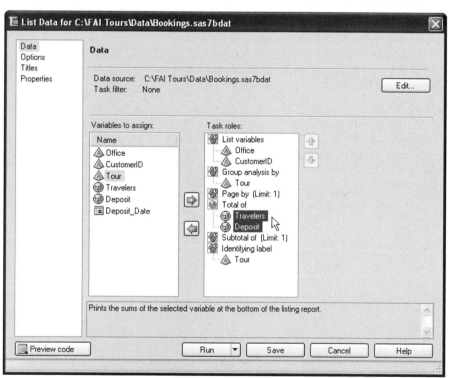

The List Data window above shows the task roles for the Bookings data. The variables Travelers and Deposit have been assigned to the Total of role. In addition, the variables Office and CustomerID have been assigned to serve as list variables, and Tour has been assigned as both a grouping and identifying variable. When you are satisfied with the variables and their roles, click **Run**.

Results Here is the list report of the Bookings data with the variables Travelers and Deposit totaled. Notice that there are totals for each value of the grouping variable, Tour, and a grand total at the bottom of the report. If this report did not have a grouping variable, then only the grand total would appear.

Bookings for Portland
July

Tour	Office	CustomerID	Travelers	Deposit
FJ12	Portland	SL34	4	200
	Portland	DE31	3	175
	Portland	WI48	2	100
FJ12			**9**	**475**
PS27	Portland	DE27	6	75
	Portland	NG17	5	65
	Portland	RA28	2	30
	Portland	ME11	2	30
PS27			**15**	**200**
SH43	Portland	SL28	10	425
	Portland	DI33	4	150
	Portland	BU12	2	75
	Portland	GI08	8	300
	Portland	HI15	4	150
	Portland	MA09	2	75
SH43			**30**	**1175**
			54	**1850**

7.5 Creating Frequency Reports

If you have ever wondered exactly how many different values a particular variable has, then a one-way frequency table is what you need. Frequencies are also called counts because you can produce a basic frequency table by simply counting the number of times each data value occurs. To produce frequencies for an individual variable in SAS Enterprise Guide, use the One-Way Frequencies task.

This example uses the Volcanoes data set to produce frequencies for the variables Activity and Type. Open the task by clicking the data icon in the Project Tree or Process Flow and select **Tasks ▶ Describe ▶ One-Way Frequencies** from the menu

	Volcano	Country	Region	Height	Activity	Type
1	Altar	Ecuador	SA	5321	Extinct	Stratovolcano
2	Arthur's Seat	UK	Eu	251	Extinct	
3	Barren Island	India	As	354	Active	Stratovolcano
4	Elbrus	Russia	Eu	5633	Extinct	Stratovolcano
5	Erebus		An	3794	Active	Stratovolcano
6	Etna	Italy	Eu	3350	Active	Stratovolcano
7	Fuji	Japan	As	3776	Active	Stratovolcano
8	Garibaldi	Canada	NA	2678		Stratovolcano
9	Grimsvotn	Iceland	Eu	1725	Active	Caldera

bar. The One-Way Frequencies window will open, displaying the Data page.

Assigning task roles For the One-Way Frequencies task, you must assign at least one variable to serve as an analysis variable. To do this, click a variable name and drag it to the **Analysis variables** role. In this example, the variables Activity and Type will be analysis variables.

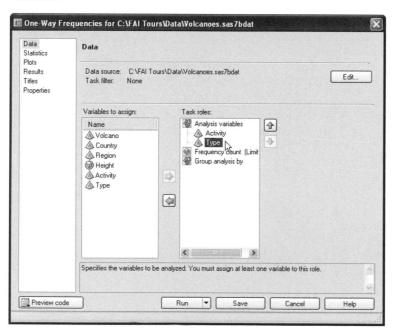

Choosing statistics If you click **Statistics** in the selection pane on the left, you will see
options for this task. By default, the results will include frequencies and percentages, along with
cumulative frequencies and percentages. You can choose among different combinations of
statistics. By default, the results exclude any missing values. If you want to include missing
values in the resulting table, then check the option **Include in calculations** in the **Missing values**
section. When you are satisfied with the options, click **Run**.

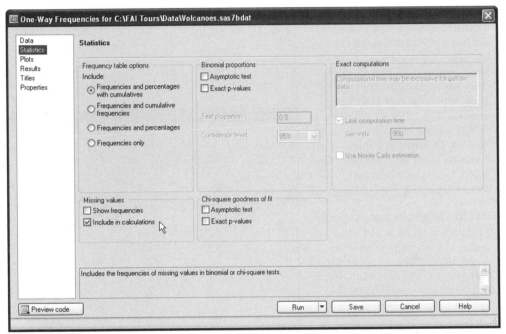

Results Here are the one-way
frequencies for Activity and Type. Notice
that there are two separate tables (one for
each analysis variable), and that
frequencies for missing values are
included.

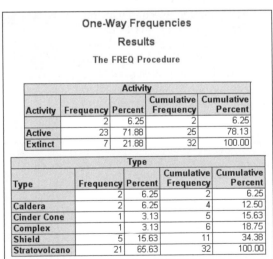

One-Way Frequencies

Results

The FREQ Procedure

Activity				
Activity	Frequency	Percent	Cumulative Frequency	Cumulative Percent
	2	6.25	2	6.25
Active	23	71.88	25	78.13
Extinct	7	21.88	32	100.00

Type				
Type	Frequency	Percent	Cumulative Frequency	Cumulative Percent
	2	6.25	2	6.25
Caldera	2	6.25	4	12.50
Cinder Cone	1	3.13	5	15.63
Complex	1	3.13	6	18.75
Shield	5	15.63	11	34.38
Stratovolcano	21	65.63	32	100.00

7.6 Creating Crosstabulations

When you have counts for one variable, they are called one-way frequencies. When you create counts by crossing two or more variables, they are called two-way, three-way, and so on, up to *n*-way frequencies, or simply crosstabulations. To produce crosstabulations, use the Table Analysis task.

As in the previous section, this example uses the Volcanoes data set, but, instead of having one table for Activity and one for Type, it produces a single table showing Activity crossed with Type. Open the task by clicking the data icon in the Project Tree or Process Flow and select **Tasks ▶ Describe ▶ Table Analysis** from the menu bar. The Table Analysis window will open, displaying the Data page.

	Volcano	Country	Region	Height	Activity	Type
1	Altar	Ecuador	SA	5321	Extinct	Stratovolcano
2	Arthur's Seat	UK	Eu	251	Extinct	
3	Barren Island	India	As	354	Active	Stratovolcano
4	Elbrus	Russia	Eu	5633	Extinct	Stratovolcano
5	Erebus		An	3794	Active	Stratovolcano

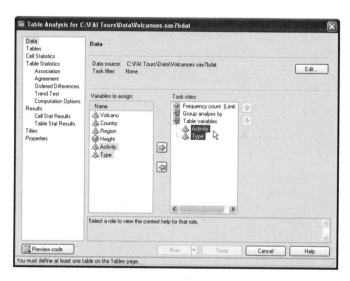

Assigning task roles   In the Table Analysis task, you must assign at least two variables to serve as table variables. In this example, the variables Activity and Type have been dragged to the **Table variables** role.

Arranging tables   Click **Tables** in the selection pane on the left to display the Tables page. In this page, you will see an area labeled **Variables permitted in table**, and an area labeled **Preview**. To arrange your table, click the name of a variable and drag it to the Preview area. The values of the first variable dragged over will be used for rows, the second for columns, and the third for pages, but you can switch them around by dragging them within the Preview area. In this window, the variable Type has been assigned to the rows, and Activity to the columns.

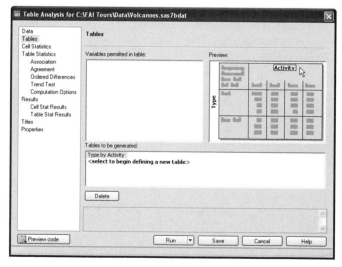

When you drag a variable to the Preview area, its name will disappear from the list of variables permitted in the table. (That way you can't accidentally cross a variable with itself.) However, if you click the words **<select to begin defining a new table>** in the area labeled **Tables to be generated**, then the variable names will appear again. This allows you to define multiple tables in a single task.

Choosing cell statistics

If you click **Cell Statistics** in the selection pane on the left, you will see options for basic statistics. By default, the results include column percentages and cell frequencies. The Table Analysis task also offers more advanced statistics, such as the chi-square test. See section 9.3 for a discussion of other options. For this report, **Cell frequencies** and **Cell percentages** have been selected. When you are satisfied with the options, click **Run**.

Results

Here is the two-way frequency table for Activity by Type. Because two volcanoes have missing values for Activity and two have missing values for Type, there is a note at the bottom saying that four observations are missing.

Table Analysis

Results

The FREQ Procedure

Table of Type by Activity		Activity		
		Active	Extinct	Total
Type				
Caldera	**Frequency**	2	0	2
	Percent	7.14	0.00	7.14
Cinder Cone	**Frequency**	0	1	1
	Percent	0.00	3.57	3.57
Complex	**Frequency**	1	0	1
	Percent	3.57	0.00	3.57
Shield	**Frequency**	4	1	5
	Percent	14.29	3.57	17.86
Stratovolcano	**Frequency**	16	3	19
	Percent	57.14	10.71	67.86
Total	**Frequency**	23	5	28
	Percent	82.14	17.86	100.00
Frequency Missing = 4				

7.7 Creating Simple Summary Reports

Statistics like the mean, standard deviation, and minimum and maximum values not only give you a feel for your data, but can alert you to unexpected values or errors. You can compute summary statistics with the Summary Statistics task or wizard. This section describes the task.

Here is a sample of the Volcanoes data set. To open the task, click the data icon in the Project Tree or Process Flow and select **Tasks ▶ Describe ▶ Summary Statistics** from the menu bar. The Summary Statistics window will open, displaying the Data page.

	Volcano	Country	Region	Height	Activity	Type
1	Altar	Ecuador	SA	5321	Extinct	Stratovolcano
2	Arthur's Seat	UK	Eu	251	Extinct	
3	Barren Island	India	As	354	Active	Stratovolcano
4	Elbrus	Russia	Eu	5633	Extinct	Stratovolcano
5	Erebus		An	3794	Active	Stratovolcano
6	Etna	Italy	Eu	3350	Active	Stratovolcano
7	Fuji	Japan	As	3776	Active	Stratovolcano
8	Garibaldi	Canada	NA	2678		Stratovolcano
9	Grimsvotn	Iceland	Eu	1725	Active	Caldera

Assigning task roles For the Summary Statistics task, you must assign at least one variable to the **Analysis variables** role, and all analysis variables must be numeric. Classification variables, on the other hand, are optional and may be numeric or character.

If you assign a variable to the **Classification variables** role, then SAS Enterprise Guide will produce separate summary statistics for each combination of the classification variables. When you drag a variable to the classification role, options will appear on the right. You can choose the sort order (Ascending or Descending) and whether to include missing values. The default is to exclude any observations with missing values for the classification variables. The **Group analysis by** role is similar to the classification role, but it produces a separate table for each combination of the grouping variables.

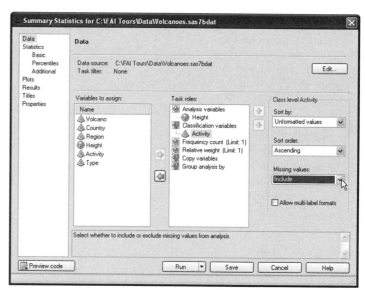

In this example, the variable Height has been designated as an analysis variable, and Activity as a classification variable. The option **Missing values** has been set to **Include**.

Choosing statistics Click **Basic** under the **Statistics** group of options in the selection pane on the left to display the Basic page. Here you can choose statistics and set the number of decimal places to be displayed in the report. The Summary Statistics task offers many other statistics, including the coefficient of variation and percentiles. See section 9.2 for a discussion of more advanced options. In this case, **Variance** has been selected along with the default statistics, and the number of decimal places has been set to four. When you are satisfied with the settings, click **Run**.

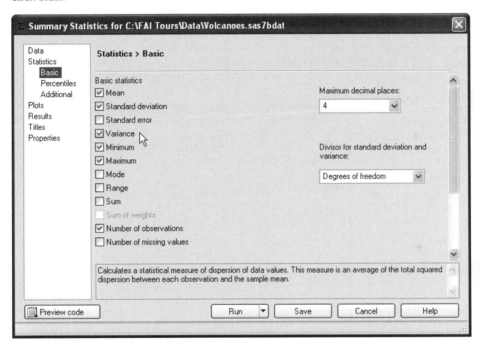

Results Here is the report showing summary statistics for Height by Activity. Notice that, because missing values were included, there is a separate line for volcanoes with a missing value for the variable Activity.

Summary Statistics

Results

The MEANS Procedure

Analysis Variable : Height						
Activity	N Obs	Mean	Std Dev	Variance	Minimum	Maximum	N
	2	4286.5000	2274.7625	5174544.5000	2678.0000	5895.0000	2
Active	23	2852.6087	1508.0614	2274249.1581	354.0000	5976.0000	23
Extinct	7	3635.8571	2572.7682	6619136.1429	251.0000	6458.0000	7

7.8 ▶ Creating Summary Data Sets in a Task

Sometimes you may want to save summary data so you can use it for further analysis or join it with other data. Many tasks can save summary data, including Table Analysis, Summary Tables, and Summary Statistics.

The previous section used the Volcanoes data set to produce a report showing summary statistics. These summary statistics can be saved in a data set. To re-open a task, right-click the task icon in the Project Tree or Process Flow and select **Modify Summary Statistics** from the pop-up menu. The task window will open. Click **Results** in the selection pane on the left to display the Results page.

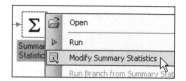

Results page In the Results page, you will see options that affect both your printed report and output data set. To save an output data set, check the **Save statistics to data set** option. SAS Enterprise Guide gives the data set a name beginning with MEAN and stores it in a default location. To specify a different name or location, click **Browse**. This opens the Save As window.

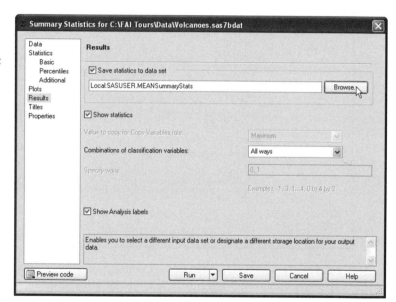

Save As window First, choose a library from the box labeled **Save in**, and then type a name for your file in the **File name** box. In this window, the data set has been named VolcanoStats and will be saved in the SASUSER library. When you are satisfied, click **Save** to return to the Results page.

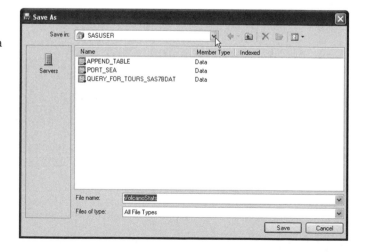

Choosing options In the Results page, you will see the new data set name. Before you run the report, you may want to make some other changes. Because you are creating an output data set, you may not care about the standard Summary Statistics report. To turn off the report, uncheck the **Show statistics** box.

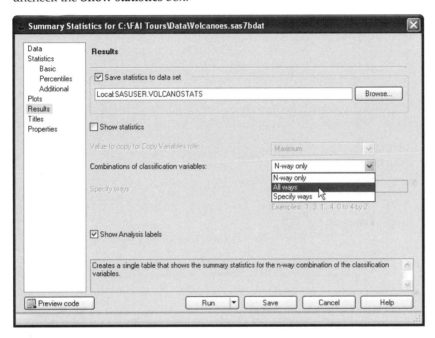

You can also select the **Combinations of classification variables** that will be included in the results. **N-way only** (the default) includes only the highest interaction of the classification variables. The option **All ways** gives you summary data for all combinations of the classification variables including the grand total. If you choose **Specify ways**, then you can select just the combinations you want. If you have many classification variables, then you will have many possible combinations. In this example, **All ways** is being selected. When you are satisfied with the settings, click **Run**.

Results Here is the output data set displayed in a Data Grid. The first row contains summary statistics for the grand total, while the following rows contain statistics for each level of Activity (missing, Active, and Extinct). Notice that SAS Enterprise Guide has created new variables for the summary statistics (Height_Mean, Height_StdDev, Height_Var, Height_Min, Height_Max, and Height_N). In addition, there are three automatic variables. _FREQ_ tells you how many observations contributed to each group, while _WAY_ and _TYPE_ reflect the type of combination. The _WAY_ and _TYPE_ are the same except that _WAY_ is a numeric variable while _TYPE_ is character.

	Activity	_WAY_	_TYPE_	_FREQ_	Height_Mean	Height_StdDev	Height_Var	Height_Min	Height_Max	Height_N
1		0	0	32	3114	1806	3262908.96	251	6458	32
2		1	1	2	4287	2275	5174544.5	2678	5895	2
3	Active	1	1	23	2853	1508	2274249.16	354	5976	23
4	Extinct	1	1	7	3636	2573	6619136.14	251	6458	7

7.9 Creating Grouped Reports with User-Defined Formats

Often you want to summarize your data by groups. For example, if you had a variable for age, you might want to see separate summary statistics for children and adults. If you did not have a variable for age group, you could compute it in a Data Grid, or use the Query Builder to recode your data. Both of these methods add a new variable to your data set. If you don't want to add a new variable, then you can group your data with a user-defined format.

Many tasks allow you to group data using a format. These include List Data, One-Way Frequencies, Table Analysis, Summary Statistics, and Summary Tables. This section groups the Volcanoes data set in a One-Way Frequencies task using the HeightGroup. format created in section 3.4. The HeightGroup. format assigns volcanoes with heights of 0-499 meters to the group Pip-squeak, 500-3999 meters to Middling, and 4000 meters and above to Stupendous.

Here is a sample of the Volcanoes data set. To open the task, click the data icon in the Project Tree or Process Flow and select **Tasks ▶ Describe ▶ One-Way Frequencies** from the menu bar.

	Volcano	Country	Region	Height	Activity	Type
1	Altar	Ecuador	SA	5321	Extinct	Stratovolcano
2	Arthur's Seat	UK	Eu	251	Extinct	
3	Barren Island	India	As	354	Active	Stratovolcano
4	Elbrus	Russia	Eu	5633	Extinct	Stratovolcano
5	Erebus		An	3794	Active	Stratovolcano

The One-Way Frequencies window will open, displaying the Data page.

Opening the Properties window To apply a format in a task, right-click the name of the variable you want to be grouped in the Data page (in either the **Variables to assign** area or the **Task roles** area), and select **Properties** from the pop-up menu. In this example, **Properties** is being selected for the variable Height.

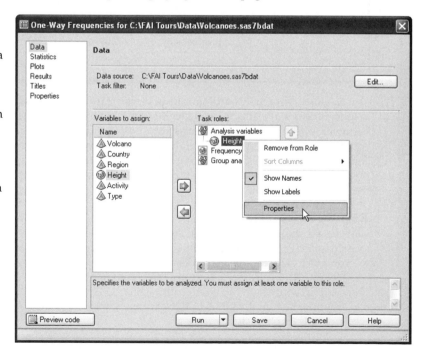

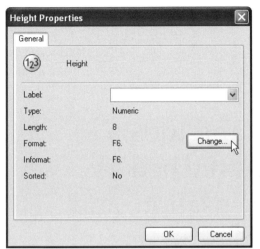

Using custom formats In the Properties window, click **Change** to open the Formats window for that variable.

Then in the Formats window, select the category **User Defined**. All the formats you have created will be listed. Here is the Formats window for the variable Height. Because Height is numeric, only numeric formats are listed. In this example, HEIGHTGROUP. is being selected.

Once you have selected the correct format, click **OK** in the Formats window and click **OK** in the Properties window. Then click **Run** in the task window.

Results Here is the grouped report. Notice that the user-defined format was applied to the variable before it was summarized. Instead of counts for data values like 251 and 5321, the report shows counts for the formatted values, Pip-squeak, Middling, and Stupendous.

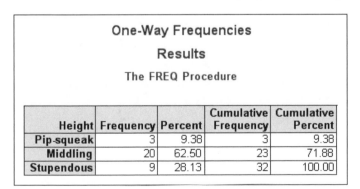

One-Way Frequencies

Results

The FREQ Procedure

Height	Frequency	Percent	Cumulative Frequency	Cumulative Percent
Pip-squeak	3	9.38	3	9.38
Middling	20	62.50	23	71.88
Stupendous	9	28.13	32	100.00

Chapter 7

"Every now and then a man's mind is stretched by a new idea or sensation, and never shrinks back to its former dimensions."

OLIVER WENDELL HOLMES, SR.

From *The Autocrat of the Breakfast Table*, 1858.

CHAPTER 8

Producing Complex Reports in Summary Tables

8.1 Creating Summary Tables with Frequencies

The Summary Tables task is the most powerful and flexible of the reporting tasks in SAS Enterprise Guide. It gives you control not only over which data appear in a report, but also over how data are arranged, summarized, labeled, and even colored. You can access some of these features using the Summary Tables wizard. This chapter shows the task.

This example uses the Volcanoes data set to create a report showing the number of active and extinct volcanoes for each region. To open the task, click the data icon in the Project Tree or Process Flow, and select **Tasks ▶ Describe ▶ Summary Tables** from the menu bar. The Summary Tables window will open, displaying the Data page.

	Volcano	Country	Region	Height	Activity	Type
1	Altar	Ecuador	SA	5321	Extinct	Stratovolcano
2	Arthur's Seat	UK	Eu	251	Extinct	
3	Barren Island	India	As	354	Active	Stratovolcano
4	Elbrus	Russia	Eu	5633	Extinct	Stratovolcano
5	Erebus		An	3794	Active	Stratovolcano
6	Etna	Italy	Eu	3350	Active	Stratovolcano
7	Fuji	Japan	As	3776	Active	Stratovolcano
8	Garibaldi	Canada	NA	2678		Stratovolcano
9	Grimsvotn	Iceland	Eu	1725	Active	Caldera

Assigning task roles To produce a summary table showing frequencies, assign one or more variables to the **Classification variables** role. These variables may be character or numeric. SAS Enterprise Guide will divide the data into categories based on the values of the classification variables. The following window shows the Volcanoes data set with the variables Region and Activity serving as classification variables.

When you drag a variable to the classification role, a box appears on the right. In this box, you can select options for that variable, including how to handle missing data. By default, missing values are included as valid rows and columns, which may or may not be what you want. In this case, two volcanoes have a missing value for Activity. To avoid having an entire row devoted to

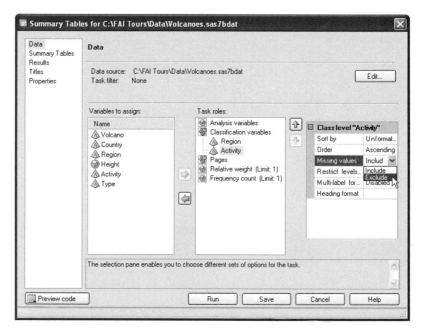

missing values, click **Missing values** and select **Exclude** for the variable Activity.

Once you exclude missing values for a variable, observations with missing values will be excluded from the report even if you decide not to use that particular variable. Because of this, it's a good idea to assign variables to the classification role only if you intend to use them in the current report.

Arranging your table Before you can run a report, you must tell SAS Enterprise Guide how to arrange the report table. Start by clicking the **Summary Tables** option in the selection pane on the left. In the Summary Tables page, you will see areas labeled **Available variables** and **Preview**. To assign a variable to serve as a row or column in your report, drag the variable name from the list of available variables to the Preview area. It may take a little practice to get variables where you want them. The trick is to watch the cursor. If the cursor looks like the universal not-allowed symbol, ⊘, then you cannot drop the variable. When the cursor turns into an arrow, then you can drop the variable.

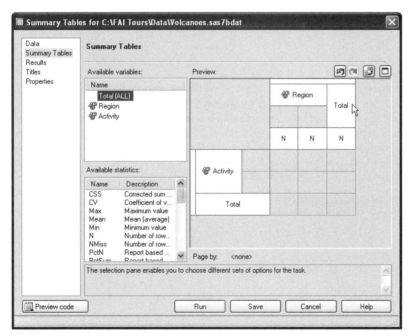

The undo ↺ and redo ↻ buttons in the upper-right corner of the Preview area can be quite useful. If you want to switch the row variables with the column variables, use the pivot ▦ button. To enlarge the Preview area, click the maximize button ▢. You can drag the **Total(ALL)** variable to the Preview area to tell SAS Enterprise Guide where to insert totals. In this window, the values of the variable Activity form the rows, while the values of Region form the columns. When you are satisfied with the arrangement of your table, click **Run**.

Results Here is the report of Activity by Region. Notice that the value in each cell is simply the number of volcanoes in that category. N (the number of non-missing values) is the default statistic for classification variables.

Summary Tables

	Region							Total (ALL)
	AP	Af	An	As	Eu	NA	SA	
	N	N	N	N	N	N	N	N
Activity								
Active	3	2	1	5	4	5	3	23
Extinct	1	1	.	.	3	.	2	7
Total (ALL)	4	3	1	5	7	5	5	30

8.2 Adding Statistics to Summary Tables

The previous section showed how to produce a table containing simple counts. Sometimes that's all you need, but often you want more. You might want to know total sales by region, or the mean test score for each class. In summary tables, you can compute sums and means, plus a long list of other statistics, including maximum and minimum values, percentages, medians, quartiles, standard deviations, and variances.

This example uses the Tours data set to create a report with statistics. To open the task, click the data icon in the Project Tree or Process Flow to make it active, and select **Tasks ▶ Describe ▶ Summary Tables** from the menu bar. The Summary Tables window will open, displaying the Data page.

	Volcano	Departs	Days	Price	Difficulty
1	Etna	Catania	7	$1,075	m
2	Fuji	Tokyo	2	$225	c
3	Kenya	Nairobi	6	$830	m
4	Kilauea	Hilo	1	$55	e
5	Kilimanjaro	Nairobi	9	$1,310	c
6	Krakatau	Jakarta	7	$895	e
7	Poas	San Jose	1	$65	e
8	Reventador	Quito	4	$575	m
9	St. Helens	Portland	2	$167	e
10	Vesuvius	Rome	6	$985	e

Assigning task roles There are a few statistics you can compute for classification variables. These include N and PctN (the percentage of frequency). However, most statistics can be computed only for analysis variables. Analysis variables must be numeric. (It's simply not possible to compute a mean using character values like Active and Extinct.) To produce a summary report containing sums and means, assign one or more variables to the analysis role. The following window shows the Tours data set with the variable Difficulty serving as a classification variable, and the variables Days and Price serving as analysis variables.

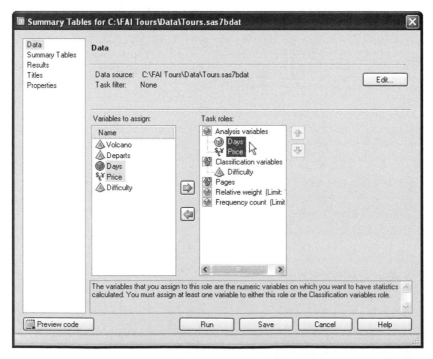

Arranging your table You arrange analysis variables in your table the same way you arrange classification variables. First, click the **Summary Tables** option in the selection pane on the left. In the Summary Tables page, you will see areas labeled **Available variables** and **Preview**. To assign a variable to serve as a row or column in your report, drag the variable name from the list of available variables to the Preview area. In the following window, the values of Difficulty form the rows, and the values of Days and Price form the columns.

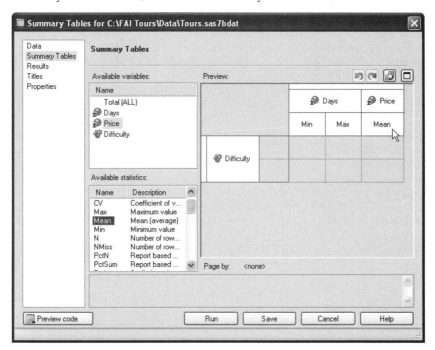

Choosing statistics The default statistic for classification variables is N (the number of non-missing values). The default statistic for analysis variables is Sum. You can choose many other statistics from the box labeled **Available statistics**. To add a statistic to your report, click the name of the statistic and drag it to the **Preview** area. Be sure to watch your cursor carefully. If the cursor looks like the universal not-allowed symbol, $\oslash$, then you cannot drop the statistic. When the cursor turns into an arrow, then you can drop the statistic.

In the preceding window, the statistics Min and Max have been placed under the variable Days, and the statistic Mean has been placed under the variable Price. When you are satisfied with the arrangement of your table, click **Run**.

Results Here is the report of Difficulty by Days and Price. Notice that the values in the cells are the minimum and maximum number of Days, and the mean Price.

Summary Tables

	Days		Price
	Min	Max	Mean
Difficulty			
c	2.00	9.00	767.50
e	1.00	7.00	433.40
m	4.00	7.00	826.67

8.3 Changing Heading Properties in Summary Tables

Once you've constructed a summary table, put each variable in its proper place, and selected statistics, you may want to change the way the table looks. In the Preview area of the Summary Tables window, you can change many properties of headers and data values.

To modify an existing report, right-click the Summary Tables task icon in the Project Tree or Process Flow, and select **Modify Summary Tables** from the pop-up menu. The Summary Tables window will open. To display the Preview area, click the **Summary Tables** option in the selection pane on the left.

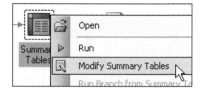

Heading Properties To change headings that are the names of variables or statistics, use the Heading Properties window. For example, to change the heading Min to Minimum, you would right-click **Min** in the **Preview** area and select **Heading Properties** from the pop-up menu. The Heading Properties window will open.

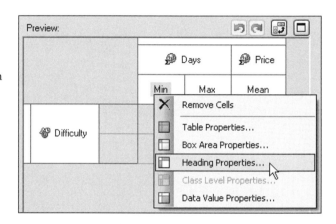

Using the **General** tab of the Heading Properties window, you can type a new label for the variable or statistic you have selected. In this window, the word Minimum has been typed in the **Label** box. Using the **Font** tab, you can change the font, font style, size, foreground color, background color, and other attributes of headings. When you are satisfied with the changes, click **OK**.

You can now change other properties. For this example, you should also change the statistic name Max to Maximum using the Heading Properties window for Max.

Box Area Properties Summary Tables reports always contain a box in the upper-left corner. By default, this box is empty. But you can put a label in that box to give your reports a nicely polished look. To do this, right-click anywhere in the **Preview** area and select **Box Area Properties** from the pop-up menu.

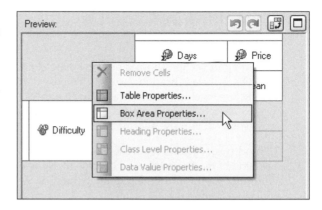

Using the **General** tab of the Box Area Properties window, you can specify the text you want printed in the box area. In this example, the words Volcano Tours have been typed in the text box. Using the **Font** tab, you can change the font, font style, size, foreground color, background color, and other attributes of the text to be printed in the box area.

When you are satisfied with the changes, click **OK**. You can then change other properties, or click **Run** to see the new results.

Results Here is the report. Notice that the labels Min and Max have been replaced with Minimum and Maximum, and the phrase Volcano Tours has been inserted in the box area.

Summary Tables			
Volcano Tours	**Days**		**Price**
	Minimum	**Maximum**	**Mean**
Difficulty			
c	2.00	9.00	767.50
e	1.00	7.00	433.40
m	4.00	7.00	826.67

8.4 Changing Class Level Headings and Properties in Summary Tables

The previous section showed how to change headings that are the names of variables or statistics, but classification variables also use data values as headings. These data values are called class level headings. When you change class level headings, you are changing the way those data values are displayed. To change the way data values are displayed, you use a format.

To modify an existing report, right-click the Summary Tables task icon in the Project Tree or Process Flow, and select **Modify Summary Tables** from the pop-up menu. The Summary Tables window will open.

Applying a format to a classification variable

To change headings that are data values, you specify a format in the Data page. Click the name of the classification variable you want to change. A box will open on the right, listing options for that variable. Click the words **Heading format** and the ellipsis button will appear

. Click the button to open a Format window for that variable. In this example, the heading format for the variable Difficulty is being selected.

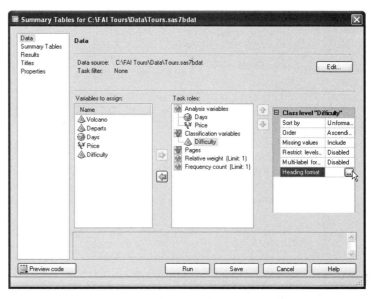

In the Select Column Format window, choose the category of formats you want to see, and then choose the name of the format you want to use. In most cases, to change a class level heading you will need a user-defined format. In this example, the user-defined format $DIFF. has been selected. The $DIFF. format was created in Tutorial B. Sections 3.3 and 3.4 also show how to create user-defined formats. Once you are satisfied, click **OK** to return to the Summary Tables window.

Class Level Properties To change other properties of class level headings, click the **Summary Tables** option in the selection pane on the left. Then right-click the name of the classification variable in the **Preview** area and select **Class Level Properties** from the pop-up menu. This example shows Class Level Properties being selected for the variable Difficulty. The Class Level Properties window will open.

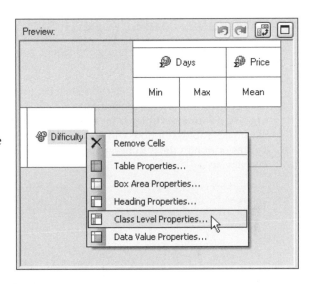

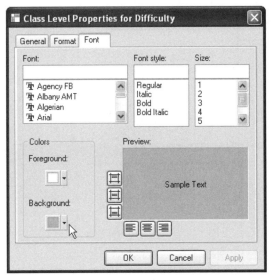

Using the **Font** tab, you can change the font, font style, size, foreground color, background color, and other attributes of headings. For this report, the background color has been changed to Gray–25%. When you are satisfied with the changes, click **OK**. Click **Run** to see the new results.

Results Here is the report. Notice that the labels c, e, and m have been replaced with Challenging, Easy, and Moderate (the values of the $DIFF. format), and have a medium gray background.

Summary Tables			
Volcano Tours	**Days**		**Price**
	Minimum	**Maximum**	**Mean**
Difficulty			
Challenging	2.00	9.00	767.50
Easy	1.00	7.00	433.40
Moderate	4.00	7.00	826.67

Chapter 8

8.5 Changing Table Properties in Summary Tables

In addition to changing headers and labels, you can make changes to the data cells in a table. To make a change that will apply to all the cells, use the Table Properties window.

To modify an existing report, right-click the Summary Tables task icon in the Project Tree or Process Flow, and select **Modify Summary Tables** from the pop-up menu. The Summary Tables window will open. Click the **Summary Tables** option in the selection pane on the left to display the Preview area.

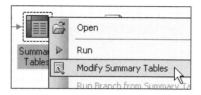

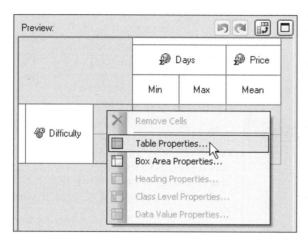

To make changes to all the data cells of a table, right-click anywhere in the **Preview** area and select **Table Properties** from the pop-up menu.

General tab Using the **General** tab of the Table Properties window, you can specify options for the treatment of missing values and class variable levels. By default, missing values are displayed as a period (.). You can specify a more meaningful label. In this example, the label none has been assigned to missing values.

Format tab Using the **Format** tab of the Table Properties window, you can choose a format for the data in the cells of the table. Here the basic numeric format, *w.d*, has been specified with an overall width of 4 characters, and no decimal places.

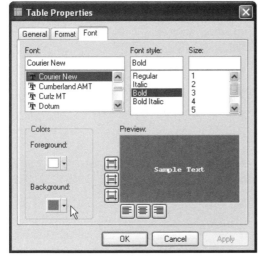

Font tab Using the **Font** tab of the Table Properties window, you can change the font, font style, size, foreground color, background color, and other attributes of the data cells in your table. In this case, the font has been set to Courier New, the style to Bold, the foreground color to white, and the background color to Gray–50%.

When you are satisfied with the changes, click **OK**. You can then change other properties, or click **Run** to see the new results.

Results Here is the new report. Notice that the data cells have a dark gray background and white foreground. Also, the data are displayed in bold Courier New, and with no decimal places.

Summary Tables

Volcano Tours	Days		Price
	Minimum	Maximum	Mean
Difficulty			
Challenging	2	9	768
Easy	1	7	433
Moderate	4	7	827

Chapter 8

8.6 ▶ Changing Data Value Properties in Summary Tables

Using the Table Properties window, you can make changes to all the data cells in a report, but sometimes you may want to choose different formats or fonts for different variables or statistics. To do that, use the Data Value Properties window.

To modify an existing report, right-click the Summary Tables task icon in the Project Tree or Process Flow, and select **Modify Summary Tables** from the pop-up menu. The Summary Tables window will open. Click the **Summary Tables** option in the selection pane on the left to display the Preview area.

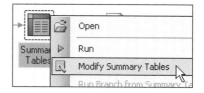

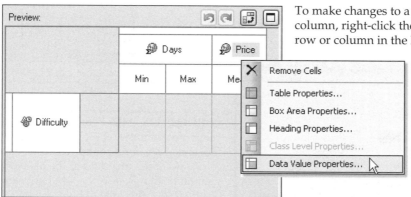

To make changes to a particular row or column, right-click the header for that row or column in the **Preview** area and select **Data Value Properties** from the pop-up menu. In this Preview area, Data Value Properties is being selected for the column Price.

Format tab Using the **Format** tab of the Data Value Properties window, you can choose a format for the data values in the row or column. In this example, the category Currency has been selected, and SAS Enterprise Guide has listed all the available formats for currency data. The format DOLLAR*w.d* is selected, with an overall width of **7** characters, and **2** decimal places.

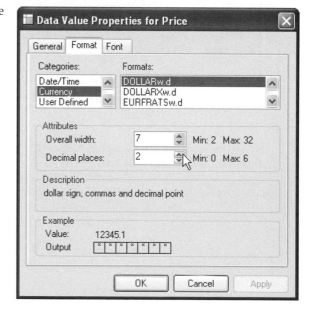

Font tab Using the **Font** tab of the Data Value Properties window, you can change the font, font style, size, foreground color, background color, and other attributes of the data cells in the row or column. In this example, the font for Price has been set to Courier New, the style to Bold, the foreground color to white, and the background color to black.

When you are satisfied with the changes, click **OK**. You can now change other properties, or click **Run** to see the new results.

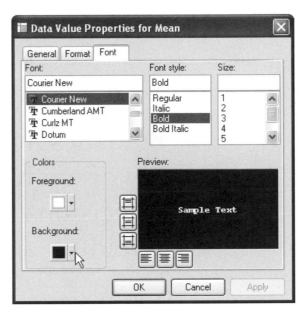

Summary Tables

Volcano Tours	Days		Price
	Minimum	Maximum	Mean
Difficulty			
Challenging	2	9	$767.50
Easy	1	7	$433.40
Moderate	4	7	$826.67

Results Here is the report. Notice that the column for Mean Price looks different from the columns for Minimum and Maximum Days. The background color is black instead of gray, and the numbers have dollar signs in front of them and two decimal places.

"Statistics may be defined as a body of methods for making wise decisions in the face of uncertainty."

W. ALLEN WALLIS AND HARRY V. ROBERTS

From *The Nature of Statistics*, 1956.

CHAPTER 9

Basic Statistical Analysis

Chapter 9

9.1 Distribution Analysis

When you are doing statistical analysis, generally your goal is to examine the relationship between two or more variables. You may want to know how length of day affects the growth of plants, or how an advertising campaign influences sales. But before you start testing hypotheses, it's a good idea to pause and do a little exploration. The Distribution Analysis task is a good place to start. Distribution Analysis produces statistics describing the distribution of a single variable.

This example explores the distribution of the variable Height in the Volcanoes data set. In the Project Tree or Process Flow, click the data icon to make it active. Then select **Tasks ▶ Describe ▶ Distribution Analysis** from the menu bar. The Distribution Analysis window will open, displaying the Data page.

	Volcano	Country	Region	Height	Activity	Type
1	Altar	Ecuador	SA	5321	Extinct	Stratovolcano
2	Arthur's Seat	UK	Eu	251	Extinct	
3	Barren Island	India	As	354	Active	Stratovolcano
4	Elbrus	Russia	Eu	5633	Extinct	Stratovolcano
5	Erebus		An	3794	Active	Stratovolcano
6	Etna	Italy	Eu	3350	Active	Stratovolcano
7	Fuji	Japan	As	3776	Active	Stratovolcano
8	Garibaldi	Canada	NA	2678		Stratovolcano
9	Grimsvotn	Iceland	Eu	1725	Active	Caldera
10	Illimani	Bolivia	SA	6458	Extinct	Stratovolcano

Assigning task roles For Distribution Analysis, you must assign at least one variable to serve as an analysis variable, and that variable must be numeric. In this example, the variable Height has been assigned to the **Analysis variables** role.

Distributions and Plots In the Summary page, choose the distributions (if any) that you want to fit to your data. Then, when you open the pages for the distributions you

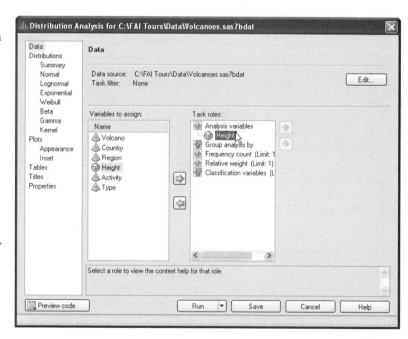

selected, you can see the available options for the distribution. The plot style (traditional or ODS) is selected in the Summary page while the desired plots are selected in the Appearance page. The Inset page allows you to add insets to some plot types that show statistics you select. You can also control the location and format for the inset.

Choosing statistics

In the Tables page, you can choose sets of statistics. For this example, select **Basic confidence intervals**, **Basic measures**, **Tests for location**, **Moments**, and **Quantiles**. When you are satisfied with your selections, click **Run**.

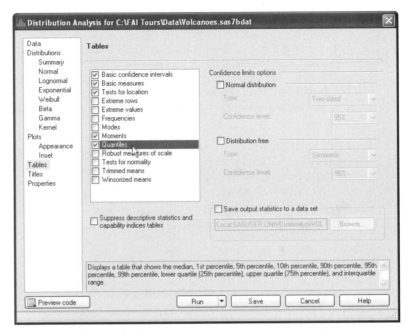

Distribution Analysis for C:\FAI Tours\Data\Volcanoes.sas7bdat

Data
Distributions
  Summary
  Normal
  Lognormal
  Exponential
  Weibull
  Beta
  Gamma
  Kernel
Plots
  Appearance
  Inset
Tables
Titles
Properties

Tables

- ☑ Basic confidence intervals
- ☑ Basic measures
- ☑ Tests for location
- ☐ Extreme rows
- ☐ Extreme values
- ☐ Frequencies
- ☐ Modes
- ☑ Moments
- ☑ Quantiles
- ☐ Robust measures of scale
- ☐ Tests for normality
- ☐ Trimmed means
- ☐ Winsorized means

Confidence limits options

☐ Normal distribution
  Type: Two-sided
  Confidence level: 95%

☐ Distribution free
  Type: Symmetric
  Confidence level: 95%

☐ Save output statistics to a data set
Local.SASUSER.UNIVDistAnalysis.VOL Browse...

☐ Suppress descriptive statistics and capability indices tables

Displays a table that shows the median, 1st percentile, 5th percentile, 10th percentile, 90th percentile, 95th percentile, 99th percentile, lower quartile (25th percentile), upper quartile (75th percentile), and interquartile range.

Preview code   Run   Save   Cancel   Help

Results The resulting report starts with basic information about the distribution of the variable: the number of observations (N), mean, and standard deviation. Skewness indicates how symmetrical the distribution is (whether it is more spread out on one side than the other), while kurtosis indicates how flat or peaked the distribution is. Other sections of the report contain the mean, the median, and the mode (in this case, there is no mode because no two volcanoes had the same value of Height); confidence limits assuming normality; tests of the hypothesis that the mean is zero; and quantiles.

Distribution analysis of: Height

The UNIVARIATE Procedure

Variable: Height

Moments			
N	32	Sum Weights	32
Mean	3113.5625	Sum Observations	99634
Std Deviation	1806.35239	Variance	3262908.96
Skewness	0.16096928	Kurtosis	-0.9518867
Uncorrected SS	411366864	Corrected SS	101150178
Coeff Variation	58.0156137	Std Error Mean	319.321006

Basic Statistical Measures			
Location		**Variability**	
Mean	3113.563	Std Deviation	1806
Median	2957.500	Variance	3262909
Mode	.	Range	6207
		Interquartile Range	3028

Basic Confidence Limits Assuming Normality			
Parameter	Estimate	95% Confidence Limits	
Mean	3114	2462	3765
Std Deviation	1806	1448	2402
Variance	3262909	2097164	5767244

Tests for Location: Mu0=0				
Test		Statistic	p Value	
Student's t	t	9.750572	Pr > |t|	<.0001
Sign	M	16	Pr >= |M|	<.0001
Signed Rank	S	264	Pr >= |S|	<.0001

Quantiles (Definition 5)	
Quantile	Estimate
100% Max	6458.0
99%	6458.0
95%	5976.0
90%	5633.0
75% Q3	4502.5
50% Median	2957.5
25% Q1	1475.0
10%	813.0
5%	354.0
1%	251.0
0% Min	251.0

9.2 Summary Statistics

There are many ways to summarize data in SAS Enterprise Guide. The Summary Statistics task gives you basic descriptive statistics like the mean, minimum, and maximum. You can also request more advanced statistics such as the coefficient of variation and quartiles. The Distribution Analysis task produces many of the same statistics, but the Summary Statistics task gives you more control over which specific statistics are produced and formats the results differently.

The Fire and Ice Tours company has weather data by month for both its Seattle and Portland offices, along with the number of tour bookings for each month. Here is a sample of the data set, NWweather. To produce summary statistics, click the data icon in the Project Tree or

	City	Month	AvgTemp	FromNormal	InchesRain	Bookings
7	Seattle	7	67.9	2.6	0.06	17
8	Seattle	8	66.4	0.8	0.32	17
9	Seattle	9	62.6	1.5	0.89	22
10	Seattle	10	54.3	1.6	8.96	20
11	Seattle	11	42.8	-2.4	6.77	25
12	Seattle	12	41.8	1.1	3.88	31
13	Portland	1	44.8	4.9	7.64	22
14	Portland	2	44.3	1.2	2.37	19
15	Portland	3	49	1.8	5.75	17
16	Portland	4	50.8	-0.4	4.37	18

Process Flow to make it active. Then select **Tasks ▶ Describe ▶ Summary Statistics** from the menu bar. The Summary Statistics window will open, displaying the Data page.

Assigning task roles You should assign to the **Analysis variables** role all the numeric variables you want summarized. If you choose a classification variable, then you will get separate analyses for each value of the classification variable. The **Group analysis by** role produces the same result as the **Classification variables** role, but the output is formatted differently. In this example, the variables InchesRain and Bookings have been

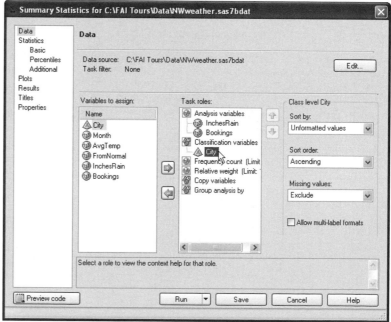

assigned to the **Analysis variables** role, and the variable City has been assigned to the **Classification variables** role.

Choosing statistics

The statistics are grouped into Basic, Percentiles, and Additional. Several statistics in the Basic page (not shown) are chosen by default: mean, standard deviation, minimum, maximum, and number of observations. In the Basic page you can also choose the maximum number of decimal values used to display the results. In the Percentiles page, you can choose from various percentile statistics, including the median and the upper and lower quartiles. The Additional page has five more statistics, including confidence limits of the mean. In the Plots page (not shown), you can request histograms and box plots of your data. In this example, the mean and number of observations have been selected in the Basic page, the median and quartiles in the Percentiles page, and the confidence limits of the mean in the Additional page. Also, the

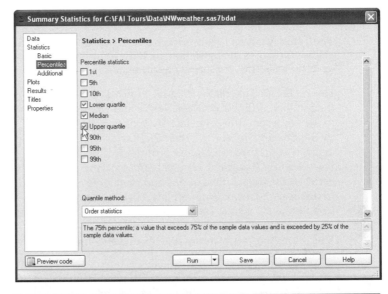

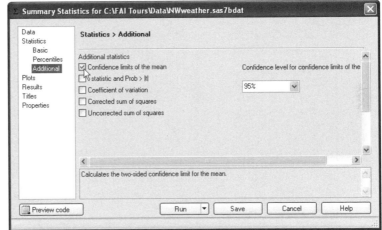

maximum decimal places have been set to 2 in the Basic page.

Results In the result, each analysis variable will have its own entry in the table, and a separate entry for each level of any classification or grouping variables. In this example, City is a classification variable so there are separate statistics for Portland and Seattle.

Summary Statistics
Results
The MEANS Procedure

City	N Obs	Variable	Mean	N	Lower Quartile	Median	Upper Quartile	Lower 95% CL for Mean	Upper 95% CL for Mean
Portland	12	InchesRain	3.13	12	0.58	2.69	5.06	1.38	4.87
		Bookings	20.92	12	17.50	20.00	23.50	17.45	24.38
Seattle	12	InchesRain	3.48	12	0.70	2.25	6.56	1.39	5.57
		Bookings	21.92	12	18.00	20.50	24.00	18.67	25.16

9.3 Table Analysis

The Table Analysis task produces crosstabulations and statistics for categorical data. You can choose measures of association, including chi-square, and you can request additional tests such as trend tests and measures of agreement.

Here is the OnTimeStatus data set, which shows the number of flights between Seattle and Chicago in the winter months. The data are broken down by the time of day, and whether flights had a delayed departure of 15 minutes or more. The objective is to determine if there is an association between the flights' time of day and punctuality. In the Project Tree or Process Flow, click the data icon to make it active. Then select **Tasks ▶ Describe ▶ Table Analysis** from the menu bar. The Table Analysis window will open, displaying the Data page.

	Month	Departure	TimeOfDay	NumOfFlights
1	Dec	OnTime	AfterNoon	25
2	Dec	Late	AfterNoon	33
3	Dec	OnTime	BeforeNoon	80
4	Dec	Late	BeforeNoon	13
5	Jan	OnTime	AfterNoon	15
6	Jan	Late	AfterNoon	12
7	Jan	OnTime	BeforeNoon	30
8	Jan	Late	BeforeNoon	13
9	Feb	OnTime	AfterNoon	20
10	Feb	Late	AfterNoon	8
11	Feb	OnTime	BeforeNoon	43
12	Feb	Late	BeforeNoon	1

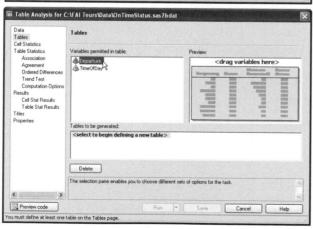

Assigning task roles For a two-way table, you must have two table variables. In this example, the variables TimeOfDay and Departure have been assigned to the **Table variables** role. Because each row in this table represents multiple flights, the variable NumOfFlights has been assigned to the **Frequency count** role. If each row in your data represents one count, then do not use the **Frequency count** role.

Creating the table To arrange your table, click the **Tables** option in the selection pane on the left. The first variable you drag to the **Preview** area will form the columns of the table. The second variable you drag will form the rows. In this example, Departure is on the top, and TimeOfDay on the side.

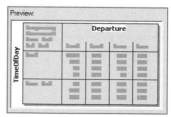

Choosing statistics You can choose many different statistics in the Table Analysis task. The different categories of statistics are listed under **Table Statistics** in the selection pane on the left. Click **Association** and choose the tests you want. In this example, **Chi-square tests** has been chosen.

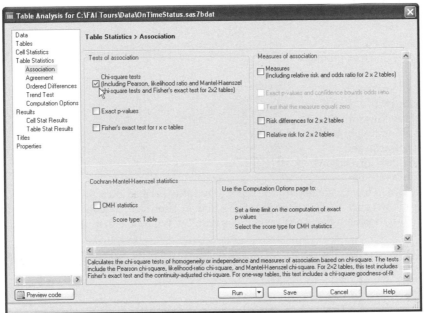

Results The output starts with a frequency table and is followed by the tests of association, including a table for Fisher's Exact Test since this is a 2x2 table. In this example, it appears that late departures tend to be more frequent in the afternoon hours. The probability of obtaining a chi-square value this large or larger by chance alone is less than 0.0001.

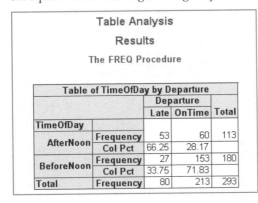

Table Analysis

Results

The FREQ Procedure

Table of TimeOfDay by Departure

TimeOfDay		Late	OnTime	Total
AfterNoon	Frequency	53	60	113
	Col Pct	66.25	28.17	
BeforeNoon	Frequency	27	153	180
	Col Pct	33.75	71.83	
Total	Frequency	80	213	293

Statistics for Table of TimeOfDay by Departure

Statistic	DF	Value	Prob
Chi-Square	1	35.5961	<.0001
Likelihood Ratio Chi-Square	1	35.1538	<.0001
Continuity Adj. Chi-Square	1	34.0070	<.0001
Mantel-Haenszel Chi-Square	1	35.4746	<.0001
Phi Coefficient		0.3486	
Contingency Coefficient		0.3291	
Cramer's V		0.3486	

Fisher's Exact Test

Cell (1,1) Frequency (F)	53
Left-sided Pr <= F	1.0000
Right-sided Pr >= F	3.428E-09
Table Probability (P)	2.772E-09
Two-sided Pr <= P	3.966E-09

Sample Size = 293

9.4 ▶ Correlations

The Correlations task produces correlation coefficients that measure relationships between numeric variables. A correlation coefficient of one means that two variables are perfectly correlated, while a correlation coefficient of zero means that there is no relationship between the two variables.

Here is a portion of the NWweather data set showing the average temperature, the deviation from the normal average temperature, the inches of rain, and the number of bookings for the Fire and Ice Tours company for each month for both Seattle and Portland. Using the Correlations task, you can measure the

	City	Month	AvgTemp	FromNormal	InchesRain	Bookings
8	Seattle	8	66.4	0.8	0.32	17
9	Seattle	9	62.6	1.5	0.89	22
10	Seattle	10	54.3	1.6	8.96	20
11	Seattle	11	42.8	-2.4	6.77	25
12	Seattle	12	41.8	1.1	3.88	31
13	Portland	1	44.8	4.9	7.64	22
14	Portland	2	44.3	1.2	2.37	19
15	Portland	3	49	1.8	5.75	17
16	Portland	4	50.8	-0.4	4.37	18
17	Portland	5	57.3	0.2	1.49	21

relationship between local weather and the number of tours booked each month. In the Project Tree or Process Flow, click the data icon to make it active. Then select **Tasks ▶ Multivariate ▶ Correlations** from the menu bar. The Correlations window will open, displaying the Data page.

Assigning task roles For correlations, variables assigned to the **Analysis variables** role will appear across the top of the table, while variables assigned to the **Correlate with** role will appear down the side of the table. If there are no Correlate with variables, then the Analysis variables will appear both across the top and down the side of the table. In this example, the three weather variables AvgTemp, FromNormal, and

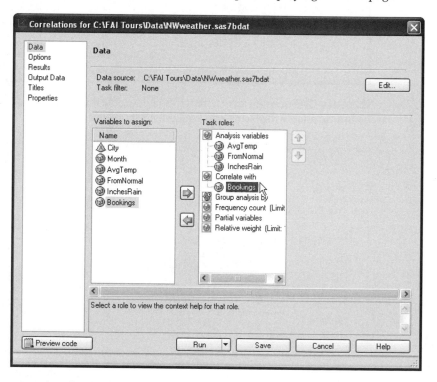

InchesRain have been assigned to the **Analysis variables** role, and Bookings has been assigned to the **Correlate with** role.

Choosing statistics and plots To run a correlation, all you need to do is assign variables to the task roles. However, you may want to choose some additional statistics. The Options page allows you to choose the type of correlation: Pearson (the default), Hoeffding, Kendall, or Spearman. There are additional options for Pearson correlations. For this example, the type of correlation is set to Pearson.

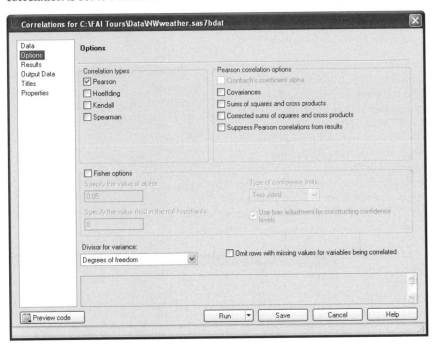

If you click **Results** in the selection pane on the left, you can request plots and choose the statistics to be included in the results. When you are satisfied with all the settings, click **Run**.

Results The output starts with a list of the analysis variables, followed by simple statistics. Next are the correlation coefficients. In this example, two variables— AvgTemp and InchesRain—are correlated with the number of bookings. AvgTemp is negatively correlated (higher temperatures correspond with lower bookings), while InchesRain is positively correlated (more rain corresponds with more bookings). The FromNormal variable is not significantly correlated with Bookings.

Correlation Analysis

The CORR Procedure

1 With Variables:	Bookings
3 Variables:	AvgTemp FromNormal InchesRain

Simple Statistics						
Variable	N	Mean	Std Dev	Sum	Minimum	Maximum
Bookings	24	21.41667	5.19127	514.00000	13.00000	33.00000
AvgTemp	24	54.30417	10.21284	1303	41.70000	71.60000
FromNormal	24	1.41250	1.99659	33.90000	-2.40000	4.90000
InchesRain	24	3.30417	2.97348	79.30000	0	8.96000

Pearson Correlation Coefficients, N = 24 Prob > |r| under H0: Rho=0			
	AvgTemp	FromNormal	InchesRain
Bookings	-0.60049	0.09931	0.57642
	0.0019	0.6443	0.0032

9.5 Linear Regression

In SAS Enterprise Guide, you can perform many different types of regression analysis, and the models that you build can be quite complex. You can choose linear, nonlinear, logistic, and generalized linear models. In addition, within each type of regression, there are many options for customizing your analysis. This section shows how to do a simple linear regression with one dependent and one explanatory variable. You must have SAS/STAT software installed on your SAS server to perform regression analysis.

The Fire and Ice Tours company started a local advertising campaign in both Seattle and Portland. It wants to see if the money spent on advertising is increasing the number of tour bookings. Here is a sample of the AdResults data set with data for the dollars spent on advertising and the number of bookings for each month and city. A linear regression analysis will show if there is a relationship between dollars spent and bookings. In the Project Tree or Process Flow, click the data icon

	City	Month	AdDollars	Bookings
8	Seattle	8	250	17
9	Seattle	9	250	22
10	Seattle	10	325	20
11	Seattle	11	400	25
12	Seattle	12	500	31
13	Portland	1	325	25
14	Portland	2	290	19
15	Portland	3	250	17
16	Portland	4	300	18

to make it active. Then select **Tasks ▶ Regression ▶ Linear** from the menu bar. The Linear Regression window will open, displaying the Data page.

Assigning task roles

For a simple linear regression, you must assign one variable to the **Dependent variable** role, and one to the **Explanatory variables** role. Both the dependent and the explanatory variables must be numeric. This example tests whether the number of bookings can be explained by the dollars spent on advertising. So, the variable Bookings has been assigned to the **Dependent variable** role, and the variable AdDollars has been

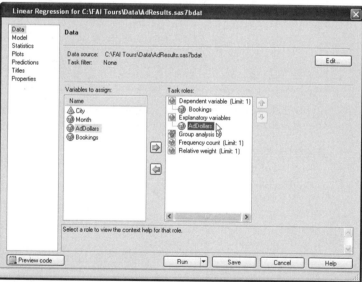

assigned to the **Explanatory variables** role.

Choosing statistics

Because you can perform many different types of regression analysis using this task, there are a lot of options listed in the selection pane on the left. In the Model page, you can choose the model selection method, including forward, backward, stepwise, and several methods based on R-squared. The Statistics page gives choices for additional statistics, including details on estimates, correlations, and diagnostics. For this simple example, there is no need to change the model type, or to request additional statistics.

Selecting plots By default, all appropriate plots are produced for your data and model. To control which plots are produced, select **Custom list of plots** in the Plots page to display all available plots. Then check the desired plots. Diagnostic plots are selected by default.

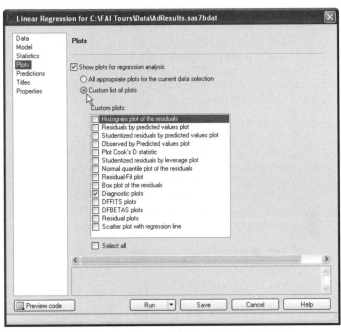

Results The results of the regression analysis start with the number of observations used for the analysis, followed by the Analysis of Variance table, statistics, and Parameter Estimates. In this example, the model is significant with a *p*-value of less than 0.0001, which means that the number of dollars spent on advertising can be used to explain some of the variation in Bookings. The diagnostic plots show eight different plots on the same page along with basic regression statistics.

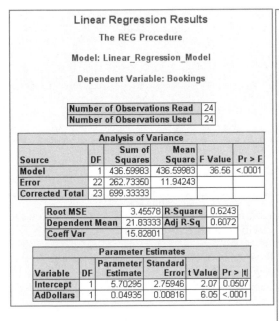

Linear Regression Results

The REG Procedure

Model: Linear_Regression_Model

Dependent Variable: Bookings

Number of Observations Read	24
Number of Observations Used	24

Analysis of Variance

Source	DF	Sum of Squares	Mean Square	F Value	Pr > F
Model	1	436.59983	436.59983	36.56	<.0001
Error	22	262.73350	11.94243		
Corrected Total	23	699.33333			

Root MSE	3.45578	R-Square	0.6243
Dependent Mean	21.83333	Adj R-Sq	0.6072
Coeff Var	15.82801		

Parameter Estimates

Variable	DF	Parameter Estimate	Standard Error	t Value	Pr > |t|
Intercept	1	5.70295	2.75946	2.07	0.0507
AdDollars	1	0.04935	0.00816	6.05	<.0001

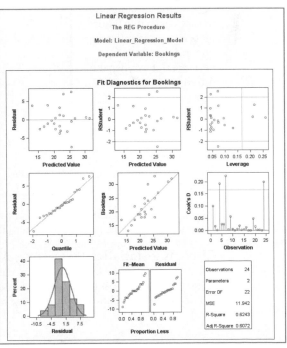

9.6▶ Analysis of Variance

SAS Enterprise Guide can perform several types of analysis of variance, including one-way ANOVA and nonparametric one-way ANOVA, as well as mixed and linear models. This section shows the One-Way ANOVA task, which performs analysis of variance tests, and comparisons of means. You must have SAS/STAT software installed on your SAS server to use any of the ANOVA tasks.

The Fire and Ice Tours company wants to know if the tours it offers, with the three difficulty ratings, attract customers from different age groups. Ten customers were surveyed in each of the three difficulty categories to find their ages. Here is a sample of the resulting data set, Ages. In the Project Tree or Process Flow, click the data icon to make it active. Then select **Tasks ▶ ANOVA ▶ One-Way ANOVA** from the menu bar. The One-Way ANOVA window will open, displaying the Data page.

	Difficulty		Age
7	e		66
8	e		57
9	e		39
10	e		33
11	m		26
12	m		37
13	m		42
14	m		27

Assigning task roles For one-way ANOVA, you must assign one variable to the **Dependent variables** role, and one to the **Independent variable** role. The dependent variable is a numeric variable whose means you want to test. The independent variable determines the different categories. In this example, the variable Age has been assigned to the Dependent variables role. The variable Difficulty has been assigned to the Independent variable role. If you want to test more than one variable at a time, you can assign several variables to the Dependent variables role, but each variable will be analyzed separately.

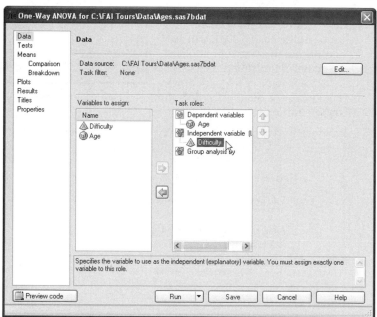

Choosing statistics The One-Way ANOVA task offers several groups of options in the selection pane on the left. In the Tests page, you can select tests for equal variance. In the Plots page, you can request box-and-whisker or means plots. You can choose descriptive statistics for the dependent variables in the Breakdown page.

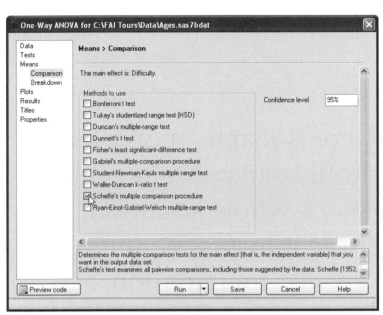

Comparison of means To do any comparison of means tests, choose them in the Comparison page. In this example, **Scheffe's multiple comparison procedure** has been selected.

Results The output starts with a table giving the number of classes (categories) and the number of observations in the data. Next is the result of the analysis of variance, followed by the results of Scheffe's test. Scheffe's test includes the comparison of the means between the three levels of difficulty. Letters are used to group the means, where means labeled with different letters are significantly different from each other. In this case, people in the challenging tours are significantly older than people in the moderate tours. However, while people in the challenging tours are also older than people in the easy tours, they are not significantly older. In this example, the *p*-value of 0.0053 shows that the overall model is also significant.

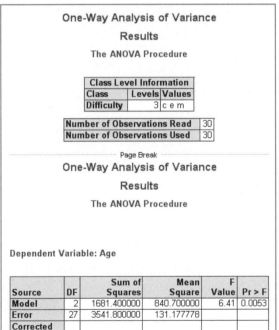

One-Way Analysis of Variance
Results
The ANOVA Procedure

Class Level Information		
Class	Levels	Values
Difficulty	3	c e m

Number of Observations Read	30
Number of Observations Used	30

— Page Break —

One-Way Analysis of Variance
Results
The ANOVA Procedure

Dependent Variable: Age

Source	DF	Sum of Squares	Mean Square	F Value	Pr > F
Model	2	1681.400000	840.700000	6.41	0.0053
Error	27	3541.800000	131.177778		
Corrected Total	29	5223.200000			

R-Square	Coeff Var	Root MSE	Age Mean
0.321910	24.68381	11.45329	46.40000

Source	DF	Anova SS	Mean Square	F Value	Pr > F
Difficulty	2	1681.400000	840.700000	6.41	0.0053

Scheffe's Test for Age

Note: This test controls the Type I experimentwise error rate.

Alpha	0.05
Error Degrees of Freedom	27
Error Mean Square	131.1778
Critical Value of F	3.35413
Minimum Significant Difference	13.266

Means with the same letter are not significantly different.			
Scheffe Grouping	Mean	N	Difficulty
A	54.200	10	c
A			
B A	48.700	10	e
B			
B	36.300	10	m

" There is magic in graphs.
The profile of a curve reveals
in a flash a whole situation....
The curve informs the mind,
awakens the imagination,
convinces. "

HENRY D. HUBBARD

From *Graphic Presentation* by Willard Cope Brinton, 1939.

CHAPTER 10

Producing Graphs

10.1 Bar Charts

Bar charts can be an effective way to present data when you want to show the frequency, percentage, sum, or mean of values in your data, broken into groups. Bar charts can be created using the Bar Chart task or wizard. This section describes the task. You must have SAS/GRAPH software installed on your SAS server to create any of the graphs shown in this chapter.

The Eruptions data set contains the volcano name and the Volcanic Explosivity Index (VEI) for selected eruptions. Here is a sample of the data. Notice that the column VEI ranges in value from 0 to 6. From these data, you can create a bar chart showing the number of eruptions for each value of VEI. In the Project Tree or Process Flow, click the data icon to make it active, and then select **Tasks ▶ Graph ▶ Bar Chart**. The Bar Chart window will open, displaying the Bar Chart page.

Choosing the type of bar chart There are many different types of bar charts you can create. Scroll down to see all the available types. For this example, select **Simple Vertical Bar,** then click **Data** in the selection pane on the left to assign columns to roles.

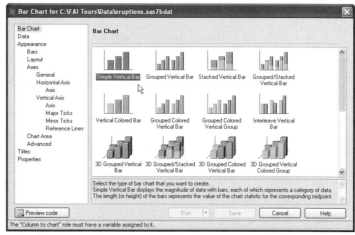

Assigning task roles For all kinds of bar charts, you must assign a column to the **Column to chart** role. For stacked or grouped bar charts, you also need to assign columns to stacking and grouping roles. In this example, the VEI column is the Column to chart. This will produce bars whose lengths are determined by the frequency of eruptions for each value of VEI. If you choose a Sum of column, then instead of getting frequencies, you will get the sum of whichever column you choose.

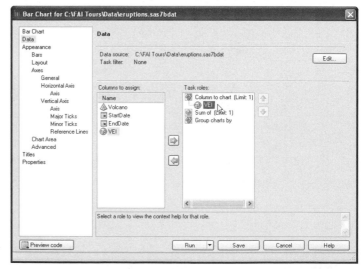

Customizing a bar chart As you can see from the list of options in the selection pane on the left, there are many options for bar charts. You can make changes to the axes and tick marks, add or remove reference lines, specify the size of your chart, change the background color, choose the shape and size of the bars in your chart, and change the order of the bars. If you want to display the mean instead of the sum (or the percentage instead of the frequency), you can change the statistic in the Advanced page.

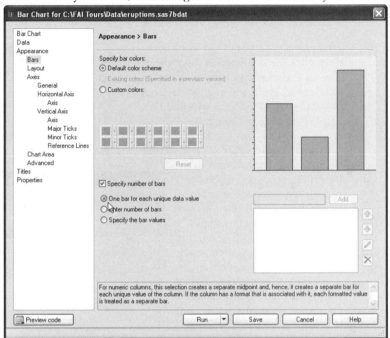

Options in the Bars page allow you to change the color of the bars, and to specify the number of bars. If the column you are charting is character, then you will get a bar for each value of the column. If your column is numeric, then SAS Enterprise Guide will determine an appropriate number of bars for your chart, and label the bars with the midpoint in the range. You can override this behavior by specifying the number of bars. In this example, the column charted—VEI—is numeric, but it has only seven discrete values. So, it makes sense to have one bar for each value. To do this, check **Specify number of bars**, and select **One bar for each unique data value**. When you are satisfied with the options, click **Run**.

Results Here is the resulting bar chart of VEI. There is a bar for each unique value of VEI, and the lengths of the bars show a simple count of eruptions for each value of VEI.

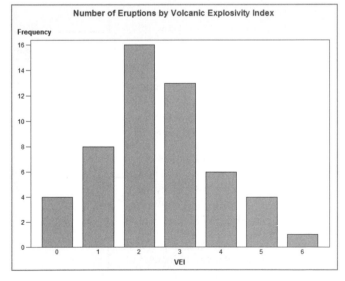

10.2   Pie Charts

Pie charts are similar to bar charts. With both types of charts, you can show the frequency, percentage, sum, or mean of values in your data, broken into groups. The type of chart you use depends on your personal preference. Pie charts can be created using the Pie Chart task or wizard. This section describes the task.

To create a pie chart of the Volcanoes data, click the data icon in the Project Tree or Process Flow to make it active. Then select **Tasks ▶ Graph ▶ Pie Chart**. This opens the Pie Chart window, displaying the Pie Chart page.

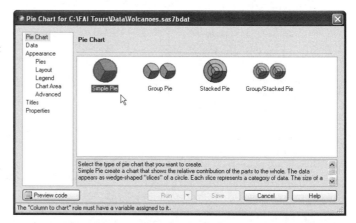

Choosing the type of pie chart

Before assigning columns to task roles, you must select the type of pie chart you want to create. If you want one pie chart that shows the frequency or percentage of rows that fall into different categories, then select Simple Pie. If you have a grouping column and you want a separate pie for each level of the group, then you may want to select Group Pie. The Stacked Pie is similar to a Group Pie, except the pies are stacked one on top of the other instead of side by side. Use a Group/Stacked Pie if you have more than one grouping column. In this example, select **Simple Pie** and then click **Data** in the selection pane on the left to assign roles to columns.

Assigning task roles

For simple pie charts, all you need is a column to chart. Drag the column you want to summarize to the **Column to chart** role. Use the **Sum of** role if you want the size of the pie slice to represent a sum or mean value, instead of simple counts or percentages. The **Group charts by** role is similar to using a Group Pie

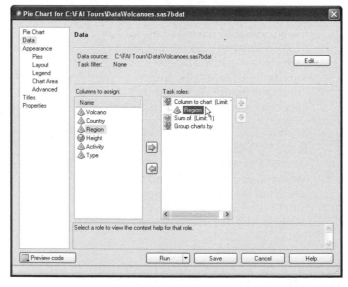

chart, except that selecting a Group Pie will produce pies side by side on the same page, whereas the Group charts by role will produce one pie per page. In this example, Region has been assigned to the Column to chart role.

Other chart options

In the Pies page, you can specify the color scheme to use for the chart, as well as the number of slices for the pie. In the Layout page, you can make the pies two- or three-dimensional, control placement of labels on the pies, specify how pies are placed on the page for grouped pies, and control the "other" slice of pie. Use options in the Legend page to control the legend, the Chart Area page to control the size and background color of the chart, and the

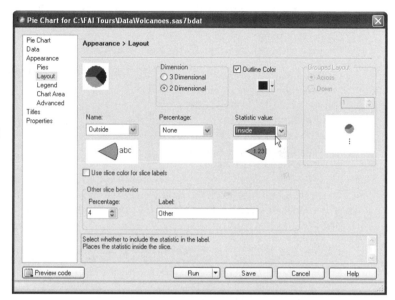

Advanced page to specify if the pie slices should be frequencies or percentages. In this example, in the Layout page, the position of the label for the **Statistic value** has been changed from Outside (the default) to Inside. When you are satisfied with the options, click **Run**.

Results Here is the result of the Pie Chart task. Because Region is the Column to chart, the size of each pie slice shows the relative number of volcanoes from the region. The label for the statistic value was specified to be inside, so the actual number of volcanoes appears inside each pie slice.

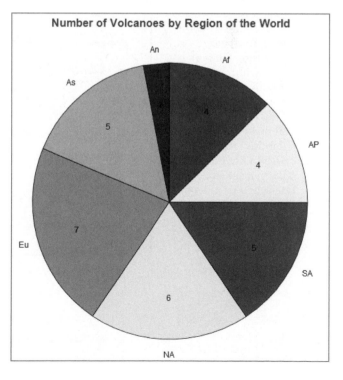

10.3 Simple Line Plots

There are many different types of line plots you can produce using SAS Enterprise Guide. You can plot one or several plots on the same graph, and you can specify different types of interpolation for your plot. If you use a type of interpolation for your plot where the points are connected, make sure that it makes sense to connect the points. Line plots can be created using the Line Plot task or wizard. This section describes the task.

Here is a portion of the NWweather data set which contains data for both Seattle and Portland. For this example, we want to use only the data for Seattle, so a filter will be applied to the data.

	City	Month	AvgTemp	FromNormal	InchesRain	Bookings
7	Seattle	7	67.9	2.6	0.06	17
8	Seattle	8	66.4	0.8	0.32	17
9	Seattle	9	62.6	1.5	0.89	22
10	Seattle	10	54.3	1.6	8.96	20
11	Seattle	11	42.8	-2.4	6.77	25
12	Seattle	12	41.8	1.1	3.88	31
13	Portland	1	44.8	4.9	7.64	22
14	Portland	2	44.3	1.2	2.37	19
15	Portland	3	49	1.8	5.75	17

To create a line plot, click the data icon in the Project Tree or Process Flow to make it active. Then select **Tasks ▶ Graph ▶ Line Plot**. This opens the Line Plot window displaying the Line Plot page.

Choosing the type of line plot

Before assigning columns to task roles, you must select the type of line plot you want to create. Choosing the plot type will automatically change other settings in the Line Plot window to fit that type of plot. For this example, select **Line Plot,** and then click **Data** in the selection pane on the left to assign columns to roles.

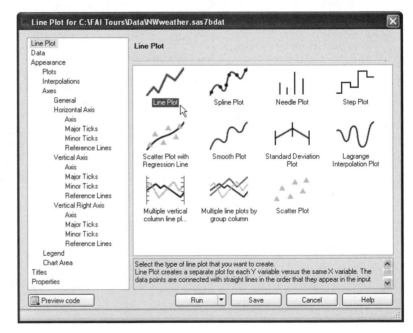

Assigning task roles For a basic line plot, you must assign one column to the **Horizontal** role and one to the **Vertical** role. In this example, Month has been assigned to the **Horizontal** role and FromNormal to the **Vertical** role. To select only rows for Seattle, click **Edit** to open the Edit Data and Filter window and apply the filter City = 'Seattle'. For more information about filtering data in a task, see section 5.1.

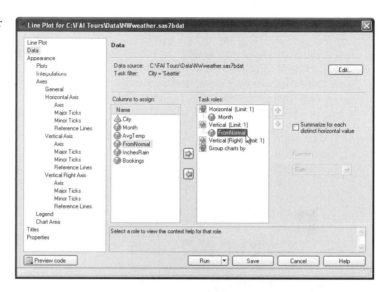

Other plot options The selection pane on the left lists many categories of options. You can specify the line style, the interpolation method, axes and tick marks, reference lines, the legend, and the size and background color of your plot. For this example, click **Reference Lines** for the Vertical Axis in the selection pane on the left. Then check the boxes labeled **Use reference lines** and **Specify values for lines**. Type the number 0 into the box next to the Add button, and click the **Add** button. When you are satisfied with the options, click **Run**.

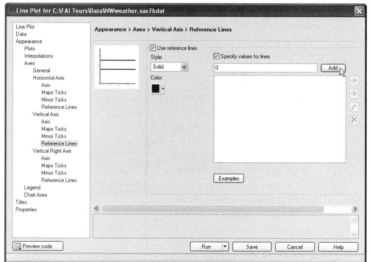

Results Here is the result of the Line Plot task. Month is on the horizontal axis and FromNormal on the vertical. The reference line on the vertical axis is set at zero.

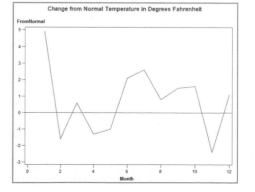

10.4 Multiple Line Plots by Group

Sometimes you may want to put more than one line on a plot. If you have a grouping column, then you can create a plot that has separate lines for each value of the grouping column. For example, you may have sales figures by month for different regions and you want one plot of sales by month with a line for each region.

Here is a portion of the NWweather data set. To create a line plot of the data with separate lines for Seattle and Portland, click the data icon in the Project Tree or Process Flow to make it active, and select **Tasks ▶ Graph ▶ Line Plot**. This opens the Line Plot window displaying the Line Plot page.

△ City	Month	AvgTemp	FromNormal	InchesRain	Bookings
7 Seattle	7	67.9	2.6	0.06	17
8 Seattle	8	66.4	0.8	0.32	17
9 Seattle	9	62.6	1.5	0.89	22
10 Seattle	10	54.3	1.6	8.96	20
11 Seattle	11	42.8	-2.4	6.77	25
12 Seattle	12	41.8	1.1	3.88	31
13 Portland	1	44.8	4.9	7.64	22
14 Portland	2	44.3	1.2	2.37	19
15 Portland	3	49	1.8	5.75	17

Choosing the type of line plot

Before assigning columns to task roles, you must select the type of line plot you want to create. In this example, select **Multiple line plots by group column,** and then click **Data** in the selection pane on the left to assign columns to roles.

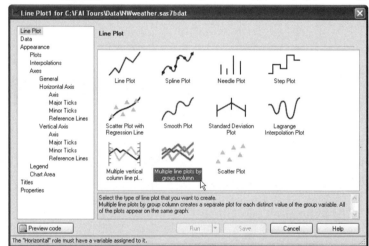

Assigning task roles

For this type of plot, you need to assign one column to the **Horizontal** role and one to the **Vertical** role. Then assign the grouping column to the **Group** role. There will be one line for each unique value of the grouping column. In this example, Month has been assigned to the Horizontal role, AvgTemp to the Vertical role, and City to the Group role.

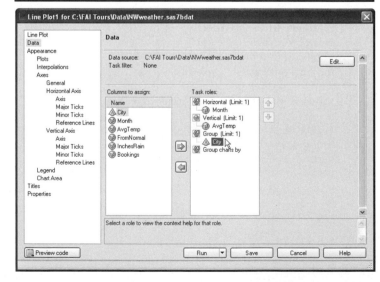

Other plot options

As with simple line plots, there are many options you can specify, such as the type of interpolation, axes and tick marks, reference lines, legends, and the size and background color of your plot. For this example, click **Plots** in the selection pane on the left. By default, all lines are solid, with no data point markers, but different colors. In the Plots page, you can assign different symbols and line styles to the

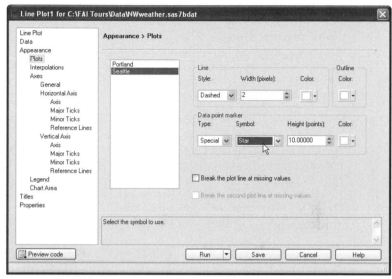

values of the grouping column, making it easier to identify the lines. There are two values for the grouping variable City: Portland and Seattle. Click the city name to choose styles for that city, and select the desired attributes for the line and data point markers. In this example, Seattle will have a dashed line with the star symbol, and Portland a solid line with the dot symbol. When you are satisfied with the options, click **Run**.

Results Here is the result of the Line Plot task. Month is on the horizontal axis and AvgTemp on the vertical. There is a separate line for each city.

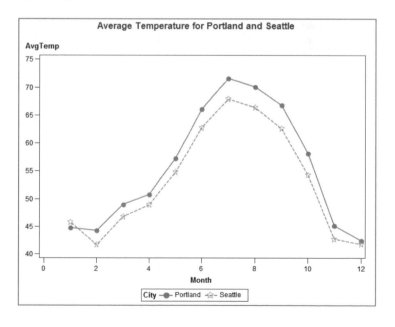

10.5 Scatter Plots

Scatter plots are similar to line plots, but in a scatter plot you do not connect the points. You may simply display the points without any interpolation, or you may add a regression line showing the relationship between two columns. You can produce scatter plots with regression lines using regression analysis, but the Scatter Plot task gives you more control over the appearance of your plot.

This example produces a simple scatter plot using the AdResults data set. This data set contains the amount spent on advertising and the number of tour bookings for each month. To create a scatter plot of the data, click the data icon in the Project Tree or Process Flow to make it active. Then select **Tasks ▶ Graph ▶ Scatter Plot**. This opens the Scatter Plot window, displaying the Scatter Plot page.

	City	Month	AdDollars	Bookings
8	Seattle	8	250	17
9	Seattle	9	250	22
10	Seattle	10	325	20
11	Seattle	11	400	25
12	Seattle	12	500	31
13	Portland	1	325	25
14	Portland	2	290	19
15	Portland	3	250	17
16	Portland	4	300	18

Choosing the type of scatter plot Before assigning columns to task roles, you must select the type of scatter plot you want to create. You can choose a two- or three-dimensional scatter plot, or a three-dimensional needle plot. For this example, select **2D Scatter Plot**, and then click **Data** in the selection pane on the left to assign columns to roles.

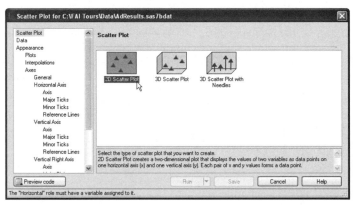

Assigning task roles For a two-dimensional scatter plot, you must assign one column to the **Horizontal** role and one to the **Vertical** role. In this example, AdDollars is assigned to the horizontal axis, and Bookings to the vertical axis.

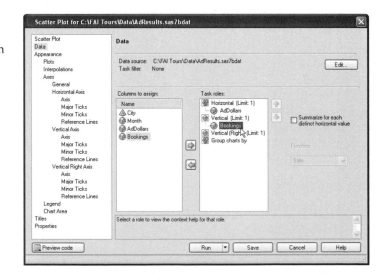

Other plot options As with line plots, there are many options you can specify, such as the type of interpolation (including regression), axes and tick marks, reference lines, and legends. Options in the Chart Area page control the size and background color of your plot. In the Plots page, you can select line styles and point markers. In this example, the data point type is set to Marker, the symbol is Left Triangle and the color is black. When you are satisfied with the options, click **Run**.

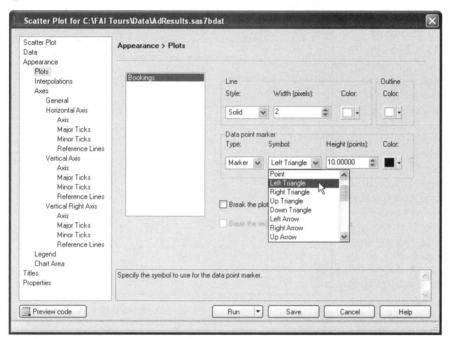

Results Here is the result of the Scatter Plot task. AdDollars is on the horizontal axis and Bookings is on the vertical. A triangle symbol is used for plotting the points instead of the default circle.

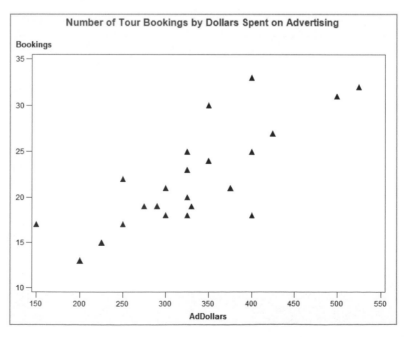

10.6 Controlling the Axes

Most types of plots produced by SAS Enterprise Guide have axes. You can control the values used for tick marks on the axes, and the style and content of the labels. There are several possible types of axes including Horizontal, Vertical, and Vertical Right. In the selection pane on the left of the task window, there will be up to four groups of options for each axis type: Axis, Major Ticks, Minor Ticks, and Reference Lines.

Changing the font, size, and style In the Axis page, you can specify the line color, width, and style for the axis. On the **Label** tab in the Axis page, you can change the label used for your axis including the font, style, and rotation. On the **Values** tab, you can control the font, style, and rotation of the text used to label the tick marks. In this example, the horizontal axis has been given a new label.

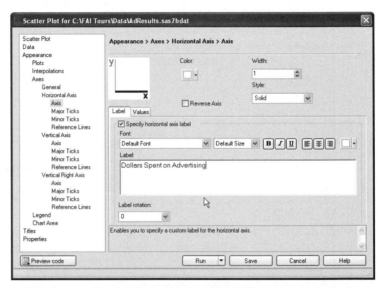

Setting the major tick marks Set the major ticks in the Major Ticks page for the axis. By default, the Automatic option is used to determine major ticks. If you select **Use**, then you can specify the number of ticks to use for the axis. Selecting **Log** will convert the axis to a log scale and you can choose which base to use for the log: base 2, 10, e, or pi. Selecting **Specify** allows you to enter your own values for the axis. In the text box to the left of the Add button, enter the desired values and click **Add**. The values you enter will appear in the text box below.

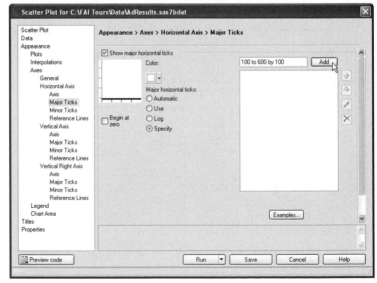

You can specify single values or ranges. Clicking the **Examples** button will display different methods for specifying values. In this example, the tick marks have been specified by typing **100 to 600 by 100** in the text box and clicking **Add**. This will produce tick marks displayed starting at 100, at each 100 interval, and ending at 600.

Adding minor tick marks By default, no minor tick marks are displayed. To set minor tick marks, open the Minor Ticks page for the axis, check **Show minor ticks**, then choose the number of minor ticks. In this example, one minor tick mark will appear on the horizontal axis.

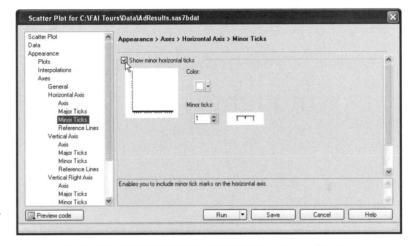

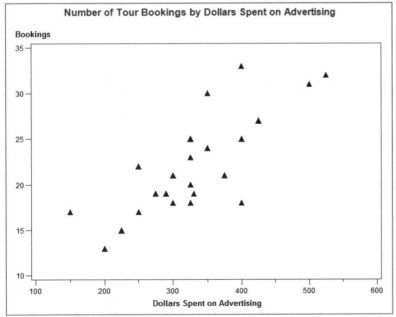

Results Here are the results of the scatter plot from the previous section with changes to the horizontal axis.

"Style is the dress of thoughts."

EARL OF CHESTERFIELD

From "On Education" in *Letters to His Son on the Art of Becoming a Man of the World and Gentleman*. Nov. 24, 1749. As quoted in *The Cyclopedia of Practical Quotations: English, Latin, and Modern Foreign Languages* by Jehiel Keeler Hoyt, 1896.

CHAPTER 11

Changing Result Styles and Formats

11.1 Changing the Result Format

When you run a task that produces output, by default the result is in SAS Report format. SAS Report format can be used to combine several results into one customized report, which can be exported to other file formats if desired. You can also create results directly in other formats. SAS Enterprise Guide can produce results in RTF, which can be opened in Microsoft Word; PDF, which can be opened using Adobe Acrobat or Adobe Reader; HTML, which can be opened in a web browser; and plain text, which can be opened in any text editor.

Setting the default result format To set the default result format for tasks, select **Tools ▶ Options** from the menu bar. This opens the Options window. Click **Results General** in the selection pane on the left to open the Results General page of options. The available result formats are listed under the heading **Result Formats** in this page. Select one or more formats by clicking the box next to the format. Once you make this change, it will affect all subsequent results. In this example, because both PDF and RTF are checked, any task that you run will produce results in both PDF and RTF format. Because PDF is selected as the default, the PDF Results tab will display on top in the workspace.

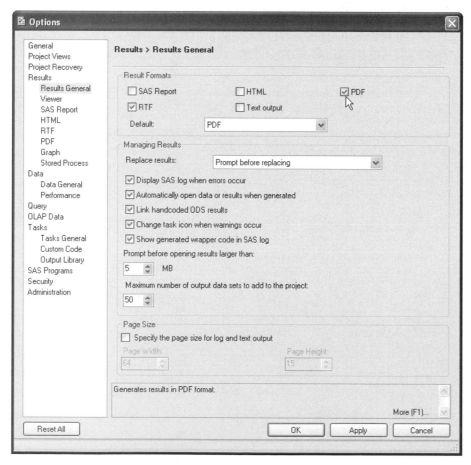

Changing the result format of a task

If you change the result format in the Options window, then the results of all tasks are affected. If you want to change result formats for individual tasks, then click **Properties** in the selection pane for the task, and then click the **Edit** button.

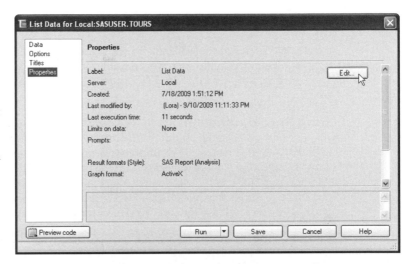

This opens the Properties window for the task. Click **Results** in the selection pane on the left to open the Results page, and then select **Customize result formats, styles, and behavior**. Now you can choose result formats and styles for the task's results. On this same page, you can select the Graph Format for any graphical output the task may produce. In this example, this task will produce results in PDF format only, and any graphs produced will be in JPEG format.

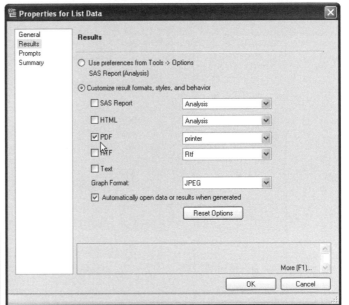

Volcano Tours				
Volcano	**Departs**	**Days**	**Price**	**Difficulty**
Etna	Catania	7	$1,075	Moderate
Fuji	Tokyo	2	$225	Challenging
Kenya	Nairobi	6	$830	Moderate
Kilauea	Hilo	1	$55	Easy
Kilimanjaro	Nairobi	9	$1,310	Challenging
Krakatau	Jakarta	7	$895	Easy
Poas	San Jose	1	$65	Easy
Reventador	Quito	4	$575	Moderate
St. Helens	Portland	2	$167	Easy
Vesuvius	Rome	6	$985	Easy

Results When you run a task that produces results in multiple formats, you get an icon in the Process Flow, and a tab in the workspace, for each result format. To open a result, click its result tab, or double-click its icon in the Process Flow. This is what the results of the List Data task look like in PDF format.

11.2 Changing the Result Style

The style determines the overall look for your results. The colors, fonts, and layout of your results are all defined in the style. Text output does not have a style associated with it, but for the other result formats—HTML, RTF, PDF, and SAS Report—you can choose from a number of styles.

Setting the default result style The default style for results in HTML and SAS Report format is Analysis. For RTF output the default style is RTF, and for PDF it is Printer. You can change the default style for any result format using the Options window. Open the Options window by selecting **Tools ▶ Options** from the menu bar. Click the type of output (SAS Report, HTML, RTF, or PDF) in the selection pane on the left to open the page for that format. Then select the style you want for that result format from the Style drop-down list. Once you make this change, every task you run will use the style you select for that format.

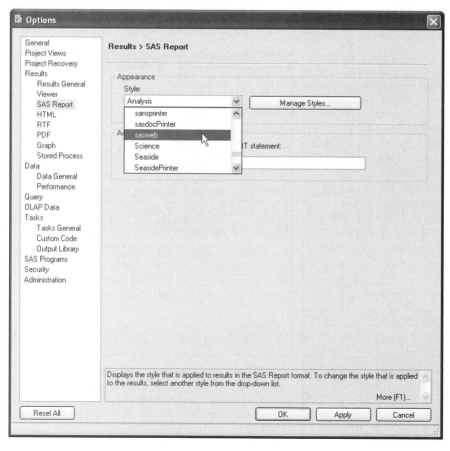

Changing the style for results of a task

To change the style for the results of a particular task, do this in the Properties window for the task. To open the Properties window, click **Properties** in the selection pane for the task, then click the **Edit** button. Click **Results** in the selection pane on the left to open the Results page of the Properties window. Check the box next to **Customize result formats, styles, and behavior**, and then select the result format and a style from the drop-down list for each format.

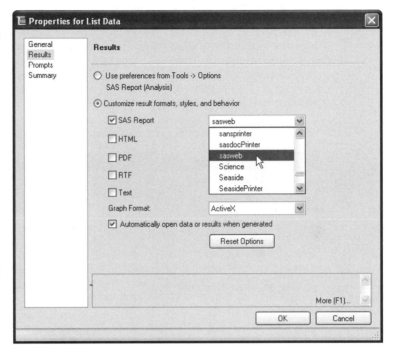

Changing the style after running a task

For results in SAS Report and HTML formats, you can change the style after you run the task. Click the **Properties** button on the workspace toolbar for the result to open the Properties window. Then choose a style from the Style drop-down

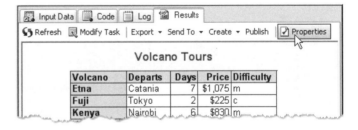

menu. Click **OK** and your result will be displayed with the selected style. You do not need to rerun the task.

Results

Here is what a SAS Report result looks like using the Sasweb style.

Volcano	Departs	Days	Price	Difficulty
Etna	Catania	7	$1,075	Moderate
Fuji	Tokyo	2	$225	Challenging
Kenya	Nairobi	6	$830	Moderate
Kilauea	Hilo	1	$55	Easy
Kilimanjaro	Nairobi	9	$1,310	Challenging
Krakatau	Jakarta	7	$895	Easy
Poas	San Jose	1	$65	Easy
Reventador	Quito	4	$575	Moderate
St. Helens	Portland	2	$167	Easy
Vesuvius	Rome	6	$985	Easy

Volcano Tours

11.3 Customizing Styles Using the Style Manager

Although SAS Enterprise Guide comes with many styles for results, you still might not find a style that fits your needs. The Style Manager allows you to modify existing styles for SAS Report and HTML results. You cannot modify styles for use with RTF or PDF result formats.

Opening the Style Manager Open the Style Manager by selecting **Tools ▶ Style Manager** from the menu bar. The Style Manager provides you with a list of available styles in the box on the left. When you click a style, you will see a preview of the style in the box on the right.

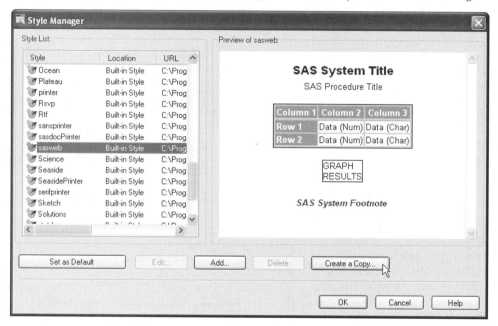

Editing an existing style To edit an existing style, first create a copy of the style. Click the style in the Style Manager window, and then click **Create a Copy**. This opens the Save Style As window where you give the new style a name and choose a storage location. Now you can edit the copy of the style you just saved. Click the new style name in the Style Manager window, and click **Edit**.

This opens the Style Editor. The preview area on the left shows the current style of various elements such as titles, headers, and data cells. Choose the element you want to edit by clicking it in the preview area on the left, or selecting it from the **Selected element** drop-down list. Then select the attributes to use for that element in the area on the right. In this example, the **SAS System Title** is given a **Bold Italic** text style, and a **14pt** font text size. In addition to changing the style of the text, you can control borders using the Borders tab, and add images to your style using the Images tab. Click **OK** when you are finished making changes to the style. Then click **OK** in the Style Manager window to save your changes.

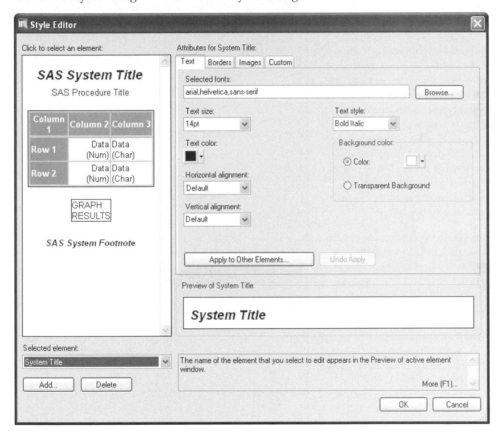

Using the new style The new style you created will appear in the **My Styles** section of the list of styles. You can select it for any SAS Report or HTML results, or set it to be the default style. See the previous section for details about changing the style for results.

11.4 Combining Results into a Single Document

The report editor allows you to combine results from multiple tasks. The task results must be in SAS Report format. You can arrange results one above the other, or side-by-side. You can also add text and images, and add headers or footers. Whenever tasks are run, the results will be automatically updated in the report. The report can then be shared with other SAS applications such as SAS Web Report Studio, or exported to an HTML, XML, or PDF file.

Selecting Items for the report From the menu bar, select **File ▶ New ▶ Report** to open the New Report window. All the results in your project produced in SAS Report format are listed in the box on the left labeled **Select SAS items**. A grid for the report layout is located on the right side of the window. Drag and drop desired results from the list on the left to one of the grid cells on the right. Results can appear side-by-side or one above the other.

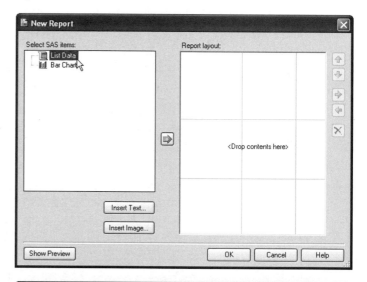

Once you have added the result to the grid, you can use the handles located on the edges of the box to expand the result to occupy multiple grid cells if desired.

In this example, a List Data result is positioned to the left of a Bar Chart result with each result occupying one grid cell. Click **OK** when you have the results positioned as desired.

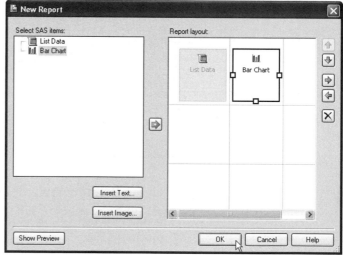

Fitting items on a page After you close the New Report window, the results will appear in the workspace. You can resize graphs and charts if necessary at this point. You cannot resize tabular results. If you want to make changes to the content of your report, click **Modify Report** on the workspace toolbar for the report. If you click the down-arrow

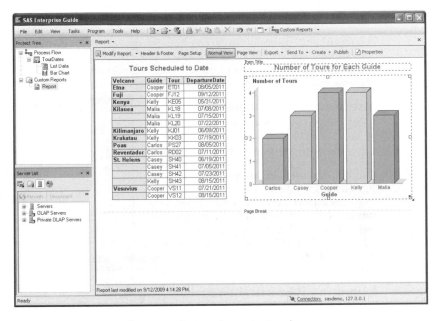

next to the Modify Report button, you can choose options to insert text or images, remove page breaks, or apply the same style to all report items.

Results To see how your result will look when printed, click the **Page View** button on the workspace toolbar. You cannot resize results or modify the report while you are in Page View. To make modifications, click **Normal View**.

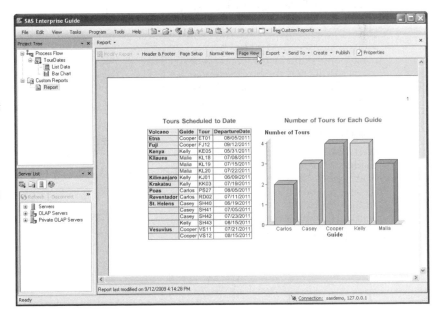

11.5   Adding Text, Images, and Headings to Reports

The report editor allows you to combine results created in the SAS Report format along with text, images, headers, and footers. To create a new report, select **File ▶ New ▶ Report** from the menu bar. To edit an existing report, click **Modify Report** on the workspace toolbar for the report. This example modifies the report created in the previous section.

Inserting text or images To insert images into your report, click the **Insert Image** button in the report contents window. This opens a window where you can navigate to your image file. Click **Open** and the image will be inserted into one of the cells in the layout window. To insert text, click **Insert Text** to open an Insert Text window (as in this example) where you can enter the desired text, and choose formatting. Click **OK** and the text will be inserted into one of the cells in the layout window.

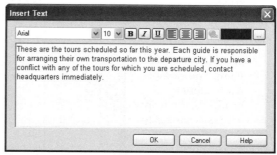

Arranging items in the report layout If the inserted text or image is not in the desired location, you can move it to a different cell by simply clicking and dragging. You can also change the relative size of any item by clicking the item and then clicking and dragging the handles on the edges of the box to change the shape. In this example, the text has been placed above the List Data and Bar Chart results and the box expanded to span both results. Click **OK** when you are satisfied with the layout of the report.

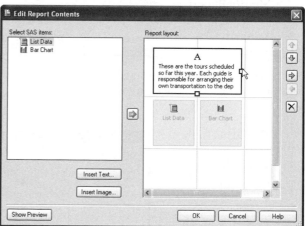

Adding headers and footers To add headers or footers to your report, click the **Header & Footer** button on the workspace toolbar for the report.

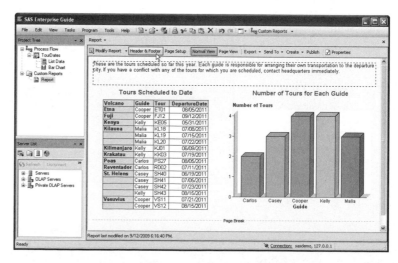

This opens the Header & Footer window. You can enter and format text in the text box, add and position images, and add lines above or below the header or footer. Any headers or footers you add to the report will appear on each page of the report. On the **Titles & Footnotes** tab, it is also possible to remove (but not edit) the titles and footnotes generated by SAS Enterprise Guide tasks. In this example, a header is added to the report, along with an image to the right of the header text and a line below. When you are finished making changes to the header and footer, click **OK**. The report will display in the workspace.

Results After arranging the items for your report and adding any headers or footers, you can preview your report by clicking **Page View** on the workspace toolbar for the report. Here is what the report will look like when printed. To print the report, choose **File ▶ Print Report** from the menu bar. All report contents generated by SAS Enterprise Guide tasks will be automatically refreshed when you rerun the tasks in the project. If you do not want the results refreshed, then create a report snapshot by right-clicking the report icon in the Project Explorer and selecting **Create Report Snapshot**.

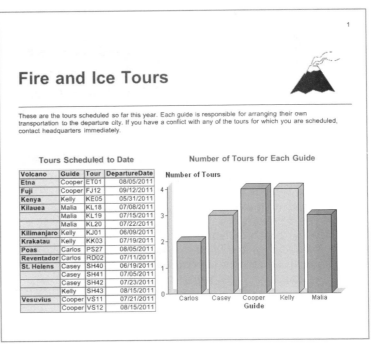

11.6   Exporting Results to a File

By default, results generated by SAS Enterprise Guide are saved inside the project. If you want, you can export your results to a file. Exporting results can be done manually or automatically each time you run the project.

Exporting results to a file

You can export any result to a file by right-clicking the result icon in the Process Flow and selecting **Export ▶ Export** *result-format – result-name* or choosing this option from the **Export** menu on the workspace toolbar for the result. This opens an Export window where you can save the file on your local computer or on a SAS server. If your result is in SAS Report format, you can export the file as a SAS Report, HTML, XML, or PDF file. All other result formats can only be exported in the original format.

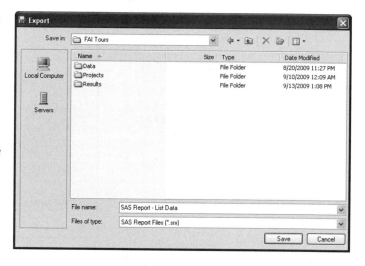

Exporting results as a step in the project

If you export results as a step in the project, then each time the project is run, the exported file will be updated. Right-click the result icon in the Process Flow and select **Export ▶ Export** *result-format – result-name* **as a step in the project** or choose this option from the **Export** menu of the workspace toolbar for the result. This opens the Export wizard. In the first window, all items in the project are listed with the selected item highlighted. Click **Next**.

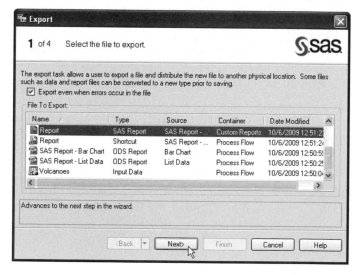

If the result you wish to export is in SAS Report format, then the second window will give you a choice for the output file type: SAS Report, HTML, or PDF. If the result format is not SAS Report, then you will not have a choice because you can only export the result in its original format, and you will not see this window. Choose the desired output file type and click **Next**.

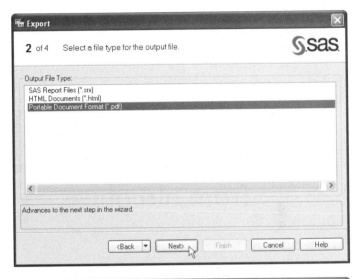

In the next window, select the location to save the file. This can be on your local computer, or on a SAS server. By default, if a file with the same name already exists, it will be overwritten. If you uncheck **Overwrite existing output**, then instead of overwriting, a new file will be created with the date and time appended to the file name. Click **Next** to view the final window of the wizard (not shown) that provides a summary of your choices. Click **Finish**.

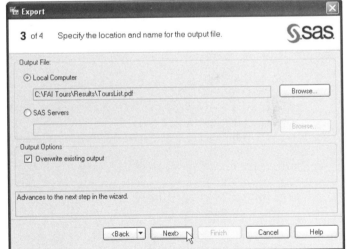

Results When you export as a step in the project, an icon will appear in the Process Flow showing the export and the result. If your export is not done as a step in the project, then no icons will appear. This example shows the Process Flow for a custom report that was exported as a step in the project to a PDF file.

> "The difficulty lies, not in new ideas, but in escaping from old ones."

JOHN KEYNES

From *The General Theory of Employment, Interest, and Money*, 1936.

CHAPTER 12

Adding Flexibility with Prompts and Conditions

12.1 Creating Prompts for Data Values

Prompts allow you to develop projects that are flexible. When you run a project that uses a prompt, a box will appear asking you to specify a value for that prompt. The project will be run using the value you enter. This allows you to create one project that can generate many different results.

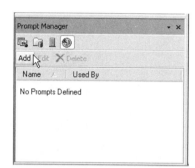

There are four ways you can use prompts: in the filter condition of a query, in a task, in a SAS program, or in the condition of a process flow. The example in this section creates a data value prompt that will be used in a query in the next section. The rest of this chapter shows how to create and use other kinds of prompts.

It may be helpful to know that prompts have other names. In SAS Enterprise Guide 4.1, prompts were called parameters. SAS programmers generally refer to prompts as macro variables.

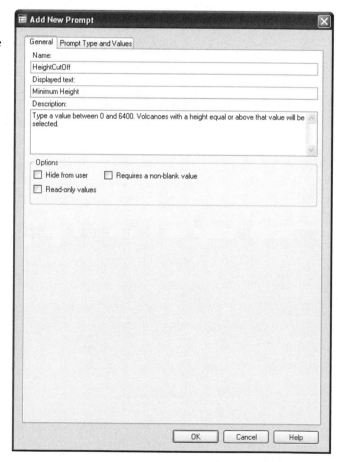

To create prompts, you use the Prompt Manager. The Prompt Manager shares the Resources pane with other windows. To open the Prompt Manager, click the Prompt Manager icon in the Resources pane. You can also open the Prompt Manager from the **View** menu, or by clicking **Prompt Manager** in the Query Builder. In the Prompt Manager, click **Add** to open the Add New Prompt window.

Naming the prompt On the **General** tab of the Add New Prompt window, you specify a **Name**, **Displayed text**, and an optional **Description** for the new prompt. The name must be 32 characters or fewer in length; start with a letter or underscore; and contain only letters, numerals, and underscores. When you use the prompt, you will see the displayed text and the description, but not the name.

In this example, the prompt has a name of **HeightCutOff**, the displayed text is **Minimum Height**, and there is a description. Next click the **Prompt Type and Values** tab.

Setting the prompt type and values

On the **Prompt Type and Values** tab, click the down-arrow on the box labeled **Prompt type,** and select an option from the pull-down list. For this example, select **Numeric**. When you select the prompt type, options for that particular type of prompt will appear in the lower part of the window. For a numeric prompt, you can enter minimum, maximum, and default values. For this example, the **Minimum value allowed** is zero, the **Maximum value allowed** is 6400, the **Default Value** is 5000, and the option **Allow only integer values** is checked. Since the tallest volcano is 6458 meters, setting the maximum value at 6400 ensures that at least one row of the Volcanoes table will always be selected after filtering. When you have set all the properties for the prompt, click **OK**.

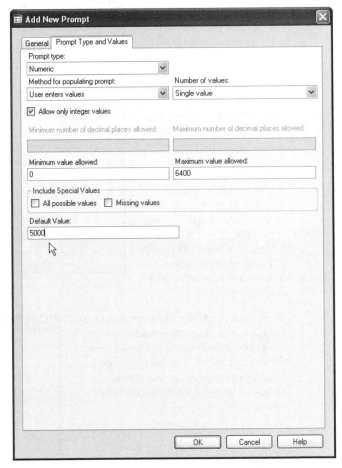

The prompt you created will appear in the Prompt Manager. If you want to make changes to the prompt, click its name to highlight it, and click **Edit**. To delete a prompt, click **Delete**.

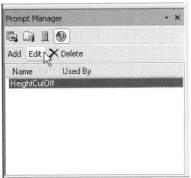

12.2 Using Prompts in Query Filter Conditions

The previous section showed how to create a prompt for a data value. This section shows how to use that prompt in the filter condition of a query.

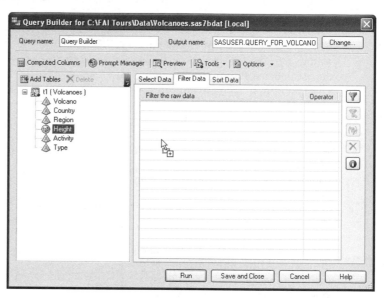

Setting the Filter Condition To open the Query Builder, click the data icon in the Project Tree or Process Flow to make it active, and select **Tasks ▶ Data ▶ Query Builder** from the menu bar. In the Query Builder, drag the columns you want to keep to the **Select Data** tab. For this example, use the Volcanoes data table, and select all the columns.

Then click the **Filter Data** tab and create the filter just like you would any other filter. Drag the desired column to the **Filter Data** tab of the Query Builder. For this example, drag the column Height. The New Filter wizard will open.

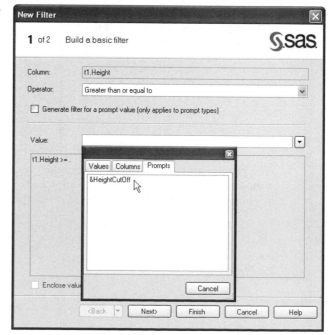

In the first window of the New Filter wizard, choose the appropriate operator for the condition, in this case **Greater than or equal to**. Click the down-arrow next to the box labeled Value. Then click the **Prompts** tab, and select the desired prompt. Notice that the prompt name is preceded by an ampersand (&). The ampersand indicates that this is the name of a prompt, not a column. In this example, the filter will select all rows where the value of the Height column is greater than or equal to the value of the **&HeightCutOff** prompt.

Click **Next** if you want to see a summary of your filter settings. To complete the filter, click **Finish** in the New Filter window. To run the new query, click **Run**.

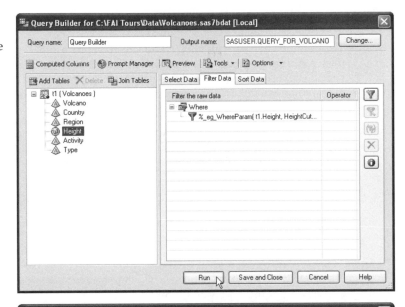

Running the query

When you run the query, a window will open, asking you to specify a value for the prompt. In this example, you must enter a value between the minimum allowed value (zero) and the maximum (6400). When you are satisfied, click **Run**. In the Process Flow, you will see that the query icon now includes a question mark, , to show that the query uses a prompt.

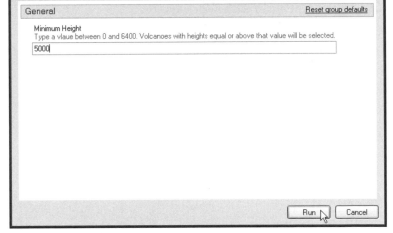

Results Here is the data table with results from selecting 5000 as the cut-off value for height. This table includes all the rows from the Volcanoes table with a height greater than or equal to 5000. Any tasks that use this data table will reflect the selection made in the

	Volcano	Country	Region	Height	Activity	Type
1	Altar	Ecuador	SA	5321	Extinct	Stratovolcano
2	Elbrus	Russia	Eu	5633	Extinct	Stratovolcano
3	Illimani	Bolivia	SA	6458	Extinct	Stratovolcano
4	Kenya	Kenya	Af	5199	Extinct	
5	Kilimanjaro	Tanzania	Af	5895		Stratovolcano
6	Popocatepetl	Mexico	NA	5426	Active	Stratovolcano
7	Sabancaya	Peru	SA	5976	Active	Stratovolcano

query. Every time you run the query, you will be asked again to specify a value for the prompt.

12.3 Creating Prompts for Variable Names

The previous two sections showed how to create a prompt for a data value and then use it in the filter condition of a query. This section shows how you can create a prompt for a variable name, and the next section shows how you can use this prompt in a task. This example creates a prompt that will allow a user to choose a grouping variable when a task is run.

To create a prompt, click the Prompt Manager icon 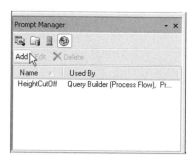 in the Resources pane, or select **View ▶ Prompts Manager** from the menu bar. The Prompt Manager will open. Click **Add** to open the Add New Prompt window.

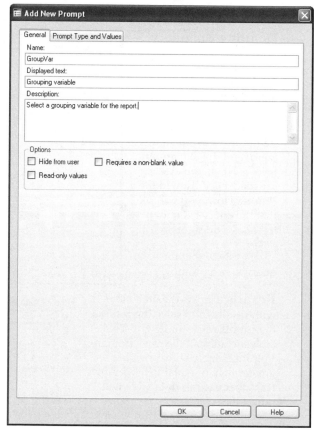

Naming the prompt On the **General** tab of the Add New Prompt window, you specify a **Name**, **Displayed text**, and an optional **Description** for the new prompt. The name must be 32 characters or fewer in length; start with a letter or underscore; and contain only letters, numerals, and underscores. When you use the prompt, you will see the displayed text and the description, but not the name. In this example, the prompt has the name **GroupVar**, the displayed text is **Grouping variable**, and there is a description. Next click the **Prompt Type and Values** tab.

Setting the prompt type and values On the **Prompt Type and Values** tab, click the down-arrow on the box labeled **Prompt type,** and select an option from the pull-down list. For this example, select **Variable**. When you select the prompt type, options for that particular type of prompt will appear in the lower part of the window.

In the section labeled **Options** on the right side of the window, you can choose the variable type. The default variable type is character.

If you click the **Load Values** button near the bottom of the window and navigate to a data set, all the variables of that type for that data set will be listed in the section labeled **Value list**. To delete unwanted variables, highlight their names, and click the delete ⊠ button. In this example, all the character variables in the Volcanoes data set were listed, but Volcano and Country are being deleted. Only the variables Region, Activity, and Type make sense as grouping variables. It is possible to choose a different variable type (such as numeric or date), and click Load Values again so that the list will include variables of more than one type. For this example, only three character variables (Region, Activity, and Type) are needed. When you have set all the properties for the prompt, click **OK**.

The prompt you created will appear in the Prompt Manager window.

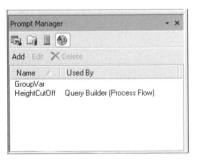

12.4 Using Prompts in Tasks

The previous section showed how to create a prompt for the name of a variable. This section shows how to assign that prompt to a task role, and how to run the new task.

This example uses the List Data task and the Volcanoes data table. To open this task, click the data icon in the Project Tree or Process Flow to make it active, and select **Tasks ▶ Describe ▶ List Data** from the menu bar.

Assigning a prompt to a task role Notice that the list of variables in the task roles page includes not only the regular variables, but also any variable prompts you have created for this project. The ampersand (&) in the data icon

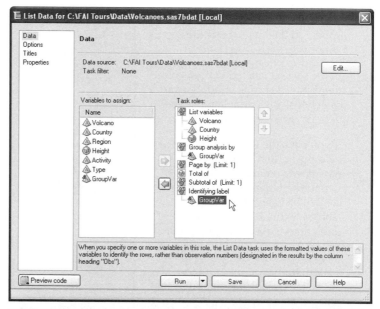

indicates that GroupVar is a prompt, not a regular variable.

You assign variables and prompts to roles by dragging them to task roles. In this example, the variables Volcano, Country, and Height have been assigned to the **List variables** role. The prompt GroupVar has been assigned to the **Group analysis by** and **Identifying label** roles.

Using prompts in titles You can use prompts to create custom titles or footnotes. Click **Titles** in the selection pane on the left to open the Titles page.

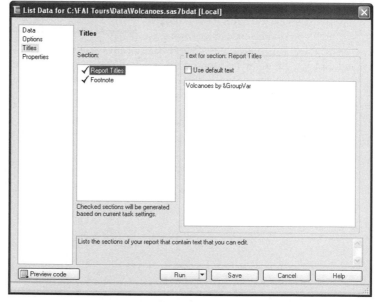

The Titles page opens, displaying the default title for that particular task. To change the title, uncheck the **Use default text** option and type the new title in the text box. In this example, the title has been changed to "Volcanoes by &GroupVar." When you are satisfied with the settings, click **Run**.

Running the task

When you run the task, a window will open, asking you to specify a value for the prompt. In this window, the variable Type is being selected from a pull-down list of three possible grouping variables. Click **Run** to run the task.

In the Process Flow, you will see that the task icon now includes a question mark, , to show that the task uses a prompt.

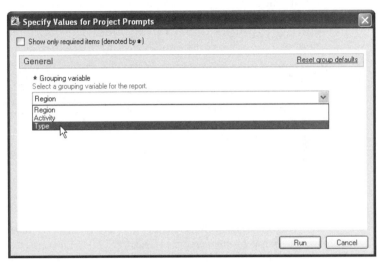

Results
Here are the results of the task. This is a List Data report organized by type of volcano. Notice that the value of the prompt (in this case Type) also appears in the title. Every time you run the task, you will be asked again to choose a grouping variable.

Volcanoes by Type

Type	Volcano	Country	Height
	Arthur's Seat	UK	251
	Kenya	Kenya	5199
Caldera	Grimsvotn	Iceland	1725
	Krakatau	Indonesia	813
Cinder Cone	Puy de Dome	France	1464
Complex	Vesuvius	Italy	1281
Shield	Kilauea	USA	1222
	Mauna Loa	USA	4170
	Nyamuragira	DRCongo	3058
	Santorini	Greece	367
	Warning	Australia	1125
Stratovolcano	Altar	Ecuador	5321
	Barren Island	India	354
	Elbrus	Russia	5633
	Erebus		3794
	Etna	Italy	3350

12.5 Using Prompts in SAS Programs

The previous sections showed how to create prompts and use them in queries or tasks. This section shows how you can create flexible SAS programs by using the same prompts. Then when you run the SAS programs, SAS Enterprise Guide will ask you to specify values for the prompts.

Adding prompts to SAS programs Here is a simple SAS program typed in a Program window in SAS Enterprise Guide.

```
PROC FREQ DATA = 'C:\FAI Tours\Data\Volcanoes';
    WHERE Height >= &HeightCutOff;
    TABLES &GroupVar;
    TITLE1 "Number of Volcanoes &HeightCutOff Meters or Higher";
    TITLE2 "For Each Value of &GroupVar";
RUN;
```

This program uses both the data value prompt created in section 12.1 (&HeightCutOff) and the variable name prompt created in section 12.3 (&GroupVar). &HeightCutOff is used in a WHERE statement to select only rows where the values of the Height column are greater than or equal to the prompt value. &GroupVar is used in a TABLES statement so the data will be summarized based on the values of the grouping variable. Then both prompts are used again in the TITLE statements so that the values of the prompts will appear in the titles for the report.

Setting the properties of the program Because the prompts have been defined outside the program, you need to associate the prompts with the program. To do this, right-click the program icon in the Project Tree or Process Flow and select **Properties** from the pop-up menu. Then, in the Properties for Program window, click **Prompts** in the selection pane on the left to display the Prompts page. Click the **Add** button. The Select Prompts window will open.

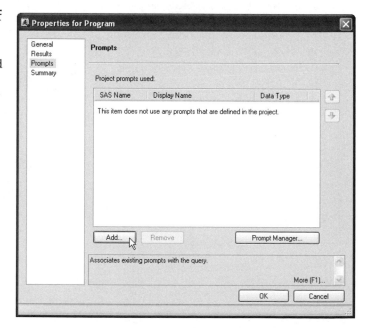

The Select Prompts window lists all the prompts currently defined in the project. Hold down the control key (CTRL), and click the names of all the prompts used in the program. Then click **OK** to return to the Properties for Program window.

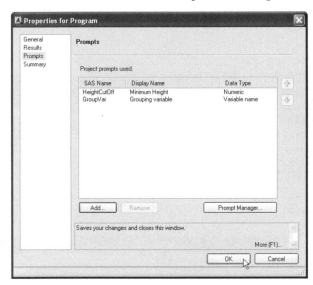

The prompts will appear in the Properties for Program window. This window shows that both the HeightCutOff and GroupVar prompts have been associated with this program. Click **OK** to save the changes and close the window.

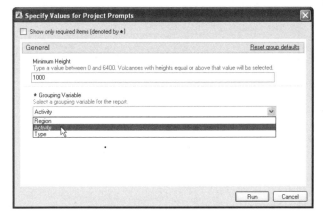

Running the SAS Program To run the program, click **Run** in the Program window, or click the program icon in the Project Tree or Process Flow, and select **Program ▶ Run** *program-name* **On** *server-name* from the menu bar. When you do this, a window will open, asking you to specify values for each prompt. In this window, the cut-off height has been set to 1000, and the grouping variable has been set to Activity. When you are satisfied, click **Run**. In the Process Flow, you will see that the program icon now includes a question mark, , to show that the program uses a prompt.

Results This report is summarized by Activity, includes all the volcanoes over 1000 meters, and has custom titles.

Number of Volcanoes 1000 Meters or Higher
For Each Value of Activity
The FREQ Procedure

Activity	Frequency	Percent	Cumulative Frequency	Cumulative Percent
Active	20	76.92	20	76.92
Extinct	6	23.08	26	100.00

Frequency Missing = 2

12.6 Creating Prompts for Text Values

Earlier sections in this chapter showed how to create a prompt for a data value or a variable name, and how to use those prompts in a query, task, or program. This section shows how to create a prompt for a text value, and the next two sections show how to use this prompt in a project condition. The text value prompt and project condition in this example allow a user to choose which of two tasks to run.

To create a prompt, click the Prompt Manager icon  in the Resources pane, or select **View ▶ Prompts Manager** from the menu bar, or click **Prompt Manager** in the Query Builder. The Prompt Manager will open. Click **Add** to open the Add New Prompt window.

Naming the prompt On the **General** tab of the Add New Prompt window, you specify a **Name, Displayed text**, and an optional **Description** for the new prompt. The name must be 32 characters or fewer in length; start with a letter or underscore; and contain only letters, numerals, and underscores. In this example, the prompt has the name **ChooseReport**, the displayed text is **Choose a report to run**, the description is **Select one option**, and the option **Requires a non-blank value** has been checked. Next click the **Prompt Type and Values** tab.

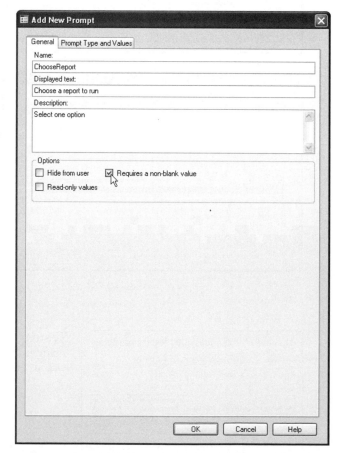

Setting the prompt type and values

On the **Prompt Type and Values** tab, click the down-arrow on the box labeled **Prompt type,** and select an option from the pull-down list. For this example, select **Text**. When you select the prompt type, appropriate options will appear in the lower part of the window.

Click the down-arrow on the box labeled **Method for populating prompt**, and select the method. Users can type in a value, or choose from a static or dynamic list. For this example, choose **User selects values from a static list**. In the box labeled **Number of values**, select **Single value**.

For a static list, you must specify possible values for the prompt. To do this, click the **Add** button. Empty cells will appear in the area labeled **List of values**. Click a cell and type in the unformatted value and the formatted value for the first choice. Then click **Add** again, and type in the values for the second choice, and so on until you have typed in all the values you want to appear in the static

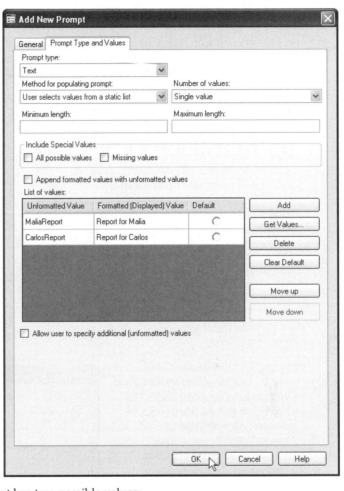

list. For this example, the text prompt has two possible values: **MaliaReport**, which has a formatted value of **Report for Malia**, or **CarlosReport**, which has a formatted value of **Report for Carlos**.

When you have set all the properties for the prompt, click **OK**. The prompt you created will appear in the Prompt Manager window.

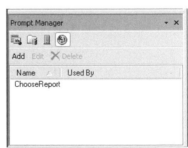

Chapter 12

12.7 Using Prompts in Project Conditions

A project condition is an expression that is evaluated by SAS Enterprise Guide at run time. Any item that you can run in SAS Enterprise Guide can have a project condition associated with it. If the condition is true, then that item will run. If it is not true, then that item will not run.

Project conditions can be based on the value of a prompt, on a data value, or on the date or time when the project runs. So, for example, you could have a query that runs only if you choose it from a list of options, or a data set that is exported whenever a particular data value appears, or a report that runs only on Wednesdays. The example in this section creates a project condition based on the text value prompt created in the preceding section.

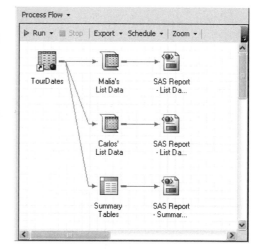

The project in this example contains three items that can be run: two List Data tasks and a Summary Tables task. The two List Data tasks have been renamed as Malia's List Data and Carlos' List Data. The project condition will prompt the user to choose which of the two List Data tasks to run.

To apply a project condition to an item in a Process Flow, right-click the icon for that item, and select **Condition ▶ Add** from the pop-up menu. A Conditional Processing window will open. For this example, the Conditional Processing window has been opened by right-clicking the icon for Malia's List Data.

In the Conditional Processing window, click **Add** to open the Add a Condition window.

Adding a condition

In the Add a Condition window, click the down-arrow in the **Based on** box, and select the type of condition. Your condition can be based on prompts, the current time or date, or a data value in your project. When you select the Based on value, options for that type of condition will appear in the lower part of the window. In this example, the condition will be based on **Prompts**. Click the down-arrow for the box labeled **Prompt** to display a list of text prompts already defined in the project, or click **New** to create a new one. Choose the operator from the box labeled **Operator**, and type the value of the prompt for this condition in the box labeled **Value**.

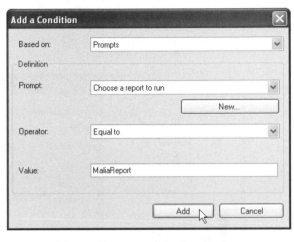

For this example, the prompt is **Choose a report to run** (the prompt created in the previous section), the operator is **Equal to**, and the value is **MaliaReport**. When you are satisfied, click **Add** to close the Add a Condition window.

Specifying an action

The condition you just created will appear under the words **If this condition is true**. Click the down-arrow on the box labeled **Then run this task**, and select the item in the project that should run when that particular condition is true.

Specifying an Else action

At this point, you must specify what to do if the first condition is not true. You have two choices. You can click **Add Else If** to create another condition, or you can click the down-arrow on the box labeled **Else run this task** and choose an alternate item to run whenever the first condition is not true. Since this project condition will include only the two List Data tasks, you do not need to specify another condition. Click the down-arrow on the box labeled **Else run this task**, and select the item that should run when the condition is not true.

In this Conditional Processing window, you can see that when the value of the prompt (named **Choose a report to run**) is **MaliaReport**, then the task named **Malia's List Data** will run. Otherwise, the task named **Carlos' List Data** will run. When you are satisfied with the settings, click **OK** to close the window and apply the condition to the project. The next section shows the Process Flow with the condition applied.

12.8 Running Projects with Conditions

When you add a condition to a project, it is illustrated in the process flow diagram. Here is what the process flow looks like for the project condition that was created in the preceding section.

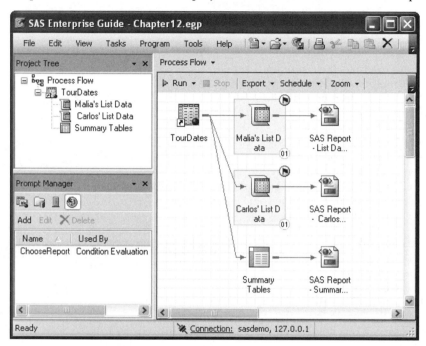

Condition indicators Boxes appear around any items associated with a condition. Numbers in the lower-right corner of each box indicate which items are part of the same condition. In this process flow, the number 01 shows that the two List Data tasks are alternate paths in the same condition, but the Summary Tables task is not. You can specify more than one condition for a process flow. If you have a second condition, then items in that condition will be marked with 02. A third condition would be marked with 03, and so on.

In the upper-right corner of a condition box appears a symbol. At first, this symbol looks like a waving flag. After the process flow has run, the symbol changes to either a check mark indicating that the branch ran, or an X indicating that the branch did not run.

Running the project You run a project with conditions in the same way that you run an ordinary project. Select **Run** from the workspace toolbar for the Process Flow, or select **File ▶ Run** *project-name* from the menu bar. You can also run one branch of a process flow by right-clicking an icon in the Process Flow window and selecting **Run Branch from** *item-name*.

Project conditions do not have to use prompts. Instead of depending on prompts, the condition could depend on the current date or time, or on a value in your data. In those cases, the Process Flow would simply run without prompting for any user input.

If the condition uses a prompt, then, when you run it, a window will open allowing you to specify a value for the prompt. In this example, the prompt is **Choose a report to run**, and it has two possible values. This is the text prompt that was created in section 12.6. The value **Report for Malia** is being selected. When you are satisfied with your choice, click **Run**.

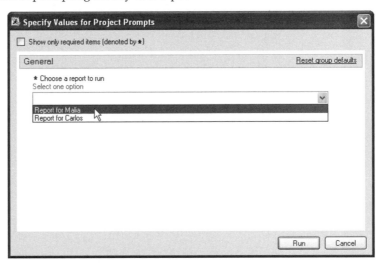

Here is the Process Flow after the project has run.

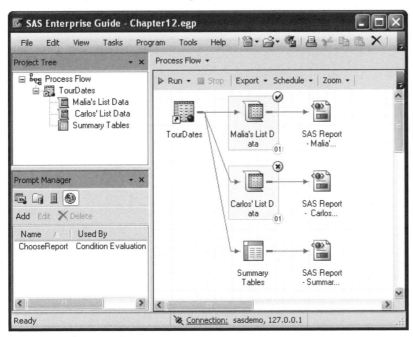

You can see that Malia's List Data task has a check mark in the corner, and that Carlos' List Data task has an X. These condition indicators show that the first task ran, but the second one did not. Since the Summary Tables task is not part of the condition, it will always run. Every time you open a project with conditions, all the condition indicators will be set back to waving flags.

APPENDIX A

"Begin at the beginning," the King said, very gravely, "and go on till you come to the end: then stop."

LEWIS CARROLL

The King speaking with the White Rabbit in *Alice's Adventures in Wonderland*, 1865.

Data Used in This Book

Reading about a topic is good, but many people learn better by doing. However, before you can do the examples in the tutorials or reference sections, you need the data. One way to get the data is to type the data shown in this appendix into a SAS Enterprise Guide Data Grid, a Microsoft Excel spreadsheet, or a text file. Another way is to download the data sets by going to

support.sas.com/authors.

Select the name of one of the authors (Susan Slaughter or Lora D. Delwiche). Then find the picture of this book, click the words **Example Code and Data** underneath the picture, and follow the instructions.

Tours Data

Filename: Tours.sas7bdat
File Type: SAS data set

Columns:

Name	Description	Possible Values
Volcano	Name of the volcano	
Departs	City from which tour departs	
Days	Length of the tour in days	
Price	Price of the tour in U.S. dollars	
Difficulty	Strenuousness of the tour	c (Challenging) m (Moderate) e (Easy)

Tours.sas7bdat

	Volcano	Departs	Days	Price	Difficulty
1	Etna	Catania	7	$1,075	m
2	Fuji	Tokyo	2	$225	c
3	Kenya	Nairobi	6	$830	m
4	Kilauea	Hilo	1	$55	e
5	Kilimanjaro	Nairobi	9	$1,310	c
6	Krakatau	Jakarta	7	$895	e
7	Poas	San Jose	1	$65	e
8	Reventador	Quito	4	$575	m
9	St. Helens	Portland	2	$167	e
10	Vesuvius	Rome	6	$985	e

Tour Dates Data

Filename: TourDates.sas7bdat
File Type: SAS data set

Columns:

Name	Description
Tour	Code for tour
Volcano	Name of the volcano
DepartureDate	Date of tour departure
Guide	Name of guide for tour

TourDates.sas7bdat

	Tour	Volcano	DepartureDate	Guide
1	PS27	Poas	08/05/2011	Carlos
2	SH40	St. Helens	06/19/2011	Casey
3	SH41	St. Helens	07/05/2011	Casey
4	SH42	St. Helens	07/23/2011	Casey
5	SH43	St. Helens	08/15/2011	Kelly
6	FJ12	Fuji	09/12/2011	Cooper
7	ET01	Etna	08/05/2011	Cooper
8	KE05	Kenya	05/31/2011	Kelly
9	KL18	Kilauea	07/08/2011	Malia
10	KL19	Kilauea	07/15/2011	Malia
11	KL20	Kilauea	07/22/2011	Malia
12	RD02	Reventador	07/11/2011	Carlos
13	VS11	Vesuvius	07/21/2011	Cooper
14	VS12	Vesuvius	08/15/2011	Cooper
15	KJ01	Kilimanjaro	06/09/2011	Kelly
16	KK03	Krakatau	07/19/2011	Kelly

Tour Bookings Data

There are two versions of the bookings data. One is a Microsoft Excel file, and the other is a SAS data set. They both contain the same columns and data values.

Filename:	Bookings.xls	Bookings.sas7bdat
File Type:	Microsoft Excel spreadsheet	SAS data set

Columns:

Name	Description
Office	Office where reservation was made
CustomerID	Customer identification number
Tour	Code for tour
Travelers	Number traveling in party
Deposit	Amount of deposit
Deposit_Date	Date of deposit

Bookings.xls

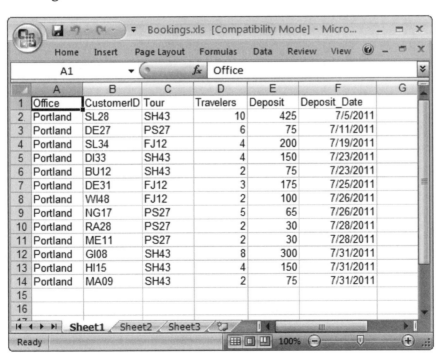

Bookings.sas7bdat

	Office	CustomerID	Tour	Travelers	Deposit	Deposit_Date
1	Portland	SL28	SH43	10	425	05JUL2011
2	Portland	DE27	PS27	6	75	11JUL2011
3	Portland	SL34	FJ12	4	200	19JUL2011
4	Portland	DI33	SH43	4	150	23JUL2011
5	Portland	BU12	SH43	2	75	23JUL2011
6	Portland	DE31	FJ12	3	175	25JUL2011
7	Portland	WI48	FJ12	2	100	26JUL2011
8	Portland	NG17	PS27	5	65	26JUL2011
9	Portland	RA28	PS27	2	30	28JUL2011
10	Portland	ME11	PS27	2	30	28JUL2011
11	Portland	GI08	SH43	8	300	31JUL2011
12	Portland	HI15	SH43	4	150	31JUL2011
13	Portland	MA09	SH43	2	75	31JUL2011

Volcanoes Data

Filename: Volcanoes.sas7bdat
File Type: SAS data set

Columns:

Name	Description	Possible Values
Volcano	Name of the volcano	
Country	Country where the volcano is located	
Region	Region where the volcano is located	Af (Africa) An (Antarctica) AP (Australia/Pacific) As (Asia) Eu (Europe) NA (North America) SA (South America)
Height	Height of the volcano in meters	
Activity	Activity of the volcano	Active Extinct
Type	Kind of volcano	Caldera Complex Shield Stratovolcano

Appendix A

Volcanoes.sas7bdat

	Volcano	Country	Region	Height	Activity	Type
1	Altar	Ecuador	SA	5321	Extinct	Stratovolcano
2	Arthur's Seat	UK	Eu	251	Extinct	
3	Barren Island	India	As	354	Active	Stratovolcano
4	Elbrus	Russia	Eu	5633	Extinct	Stratovolcano
5	Erebus		An	3794	Active	Stratovolcano
6	Etna	Italy	Eu	3350	Active	Stratovolcano
7	Fuji	Japan	As	3776	Active	Stratovolcano
8	Garibaldi	Canada	NA	2678		Stratovolcano
9	Grimsvotn	Iceland	Eu	1725	Active	Caldera
10	Illimani	Bolivia	SA	6458	Extinct	Stratovolcano
11	Kenya	Kenya	Af	5199	Extinct	
12	Kilauea	USA	AP	1222	Active	Shield
13	Kilimanjaro	Tanzania	Af	5895		Stratovolcano
14	Kliuchevskoi	Russia	As	4835	Active	Stratovolcano
15	Krakatau	Indonesia	As	813	Active	Caldera
16	Lassen	USA	NA	3187	Active	Stratovolcano
17	Mauna Loa	USA	AP	4170	Active	Shield
18	Nyamuragira	DRCongo	Af	3058	Active	Shield
19	Nyiragongo	DRCongo	Af	3470	Active	Stratovolcano
20	Pinatubo	Philippines	As	1486	Active	Stratovolcano
21	Poas	Costa Rica	NA	2708	Active	Stratovolcano
22	Popocatepetl	Mexico	NA	5426	Active	Stratovolcano
23	Puy de Dome	France	Eu	1464	Extinct	Cinder Cone
24	Reventador	Ecuador	SA	3562	Active	Stratovolcano
25	Ruapehu	NZ	AP	2797	Active	Stratovolcano
26	Sabancaya	Peru	SA	5976	Active	Stratovolcano
27	Santorini	Greece	Eu	367	Active	Shield
28	Shishaldin	USA	NA	2857	Active	Stratovolcano
29	St. Helens	USA	NA	2549	Active	Stratovolcano
30	Vesuvius	Italy	Eu	1281	Active	Complex
31	Villarrica	Chile	SA	2847	Active	Stratovolcano
32	Warning	Australia	AP	1125	Extinct	Shield

Eruptions Data

There are two versions of the eruptions data. One is a text file, and the other is a SAS data set. They both contain the same columns and data values.

Filename:	Eruptions.csv	Eruptions.sas7bdat
File Type:	Text file with comma-separated values	SAS data set

Columns:

Name	Description	Possible Values
Volcano	Name of the volcano	
StartDate	Date the eruption started in MMDDYY10. format	
EndDate	Date the eruption ended in MMDDYY10. format	
VEI	Volcanic Explosivity Index	0–8

Eruptions.csv

```
Volcano, StartDate, EndDate, VEI
Barren Island, 12/20/1795, 12/21/1795, 2
Barren Island, 12/20/1994, 06/05/1995, 2
Erebus, 12/12/1912, . , 2
Erebus, 01/03/1972, . , 1
Etna, 02/06/1610, 08/15/1610, 2
Etna, 06/04/1787, 08/11/1787, 4
Etna, 01/30/1865, 06/28/1865, 2
Etna, 12/16/2005, 12/22/2005, 1
Fuji, 12/16/1707, 02/24/1708, 5
Grimsvotn, 10/31/1603, 11/01/1603, 2
Grimsvotn, 01/08/1873, 08/01/1873, 4
Grimsvotn, 12/18/1998, 12/28/1998, 3
Kilauea, 05/30/1840, 06/25/1840, 0
Kilauea, 05/24/1969, 07/22/1974, 0
Kliuchevskoi, 09/25/1737, 11/04/1737, 2
Kliuchevskoi, 03/25/1931, 03/27/1931, 4
Kliuchevskoi, 01/20/2005, 04/07/2005, 2
Krakatau, 05/20/1883, 10/21/1883, 6
Krakatau, 07/04/1938, 07/02/1940, 3
Krakatau, 05/29/2000, 10/30/2000, 1
Lassen, 05/30/1914, 06/29/1917, 3
Mauna Loa, 06/20/1832, 07/15/1832, 0
Mauna Loa, 03/25/1984, 04/15/1984, 0
Nyamuragira, 11/07/1907, 12/05/1907, 3
Nyamuragira, 02/06/2001, 04/05/2001, 2
Nyiragongo, 06/21/1982, 10/17/1982, 1
Nyiragongo, 01/17/2002, 02/03/2002, 1
Pinatubo, 04/02/1991, 09/02/1991, 5
Poas, 12/29/1898, 12/31/1907, 1
Poas, 04/08/1996, 04/08/1996, 1
Popocatepetl, 10/13/1663, 10/19/1665, 3
Popocatepetl, 12/21/1994, 08/05/1995, 2
Reventador, 12/12/1856, 12/13/1856, 3
Reventador, 02/24/1944, 03/01/1944, 3
Reventador, 11/03/2002, 01/10/2003, 4
Ruapehu, 02/13/1861, 05/16/1861, 2
Ruapehu, 06/17/1996, 09/01/1996, 3
Sabancaya, 05/01/1997, 05/02/1997, 3
Santorini, 09/27/1650, 12/06/1650, 4
Santorini, 05/23/1707, 09/14/1711, 3
Santorini, 01/26/1866, 10/15/1870, 2
Santorini, 01/10/1950, 02/02/1950, 2
Shishaldin, 03/13/1999, 05/27/1999, 3
St. Helens, 03/26/1847, 03/30/1847, 2
St. Helens, 03/27/1980, 10/28/1986, 5
St. Helens, 10/01/2004, 01/27/2008 , 2
Vesuvius, 12/15/1631, 01/31/1632, 5
Vesuvius, 12/25/1732, 06/04/1737, 3
Vesuvius, 12/18/1875, 04/22/1906, 4
Vesuvius, 07/05/1913, 04/04/1944, 3
Villarrica, 11/07/1837, 11/21/1837, 2
Villarrica, 10/26/2008, . , 1
```

Eruptions.sas7bdat

	Volcano	StartDate	EndDate	VEI
1	Barren Island	12/20/1795	12/21/1795	2
2	Barren Island	12/20/1994	06/05/1995	2
3	Erebus	12/12/1912	.	2
4	Erebus	01/03/1972	.	1
5	Etna	02/06/1610	08/15/1610	2
6	Etna	06/04/1787	08/11/1787	4
7	Etna	01/30/1865	06/28/1865	2
8	Etna	12/16/2005	12/22/2005	1
9	Fuji	12/16/1707	02/24/1708	5
10	Grimsvotn	10/31/1603	11/01/1603	2
11	Grimsvotn	01/08/1873	08/01/1873	4
12	Grimsvotn	12/18/1998	12/28/1998	3
13	Kilauea	05/30/1840	06/25/1840	0
14	Kilauea	05/24/1969	07/22/1974	0
15	Kliuchevskoi	09/25/1737	11/04/1737	2
16	Kliuchevskoi	03/25/1931	03/27/1931	4
17	Kliuchevskoi	01/20/2005	04/07/2005	2
18	Krakatau	05/20/1883	10/21/1883	6
19	Krakatau	07/04/1938	07/02/1940	3
20	Krakatau	05/29/2000	10/30/2000	1
21	Lassen	05/30/1914	06/29/1917	3
22	Mauna Loa	06/20/1832	07/15/1832	0
23	Mauna Loa	03/25/1984	04/15/1984	0
24	Nyamuragira	11/07/1907	12/05/1907	3
25	Nyamuragira	02/06/2001	04/05/2001	2
26	Nyiragongo	06/21/1982	10/17/1982	1
27	Nyiragongo	01/17/2002	02/03/2002	1
28	Pinatubo	04/02/1991	09/02/1991	5
29	Poas	12/29/1898	12/31/1907	1
30	Poas	04/08/1996	04/08/1996	1
31	Popocatepetl	10/13/1663	10/19/1665	3
32	Popocatepetl	12/21/1994	08/05/1995	2
33	Reventador	12/12/1856	12/13/1856	3
34	Reventador	02/24/1944	03/01/1944	3
35	Reventador	11/03/2002	01/10/2003	4
36	Ruapehu	02/13/1861	05/16/1861	2
37	Ruapehu	06/17/1996	09/01/1996	3
38	Sabancaya	05/01/1997	05/02/1997	3
39	Santorini	09/27/1650	12/06/1650	4
40	Santorini	05/23/1707	09/14/1711	3
41	Santorini	01/26/1866	10/15/1870	2
42	Santorini	01/10/1950	02/02/1950	2
43	Shishaldin	03/13/1999	05/27/1999	3
44	St. Helens	03/26/1847	03/30/1847	2
45	St. Helens	03/27/1980	10/28/1986	5
46	St. Helens	10/01/2004	01/27/2008	2
47	Vesuvius	12/15/1631	01/31/1632	5
48	Vesuvius	12/25/1732	06/04/1737	3
49	Vesuvius	12/18/1875	04/22/1906	4
50	Vesuvius	07/05/1913	04/04/1944	3
51	Villarrica	11/07/1837	11/21/1837	2
52	Villarrica	10/26/2008	.	1

Latitude and Longitude Data

There are two versions of the latitude and longitude data. One is a text file, and the other is a
SAS data set. They both contain the same columns and data values.

Filename: Latlong.txt   Latlong.sas7bdat
File Type: Fixed-width text file   SAS data set

Columns:

Name	Description
Volcano	Name of the volcano
Latitude	Latitude
Longitude	Longitude

Latlong.txt

```
Volcano           Latitude Longitude
Altar             -1.67     -78.42
Barren Island     12.28      93.52
Elbrus            43.33      42.45
Erebus           -77.53     167.17
Etna              37.73      15.00
Fuji              35.35     138.73
Garibaldi         49.85    -123.00
Grimsvotn         64.42     -17.33
Illimani         -16.39     -67.47
Kenya             -0.09      37.18
Kilauea           19.43    -155.29
Kilimanjaro       -3.07      37.35
Kliuchevskoi      56.06     160.64
Krakatau          -6.10     105.42
Lassen            40.49    -121.51
Mauna Loa         19.48    -155.61
Nyamuragira       -1.41      29.20
Nyiragongo        -1.52      29.25
Pinatubo          15.13     120.35
Poas              10.20     -84.23
Popocatepetl      19.02     -98.62
Puy de Dome       45.50       2.75
Reventador        -0.08     -77.66
Ruapehu          -39.28     175.57
Sabancaya        -15.78     -71.85
Santorini         36.40      25.40
Shishaldin        54.76    -163.97
St. Helens        46.20    -122.18
Vesuvius          40.82      14.43
Villarrica       -39.42     -71.93
```

Latlong.sas7bdat

	Volcano	Latitude	Longitude
1	Altar	-1.67	-78.42
2	Barren Island	12.28	93.52
3	Elbrus	43.33	42.45
4	Erebus	-77.53	167.17
5	Etna	37.73	15
6	Fuji	35.35	138.73
7	Garibaldi	49.85	-123
8	Grimsvotn	64.42	-17.33
9	Illimani	-16.39	-67.47
10	Kenya	-0.09	37.18
11	Kilauea	19.43	-155.29
12	Kilimanjaro	-3.07	37.35
13	Kliuchevskoi	56.06	160.64
14	Krakatau	-6.1	105.42
15	Lassen	40.49	-121.51
16	Mauna Loa	19.48	-155.61
17	Nyamuragira	-1.41	29.2
18	Nyiragongo	-1.52	29.25
19	Pinatubo	15.13	120.35
20	Poas	10.2	-84.23
21	Popocatepetl	19.02	-98.62
22	Puy de Dome	45.5	2.75
23	Reventador	-0.08	-77.66
24	Ruapehu	-39.28	175.57
25	Sabancaya	-15.78	-71.85
26	Santorini	36.4	25.4
27	Shishaldin	54.76	-163.97
28	St. Helens	46.2	-122.18
29	Vesuvius	40.82	14.43
30	Villarrica	-39.42	-71.93

Portland Flights Data

Filename: Portland.sas7bdat
File Type: SAS data set

Columns:

Name	Description
Origin	City from which flight departs
Destination	City in which flight arrives
FlightNo	Flight number
FlightPrice	Price of flight in U.S. dollars

Portland.sas7bdat

	Origin	Destination	FlightNo	FlightPrice
1	Portland	Catania	L469	$779.00
2	Portland	Hilo	HA25	$703.00
3	Portland	Nairobi	KLM6034	$1,833.00
4	Portland	Rome	D1576	$644.00
5	Portland	San Jose	CA1210	$494.00
6	Portland	Tokyo	UA383	$705.00

Seattle Flights Data

Filename: Seattle.sas7bdat
File Type: SAS data set

Columns:

Name	Description
Origin	City from which flight departs
Destination	City in which flight arrives
FlightNo	Flight number
FlightPrice	Price of flight in U.S. dollars

Seattle.sas7bdat

	Origin	Destination	FlightNo	FlightPrice
1	Seattle	Catania	BA48	$802.00
2	Seattle	Hilo	HA21	$677.00
3	Seattle	Jakarta	AA119	$1,815.00
4	Seattle	Nairobi	KLM6034	$1,761.00
5	Seattle	Quito	CA1086	$833.00
6	Seattle	Rome	USA6	$596.00
7	Seattle	San Jose	CA1100	$480.00
8	Seattle	Tokyo	UA875	$721.00

Northwest Weather Data

Filename: NWweather.sas7bdat
File Type: SAS data set

Columns:

Name	Description	Possible Values
City	City	
Month	Month	1–12
AvgTemp	Average high temperature in degrees Fahrenheit	
FromNormal	Change from normal temperature in degrees Fahrenheit	
InchesRain	Amount of rain in inches	
Bookings	Number of tours booked for that month	

NWweather.sas7bdat

	City	Month	AvgTemp	FromNormal	InchesRain	Bookings
1	Seattle	1	45.8	4.9	8.39	32
2	Seattle	2	41.7	-1.6	1.76	19
3	Seattle	3	46.8	0.6	6.34	23
4	Seattle	4	48.9	-1.3	2.74	18
5	Seattle	5	54.8	-1	1.16	21
6	Seattle	6	62.8	2.1	0.51	18
7	Seattle	7	67.9	2.6	0.06	17
8	Seattle	8	66.4	0.8	0.32	17
9	Seattle	9	62.6	1.5	0.89	22
10	Seattle	10	54.3	1.6	8.96	20
11	Seattle	11	42.8	-2.4	6.77	25
12	Seattle	12	41.8	1.1	3.88	31
13	Portland	1	44.8	4.9	7.64	22
14	Portland	2	44.3	1.2	2.37	19
15	Portland	3	49	1.8	5.75	17
16	Portland	4	50.8	-0.4	4.37	18
17	Portland	5	57.3	0.2	1.49	21
18	Portland	6	66.1	3.4	0.31	19
19	Portland	7	71.6	3.5	0	13
20	Portland	8	70.1	1.6	0.19	15
21	Portland	9	66.8	3.2	0.85	23
22	Portland	10	58.2	3.9	3.01	24
23	Portland	11	45.2	-0.6	4.09	27
24	Portland	12	42.5	2.3	7.45	33

On-Time Status of Flights Data

Filename: OnTimeStatus.sas7bdat
File Type: SAS data set

Columns:

Name	Description	Possible Values
Month	Month	Dec Jan Feb
Departure	Whether delayed 15 minutes or more	OnTime Late
TimeOfDay	Whether before or after 12 p.m.	BeforeNoon AfterNoon
NumOfFlights	Number of flights in that category	

OnTimeStatus.sas7bdat

	Month	Departure	TimeOfDay	NumOfFlights
1	Dec	OnTime	AfterNoon	25
2	Dec	Late	AfterNoon	33
3	Dec	OnTime	BeforeNoon	80
4	Dec	Late	BeforeNoon	13
5	Jan	OnTime	AfterNoon	15
6	Jan	Late	AfterNoon	12
7	Jan	OnTime	BeforeNoon	30
8	Jan	Late	BeforeNoon	13
9	Feb	OnTime	AfterNoon	20
10	Feb	Late	AfterNoon	8
11	Feb	OnTime	BeforeNoon	43
12	Feb	Late	BeforeNoon	1

Advertising Results Data

Filename: AdResults.sas7bdat
File Type: SAS data set

Columns:

Name	Description	Possible Values
City	City	
Month	Month	1–12
AdDollars	Money spent on advertising in U.S. dollars	
Bookings	Number of tours booked for that month	

AdResults.sas7bdat

	City	Month	AdDollars	Bookings
1	Seattle	1	350	30
2	Seattle	2	330	19
3	Seattle	3	525	32
4	Seattle	4	400	18
5	Seattle	5	375	21
6	Seattle	6	325	18
7	Seattle	7	150	17
8	Seattle	8	250	17
9	Seattle	9	250	22
10	Seattle	10	325	20
11	Seattle	11	400	25
12	Seattle	12	500	31
13	Portland	1	325	25
14	Portland	2	290	19
15	Portland	3	250	17
16	Portland	4	300	18
17	Portland	5	300	21
18	Portland	6	275	19
19	Portland	7	200	13
20	Portland	8	225	15
21	Portland	9	325	23
22	Portland	10	350	24
23	Portland	11	425	27
24	Portland	12	400	33

Ages Data

Filename: Ages.sas7bdat
File Type: SAS data set

Columns:

Name	Description	Possible Values	
Difficulty	Strenuousness of the tour	c	(Challenging)
		m	(Moderate)
		e	(Easy)
Age	Age in years		

Ages.sas7bdat

	Difficulty	Age
1	e	45
2	e	38
3	e	65
4	e	43
5	e	29
6	e	72
7	e	66
8	e	57
9	e	39
10	e	33
11	m	26
12	m	37
13	m	42
14	m	27
15	m	31
16	m	39
17	m	35
18	m	30
19	m	41
20	m	55
21	c	65
22	c	39
23	c	59
24	c	55
25	c	50
26	c	47
27	c	42
28	c	60
29	c	58
30	c	67

Index